MW00649510

Activism through Music during the Apartheid Era and Beyond

The Lexington Series in Historical Ethnomusicology: Deep Soundings

Series Editors: David G. Hebert (Western Norway University of Applied Sciences), and Jonathan McCollum (Washington College, USA)

The Lexington Series in Historical Ethnomusicology: Deep Soundings is a series from Lexington Books envisioned to offer rigorous, cutting-edge research that probes music of the past and mechanisms of sociomusical change. We champion innovative approaches and diverse methodologies, ranging from archival and oral histories, to syntheses of organological and music-archeological findings, to computational studies of musical evolution across decades, as well as novel interpretations of non-western music philosophy. The series also features original works that synthesize the oeuvre of influential scholars whose publications are primarily in languages other than English. Books in this series offer theoretically robust presentations of unique discoveries, written in lucid prose appropriate for liberal arts colleges and universities, as well as professional researchers.

We are pleased to offer here the first volume in the series: *Activism through Music during the Apartheid Era and Beyond:* When Voices Meet, by Ambigay Yudkoff

Activism through Music during the Apartheid Era and Beyond

When Voices Meet

Ambigay Yudkoff

LEXINGTON BOOKS

Lanham • Boulder • New York • London

Published by Lexington Books
An imprint of The Rowman & Littlefield Publishing Group, Inc.
4501 Forbes Boulevard, Suite 200, Lanham, Maryland 20706
www.rowman.com

6 Tinworth Street, London SE11 5AL, United Kingdom

Copyright © 2021 by The Rowman & Littlefield Publishing Group, Inc.

All rights reserved. No part of this book may be reproduced in any form or by any
electronic or mechanical means, including information storage and retrieval systems,
without written permission from the publisher, except by a reviewer who may quote
passages in a review.

British Library Cataloguing in Publication Information Available

Library of Congress Cataloging-in-Publication Data

Names: Yudkoff, Ambigay, 1961- author.
Title: Activism through music during the apartheid era and beyond : when voices meet /
    Ambigay Yudkoff.
Description: Lanham : Lexington Books, 2021. | Series: The Lexington series in
    historical ethnomusicology : deep soundings | Includes bibliographical references
    and index. | Summary: "In Activism through Music during the Apartheid Era and
    Beyond, Ambigay Yudkoff details a compelling narrative of collaboration through
    music, travel, performances, and socialization as a vehicle for racial integration and
    intercultural exchange"— Provided by publisher.
Identifiers: LCCN 2021017943 (print) | LCCN 2021017944 (ebook) |
    ISBN 9781793630544 (cloth) | ISBN 9781793630551 (epub)
Subjects: LCSH: Music—Social aspects—South Africa. | Anti-apartheid movements—
    South Africa. | Music and race—South Africa. | Katz, Sharon (Musician)
Classification: LCC ML3917.S62 Y84 2021 (print) | LCC ML3917.S62 (ebook) | DDC
    306.4/8420968—dc23
LC record available at https://lccn.loc.gov/2021017943
LC ebook record available at https://lccn.loc.gov/2021017944

∞™ The paper used in this publication meets the minimum requirements of American
National Standard for Information Sciences—Permanence of Paper for Printed Library
Materials, ANSI/NISO Z39.48-1992.

For My Dearest Parents
. . . who voted for the first time in 1994, more than
fifty years after they were born in South Africa
and
For Tamara, Jasmin, and Brandon

Contents

List of Figures and Tables ix

Acknowledgments xiii

1 Get on the Peace Train 1

2 Creating a Platform for Musical Activism 21

3 Glimpses of Musical Activism on a Transcontinental Journey 59

4 Tracking and Triangulation through Film 99

5 Replicating the Peace Train Model in the United States 115

6 The Peace Train Rolls On 147

Glossary of Musical Styles 165

Appendices 169

    1 Compact Discs by Sharon Katz & The Peace Train 169

    2 NVivo Software Applications 171

    3 Vocal Scores 172

    4 Responses to Questionnaire: A Demographic Survey
      of Adults on Tour 186

References 187

Index 199

About the Author 209

List of Figures and Tables

FIGURES

Figure 1.1   Map of KwaZulu-Natal in South Africa Depicting
Designated Areas of the Group Areas Act of 1950
Based on Race. Image sourced from the documentary
When Voices Meet, 2015   4

Figure 1.2   Pete Seeger and Sharon Katz Performed at *Joe's Pub*
in New York City in 2009   16

Figure 2.1   John Kani and Sharon Katz—Old Friends Greet
Each Other at the Market Theatre in Johannesburg.
Photo frame from the documentary DVD, *When Voices
Meet*, 2015   31

Figure 2.2   Lyrics of a Song from the Album, *Niemandsland*,
Released May 31, 1985   36

Figure 3.1   The Upper and Lower Portions of a Salvaged
Poster Advertised the 500-Voice Concerts at the
Durban City Hall   64

Figure 3.2   An Entrance Ticket to May 26, 1993, 500-Voice Choir
Concert at the Durban City Hall   65

Figure 3.3   A Billboard at the Entrance of the Orphanage with a
Photo of Mama Mary   82

Figure 3.4   An Inspirational Mural Inside the Orphanage   88

Figure 3.5   Large Posters on the Interior Walls of the Orphanage   89

Figure 3.6   The Author Getting to Know the Caregivers and the
Children at the Orphanage   90

Figure 3.7   Sharon Katz Is Pictured with American Tourists
              (*Friends of The Peace Train*) at the KwaNgcolosi
              School with Adults and Children from the Community   92
Figure 3.8   An Acknowledgment of the Building of the Hall and
              School at KwaNgcolosi   94
Figure 4.1   Joseph Shabalala and Paul Simon Perform at the
              Library of Congress Awards Ceremony in 2007 When
              Paul Simon Received the First Gershwin Prize for
              Popular Song   105
Figure 4.2   (From Left to Right) Nonhlanhla Wanda, Sharon Katz,
              and Wendy Quick at the Screening of *When Voices
              Meet* on September 26, 2015, at the Community
              Global Film Festival in Toronto, Canada, Where the
              Film Received the "Best Documentary" Award   112
Figure 5.1   Shari Belafonte (Second from Right), Pictured with
              Sharon Katz, Wendy Quick, Nonhlanhla Wanda, and
              Marilyn Cohen, Receives an Award on July 9, 2016,
              on Behalf of Her Family for Being "Champions of
              Social Justice & The Arts, Worldwide" at the First
              Concert of the American Peace Train Tour in New York   119
Figure 5.2   Second Draft of the American Peace Train Concert of
              July 2016   121
Figure 5.3   Sharon Katz (Pictured with a Guitar in the Center of
              the Photo) and the Participants of the American Peace
              Train Tour 2016 Perform at the New York Society for
              Ethical Culture Centre in Manhattan, New York, the
              United States on July 9, 2016   123
Figure 5.4   Score for Horns for the Song, *The Time Is Right Today*,
              by Sharon Katz   127
Figure 5.5   Score for Horns for the Song, *Sanalwami*,
              by Sharon Katz   128
Figure 6.1   Nonhlanhla Wanda (Left Microphone) with Sharon
              Katz (Right Microphone) during the First American
              Peace Train Concert Performance in New York on
              July 9, 2016   159
Figure 6.2   Sharon Katz (Left Microphone) with Wendy Quick
              (Right Microphone) during the First American Peace
              Train Tour Concert in New York on July 9, 2016   159
Figure 6.3   Sharon Katz Performs as Guest Artist of *Promotora
              de las Bella's Artes* with 1,500 Children in Concert in
              Tijuana, Mexico, 2019   162
Figure 7.1   Cluster Depictions   171

Figure 7.2   Selected Keywords of Interviewees and the Frequency
             of Associated References from Highest to Lowest
             Using NVivo Software   171
Figure 7.3   The song *Shosholoza* Arranged by Sharon Katz   172
Figure 7.4   *We Are the Children* Composed by Sharon Katz in
             1993/Adapted 2016   174
Figure 7.5   *The Time Is Right Today* Composed by Sharon Katz
             1993/Adapted 2016   177
Figure 7.6   *Sanalwami* Arranged by Sharon Katz   180
Figure 7.7   *Sala Ngoana* Composed by Sharon Katz   182
Figure 7.8   *The Little We Have We Share* by Sharon Katz   184

TABLES

Table 4.1   Details of the Screenings of the Documentary and
             Awards Received   110
Table 5.1   Demographic Data of the American Peace Train Tour
             of July 2016   120
Table 6.1   Inequitable Treatment of Blacks and Whites in South
             Africa circa 1978   157
Table 7.1   Frequency of Keywords and Related References in
             Interviews   171
Table 7.2   A Demographic Survey of Adult Respondents on the
             American Peace Train Tour of 2016   186

Acknowledgments

Music is a great blessing. It has the power to elevate and liberate us. It
sets people free to dream. It can unite us to sing with one voice. Such
is the value of music.

—Nelson Mandela

Listening to the music of Sharon Katz & The Peace Train during an intimate
performance at Caffè Lena in Saratoga Springs, New York, liberated me from
my intellectual slumber. The familiarity of Katz's South African musical
style and her powerful message of social justice, unity, and peace inspired
my research into musical activism. Sharon Katz shared her vision, artistic
materials, contacts, and time with me throughout the following two years. I
am genuinely grateful for the access she provided.

This book was a journey in several ways. My research entailed extensive
travel in two countries, South Africa and the United States, tracking the
musical activism of Sharon Katz & The Peace Train. My heartfelt thanks
go to many people who assisted with my research: the participants of The
Peace Train initiatives in South Africa and the United States who shared
their personal experiences with me; Mama Mary Lwate for opening her home
to me and allowing me to visit the children at the orphanage in Mabopane;
Nonhlanhla Wanda and Wendy Quick for sharing their stories with me;
Marilyn Cohen for collating valuable data, and Marc Duby, my mentor in
South Africa, for recognizing the potential of my research and supporting my
endeavors.

The coeditors of this book, David Hebert and Jonathan McCollum, provided me with the opportunity to realize the culmination of this historical
journey in musical activism. David and Jonathan are scholars par excellence
whose intellectual depth and critical insights made me see "with new eyes"

the multidisciplinary appeal of my work. I am deeply appreciative of their guidance and experience. A special thank you to the Acquisitions Editor, Courtney Morales, for her meticulous attention to the technical aspects of this book.

My parents are an ongoing source of inspiration. As a child of color growing up in apartheid South Africa, I was always keenly aware of our country's political and social injustices. Besides my parents' sociopolitical activism within our community, they shared a rich background in music. My mother was an actress and singer in community theater, and my late father was a glorious tenor. Although my parents had limited resources, they supported my musical aspirations and encouraged my lifelong love of learning. My mother, Savitri Pillay, has always been steadfast in her support of my ventures. For this, I feel blessed.

My family—Charles, Tamara, Jasmin, and Brandon—provided feedback, encouragement, and love throughout my research and writing. I will always cherish your presence in my life.

Chapter 1

Get on the Peace Train

We need a sweet survival, love revival, Peace Train!
Make a heart connection, sweet affection, Peace Train!
Come on, get on, Come on, get on
Get on the Peace Train!
Meet the Love Conductor,
He's your brother on the Peace Train!
Choo! Choo!

—*Peace Train* by Sharon Katz
and Bolden Abrams

INTRODUCTION

The immigrant experience is exhausting. There is undoubtedly a sense of gratitude for all accomplishments despite the many obstacles, but the undeniable yearning lingers. If only you could hear someone in the neighborhood who talks like you and see perhaps a recognizable face and smell the warm ocean breeze that blows across the eastern shores of South Africa, if that's from where you have come. Seeking this familiarity, I scour the events calendar of Saratoga Springs, New York, searching for artists who will bring a piece of Africa to me here in the United States. And so, it was on a quiet Saturday afternoon in the Spring of 2013; I discovered that Sharon Katz, a South African musician, and Wendy Khetiwe Quick would be performing at Caffè Lena. The latter is an intimate and historic venue in downtown Saratoga Springs, a few miles from my home in upstate New York.

Caffè Lena, established in May 1960, is "widely recognized as the longest continuously operating folk music venue in the United States."[1] The Library of Congress calls Caffè Lena "an American treasure," and the Grammy Foundation has recognized this iconic venue for its important contributions to the development of American music (ibid.). Most of the artists who performed at this coffee house since the 1960s were folk musicians and songwriters, most notably Bob Dylan, Ani DiFranco, Arlo Guthrie, and Pete Seeger, among others. Following in their footsteps on this memorable evening in April 2013, Sharon Katz and Wendy Quick performed on the same stage as famous folk musicians' past. These two artists graced that small platform of Caffè Lena with its reddish exposed brick backdrop.

As a member of the audience seated at a table closest to the stage, I was immediately drawn in by Katz's performance, distinctly South African accent, and colorful African-print clothing. Her voice has a gentle lilting folk-like quality that contrasts with her style of guitar playing. Katz describes her music as a blend of traditional South African musical styles such as *Maskanda*, *Mbaqanga*, and Township Jive with Afro-Jazz and a little rock (see Glossary for musical styles). During her singing of the South African National Anthem, *Nkosi Sikelel' iAfrika* (lit. God [Lord] Bless Africa), Katz encouraged audience participation. At the end of the song, she smiled and declared, "There's a South African in the house!" I must admit I was an enthusiastic participant. After a brief conversation with Katz during the intermission, I was intrigued. Her musical journey and a brief description of her work warranted further investigation. It was the inspiration I needed. Within a few months, I immersed myself in research for my doctoral studies documenting the grassroots musical activism of the performer, composer, educator, therapist, and musical activist Sharon Katz and the formation of The Peace Train.

Ethnomusicology has addressed the challenges and opportunities of using the life story of an individual musician to convey a larger narrative about history and politics through music. Researchers have long been detailing the work of musicians within a global context. Veit Erlmann (1991) examines the evolution of Black musical performance from the late nineteenth century into the twentieth century. Timothy Rice (1994) traces the role of music and dance in the Bulgarian culture through a study of two musicians from the Varimezov family. Incredibly insightful is the author's interpretation of the emic/etic[2] distinction related to the ethnomusicologist. The Egyptian singer, Umm Kulthum, is the subject of Virginia Danielson's work. Danielson (1998) examines Egyptian culture and how the singer navigates the twentieth century's impact on Arabic music. An essay by Qureshi (2001) on Begum Akhtar examines the life history of a celebrated female musician well known in India and Pakistan during Hindustani music's momentous transformation in the twentieth century. In Rees (2009), the focus is on individual musicians active in different amateur and professional music scenes in mainland China, Hong Kong, and Chinese communities in Europe. The contributors use biography to deepen the understanding of Chinese music by locating these portraits of rural folk singers, urban opera singers, literati, and musicians within the context of their geographic and cultural backgrounds. These examples of studies highlight the fact that biographies in ethnomusicology are a global phenomenon. Nettl asserts (2005), "We do not privilege elite repertories . . . we must, in the end, study all of the world's music, from all people and nations, classes, sources, periods of history" (p. 13). Therefore, it is imperative that grassroots musicians such as Sharon Katz, working with children and young people, who provide rich musical, social, and political experiences, are studied to expand the reach of historical ethnomusicology.

One of the central themes explored in this study of Sharon Katz & The Peace Train is the relationship between music and nation-building. Katz's formation of The Peace Train and associated projects reveal a compelling narrative of multigenerational collaboration. This relationship occurs through music, travel, performances, and socialization as a cultural practice and vehicle for racial integration and intercultural understanding. Through extensive fieldwork in South Africa and the United States that includes interviews, recordings of musical performances, and observations, the grassroots activism of Sharon Katz & The Peace Train is documented. Among the several intersections of her work, Katz offers a vision of the possibilities of national identity and belonging amid enormous diversity in South Africa's transition from apartheid to a fully democratic dispensation. Then, Katz transplants these possibilities to the United States. Instead of the United States showing South Africa (a shift in the global North and global South dynamic of politics and power), the reverse occurs through Katz & The Peace Train project in the United States in 2016. Understanding the political and social climate of South Africa during the apartheid era provides the backdrop against which Katz's activism emerged.

Historical Backdrop to Music and Resistance in South Africa since 1948

Beginning in 1948, the Nationalistic Government in South Africa enacted laws to define and enforce racial segregation. South Africa's apartheid system was formalized and entrenched through the laws of the National Party, a White party comprising primarily Afrikaners, which came into power that year. Apartheid policies affected every sphere of South African life, from marriage and freedom of movement to education. (Yudkoff in Hebert and Kertz-Welzel 2012, 95)

Leonard Thompson's *A History of South Africa* (2001) provides a detailed chronology of the watershed events of the apartheid era. He details the organizations that originated during that time and enacted laws that secured the apartheid government's stranglehold on people of color. These laws impacted all South Africans. As a child of color growing up in South Africa, I have vivid memories of my childhood in apartheid South Africa. I was fortunate to have the wisdom and guidance of my family and community, who were all actively engaged in social justice issues at some level. Although I could not understand why we could not sit inside Durban restaurants, my mother would always explain calmly that the government created these laws. Of course, I asked too many questions, and she would sometimes become frustrated with me, as many of these laws were enacted before I was born.

The Population Registration Act of 1950 classified people by race, while the Group Areas Act of the same year designated areas where people could reside based on race. Figure 1.1 is a map that broadly depicts the separation of people along racial lines in the province of Natal (now KwaZulu-Natal) during the apartheid era.

In 1952, the African National Congress (ANC) (originating in 1912 as the South African Native National Congress), and its allies, launched a passive resistance campaign against the South African government. Several events of the next twelve years changed the face of the resistance. One of the most devastating attacks was the Sharpeville massacre of 1960. Police killed sixty-seven Black anti-pass law demonstrators. The banning of African political organizations occurred in the same year, followed by the life imprisonment of

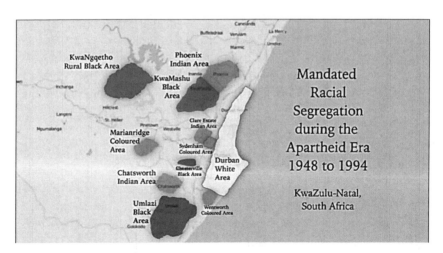

Figure 1.1   Map of KwaZulu-Natal in South Africa Depicting Designated Areas of the Group Areas Act of 1950 Based on Race. Image sourced from the documentary *When Voices Meet*, 2015. Courtesy of Sharon Katz. Used with permission.

Nelson Mandela and other ANC and PAC[3] leaders in 1964. Vershbow (2010, p. 1) describes the evolution of resistance movements during the forty-six years of apartheid as transforming from "loosely organized unions of nonviolent protestors to powerful and armed coalitions such as the African National Congress (ANC)." The various musics of this struggle against apartheid created a sense of unity and solidarity among protestors. Vershbow (ibid.) argues that the song is "a communal act of expression that shed light on the injustices of apartheid." In this context, the singing of songs is not surprising as songs have always been an integral part of African culture and its people's everyday lives.

Although a detailed discussion of indigenous musical practices is beyond the scope of this book, the profound impact of traditional music is not lost on me. My mother has often shared amusing stories of my childhood. As a baby, I was very fussy unless I was carried on my African nanny's back and rocked to sleep. I also have vivid recollections of the traditional Zulu lullaby "Thula Baba" that was sung to me during my African childhood. This experience was not in conflict with listening to the American folk lullaby "Hush Little Baby" that my mother sang to me. My music theory exams through the Royal Schools of Music in London, for example, reinforced the strong European influence in South Africa. These exams were taken while I was attending a segregated local high school. This Western influence included attending opera productions and ballets at the Alhambra Theatre in Durban. It was also not unusual for me to sing and play my guitar at school, performing African or Western folk songs, or going Christmas caroling in my neighborhood with friends from a nearby church.

Nonetheless, my enjoyment of African music was a daily part of life in South Africa: listening to African children, many of whom were my friends, on the streets walking home from school; on the radio and sometimes the television; hearing the singing of African domestic workers as they completed their chores in the yard and around the house; and most excitingly, when I watched the colorfully attired ensembles of African singers and dancers (often including children as young as four years old) on the Durban beachfront as they entertained tourists and locals, trying to earn some money.

Then there were other cultural influences. As children of Indian descent (third generation in South Africa), it was also not strange to my brother and me that our parents enrolled us in Saturday morning music classes. There, we learned to play the harmonium, a keyboard instrument commonly used in Indian music. Although we did not speak an Indian language, I found that music, song, dance, and community events such as the celebration of Hindu festivals reinforced aspects of my cultural heritage. As if this was not culturally stimulating enough, my home was in an "Indian" suburb (a designation of the apartheid system of segregation) where many of my neighbors were

Muslims (followers of Islam). Before sunrise every morning, I awoke to the early morning call to prayer in Arabic blaring through a loudspeaker, sung by the Imam of a local mosque. Four cultures (African, European, Indian [Hindu], and Muslim) reflect the complexity of growing up in a rich multicultural environment. To me, there was no confusion or conflict in negotiating these spaces. It was normal.

Significantly, in both African and Indian cultures, the vocal music I learned were rooted in tradition and taught through oral transmission. De Beer and Shitandi (2012) refer to the anthropological and archeological sources as well as oral history recordings that "provide clear evidence of a long-standing quasi-choral music culture in Africa" (p. 185) that predates colonization. The seminomadic and pastoral Maasai people of Kenya, for example, have retained their traditions and lifestyle. This resilience is remarkable since they have been displaced, and they have struggled to hold on to parts of their land against European invasion. Their homophonic and polyphonic choruses indicate the social and communal aspects of indigenous African communities such as the "Ijesha-Yoruba of Nigeria, Nguu of Tanzania, Zulu, Xhosa and Swazi of South Africa" (ibid.). Maasai music is predominantly vocal, where rhythmic harmonies of a chorus support the melody performed by the song leader/s or *olaranyani*. This call-and-response form between the *olaranyani* and the group is one of the popular forms in indigenous African music adopted by Sharon Katz for some of her compositions. The importance of bringing communities together through music is the foundation of Katz's musical activism. This community engagement bears a striking resemblance to the act of communal singing, yet another significant aspect of traditional African music. Communal singing for rituals, celebrations such as weddings, and performances continue among several African language groups from South Africa such as the Zulu, Xhosa, Pedi (Bapedi), and Sotho.

While the Maasai people from Kenya and the Bapedi people from South Africa (among the vast array of other indigenous peoples of Africa) maintain their traditions, the impact of colonialism, modernization, and the promotion of Christianity through the work of missionaries cannot be overstated. De Beer and Shitandi (2012, 186) argue that:

Africans easily adopted the Western tradition of choral music brought into Africa by missionaries because of the number of concurrences, including the social nature of singing together, polyphonic structures in music, and the function of music as an enhancement of social (religious) activity, such as the congregational singing of Christian hymns. These hymns were later transformed into new African choral styles by being adapted to African practices, including language, parallel movement between voices, responsorial elements, and rhythmic alterations, through the inclusion of dances or instrumental accompaniments.

Elements of traditional musical practices often permeate new compositions in urban settings. This practice is evident in the music of Sharon Katz & The Peace Train that developed within the boundaries of contemporary urban culture in South Africa in the 1990s. Katz's music is easily accessible to Western audiences because her compositions have been influenced, in part, by her study of Western music (both theory and form). This Eurocentric influence in music is not unusual for any South African who grew up in an urban setting during the apartheid era. The Dutch and British colonizers,[4] at various times, influenced language, education, music, and many other aspects of South African life since the arrival of the first Dutch settlers in 1652. However, it is also abundantly clear that the inspiration behind Katz's musical activism is grounded in an Afrocentric identity through both the substance of her messaging and the vital elements of African musical style in Katz's songs.

Highlights of Traveling Musical Groups in South Africa

The art of storytelling among Africa's indigenous people has also been significant, with folk tales around fires holding captive audiences, young and old. There is an inextricable link between storytelling and music—a vehicle that captures a feeling, a moment, a narrative, or a message. Over a century before the emergence of Sharon Katz & The Peace Train, in the mid-1800s, traveling minstrel shows began to visit South Africa.

The earliest of these performers were White English colonists performing in "blackface."[5] These crass performances—following the premiere of the Virginia Minstrels in New York—smacked of racism "ideally suited as a rationalization of the anxiety of White settlers in South Africa attempting to come to terms with the strength of precolonial social formations and independent African political power" (Veit Erlmann 1991, 30). The arrival of the Christy Minstrels in Cape Town in 1862 from the United States elevated the popularity of blackface minstrel shows playing a dominant role in the "popular White musical and theatrical entertainment in South Africa" (ibid.). In towns and cities such as Durban, Kimberley, and Cape Town, where English culture predominated, amateur minstrel groups flourished. The racist underpinnings of the American Minstrel troupes also permeated the culture and folk songs of both the Dutch Boer and Cape "Colored"[6] people.

This entertainment genre changed considerably when Black American minstrel troupes toured South Africa in the 1860s, singing spirituals of the American South. In the 1890s, Orpheus McAdoo and the Virginia Jubilee Singers were among the most popular visiting minstrel groups, touring the country four times. The spread in popularity of African American spirituals inspired the formation of South African Black choirs and a subculture of rehearsals and competition that is a vibrant part of the South African music experience today. It is noteworthy that Katz recruited most students out of a similar culture of choir music competitions in the 1990s for the formation of the 500-voice choir with its inaugural performance at the Durban City Hall in 1992.

The impact of Orpheus McAdoo on the history of musical traveling groups in South Africa is extraordinary. He was born in 1858, the oldest child of slave parents in North Carolina. As a young man, he attended the Hampton Institute in Virginia, founded in 1868 as a higher education institution for emancipated slaves. McAdoo worked as a teacher and toured extensively with the Hampton Male Quartette, one of the best-known Afro-American quartets at the time. He later joined the Fisk Jubilee Singers. Their first world tour lasted seven years, introducing American and European audiences to "genuine Afro-American culture: the spirituals, the 'sorrow songs' as W. E. B. DuBois[7] called them" (Veit Erlmann 1991, 24). The tours of the Fisk Jubilee Singers extended to include Australia, India, and the Far East. Upon their return, McAdoo formed the Virginia Jubilee Singers in 1890 and set sail for England. After a short run and little success, McAdoo headed for South Africa, where he and his troupe triumphed, opening at the Vaudeville Theatre in Cape Town on June 30, 1890. They enjoyed the enthusiastic reception of mostly White audiences throughout the country, elevating the music of minstrels.

Fast forward to the 1950s, and White impresarios were organizing musical variety shows like "Zonk!" "Drums of Africa," "African Jazz," and "Variety." Some of these shows ran for more than a decade. The first all-Black South African musical was *King Kong: An African Jazz* that premiered on February 2, 1959, at the Wits Great Hall. This musical that chronicles the ascent and demise of the champion boxer Ezekiel "King Kong" Dhlamini was significant in creating opportunities for Black South Africans in the arts. It expanded the scope of South African theater playing to segregated Black and White audiences in major cities from Johannesburg, Cape Town, Port Elizabeth to Durban. Working as a creative force on King Kong's production was the architect and painter Arthur Goldreich, who created the decor and costumes for this jazz musical. An explanation of his political role in the resistance and association with Nelson Mandela (who attended the show's premiere in Johannesburg) appears in Chapter 2. More broadly, the Jewish people's role (Arthur Goldreich's heritage) in the struggle for liberation in South Africa is addressed.

Among the seventy-member cast were Miriam Makeba, Phyllis Mqoma, Hugh Masekela, and others who went on to highly successful careers both in South Africa and abroad. Miriam Makeba, whose powerful and distinctive voice earned her the nickname Mama Africa, played the shebeen[8] queen of the Back of the Moon, a popular establishment in Sophiatown. In this role, Makeba attracted the attention of an English record company. She signed a contract with them, which catapulted her to finding international success. The show itself sparked the interest of a London promoter who was at the premiere in Johannesburg.

Two years after its opening in South Africa, the show headed to London's Prince Theatre with its opening night on February 23, 1961. Nathan Mdledle, the lead actor playing the role of Ezekiel Dhlamini, reportedly said, "if the London cats like it, we're in!"[9] After fifteen shows to wildly receptive audiences, *King Kong* etched itself into musical theater history with its all-Black cast from South Africa. The subject matter was apolitical and therefore helped bridge the divide between Black and White audiences. However, the song "Sad Times, Bad Times" was considered a reference to the infamous South African Treason Trial[10] in Pretoria that had begun in 1956 and dragged on for more than four years. This trial eventually collapsed, and all the accused were acquitted. *King Kong* also encouraged community theater in South Africa and created a sophisticated forum for South African storytelling.

Another form of popular musical entertainment starting in the 1950s was brought to audiences by The Golden City Dixies. They created a vaudeville-style variety spectacular show that other musicians emulated in the 1960s, with artists such as Jonathan Butler, Taliep Peterson, and Zayn Adams enjoying phenomenal success in the 1970s. In 1959, the original Golden Dixies were the first all-Black group of twenty-one entertainers to leave South Africa for England, Ireland, and Sweden. Among these performers were singers, guitarists, saxophonists, a pianist, and a drummer. In the face of financial setbacks, the group concluded their tour in Sweden. However, ten of the original performers decided to seek asylum in Sweden in the wake of the ongoing atrocities of the apartheid system in South Africa. The Swedish government granted them sanctuary. Warren Ludski (2019) interviewed one of the performers, Arthur Gillies, sixty years later in Norway. Gillies recalled his solo gigs in Sweden and Denmark playing jazz in cafés, bars, and supper clubs until a promoter offered him a contract in Norway. A work permit allowed Gillies to perform as a solo artist regularly in Norway. The immigrant journey continued for Gillies as he explains:

Then I met a man who owned a piano factory in Stavanger in Norway, and he offered me permanent work. The next thing I knew, I was applying for political asylum again, but this time for Norway. That was in the mid-'60s, and I have been in Stavanger ever since, playing jazz in the style of renowned pianist Errol Garner. If I may say so myself, I'm pretty famous in this town. I couldn't rob a bank here![11]

The most remarkable aspect of his life was that Gillies remained in exile for over thirty years as he feared that going back to South Africa would mean imprisonment. Most unexpectedly, Nelson Mandela intervened. Gillies reveals in his interview:

> In 1992, when Mandela came to Norway with de Klerk to be awarded their Nobel Peace Prize, I had the honor of playing at the SA embassy in Oslo. When I was introduced to Mandela, he said, "you're a South African, you play beautifully." I told him I hadn't been back for 30 years; I couldn't go to my father's funeral, I hadn't seen my mother, and she was going to be 100. He was surprised and angry. "My son," he said to me, "you go back to South Africa tomorrow, and if anybody hassles you at the airport, they must answer to me!" I went back later that year, and there were still "boere" behind the counter. They looked at my Norwegian passport that said I was born in Cape Town. He took it away, and I thought, "here the *kak*[12] begins." Five minutes later, a big Boer[13] comes back and says, "Arthur Gillies, the piano player!! Welcome home: your family is waiting for you." (ibid.)

The entertainment industry in South Africa played out in different ways in each of the segregated communities of South Africa, with some points of intersection when Black performers entertained White audiences. Bringing musical theater to the impoverished townships was the South African playwright, Gibson Kente, also known as "Bra[14] Gib." Born in 1932 in East London in the eastern part of Cape Province, South Africans hail Kente as the father of Black township theater. His works tackled the issues of the day: crime, poverty, love, and apartheid through laughter, song, and dance. His first play, *Manana, The Jazz Prophet*, was performed in 1963. The musical *Sikalo* followed in 1966. It was a blend of African Gospel music with township jazz.

Kente was also instrumental in nurturing and showcasing performers such as Brenda Fassie, Nomsa Nene, and the now-famous Mbongeni Ngema. Many of them rehearsed in Kente's garage at his home in Soweto. He also wrote music for Miriam Makeba and Letta Mbulu. Kente's artistic endeavors were thwarted by censorship in South Africa when three of his plays were banned because they contained anti-apartheid subject matter. His work, *How Long*, was seized following its filming in 1976. Kente was subsequently arrested and imprisoned for a year. Despite the government's attempts to stifle his work, which included a firebombing in 1989 of Kente's home in Soweto containing his early scripts and records, his output is prolific. Kente has written some twenty-three plays and four television dramas. His last work, *The Call*, written when he received an HIV diagnosis, is a musical about a man living with the disease. It explores the themes of hope and healing, reflecting his own outlook until he died in 2004.

Post-apartheid, the Bra Gibson Kente Theatre opened in Sharpeville in 1997, and the Civic Theatre presented *A Tribute to Gibson Kente* in 1998. Associate Professor Emeritus Rolf Solberg of Norway captured the playwright's life and contribution to music in *Bra Gib: Father of South Africa's Township Theatre.*[15] In contrast to Kente's homegrown township theater, some playwrights tackled subjects and themes that would have broader audience appeal.

The fascinating appropriation and overlapping of cultures, typical of growing up in a country like South Africa, is no more apparent than in the adaptation of William Shakespeare's tragedy *Macbeth* by Welcome Msomi in 1970. Called *Umabatha*, Msomi tells the nineteenth-century story of how Mabatha overthrew Dangane. He wrote this play when Msomi was attending the then-University of Natal as a student. After its first performance at the University's open-air theater in 1971—Msomi played the title role—the play was staged in 1972 at London's Royal Shakespeare Company's Aldwych Theatre as part of that year's World Theatre Season. Tours to Italy, Scotland, Zimbabwe, and the United States followed with a very successful off-Broadway season in 1978. *Umabatha* played in New York again in 1997 at the Lincoln Center Festival to glowing reviews with a Johannesburg Civic Theater production. An excerpt of Ben Brantley's July 23, 1997, in a *New York Times* review attests to the quality of Msomi's work:

> Mr. Msomi has pointed out that there are natural, historical parallels between Shakespeare's medieval Scotland, with its elaborate network of rival clans, and the era of emerging nations in the Africa of the last century. But you needn't be aware of this to enjoy "Umabatha." Nor should the piece, which will continue on a tour of the United States and Europe when it concludes its run at Lincoln Center on Sunday, be regarded as merely an exotic cultural curiosity.
>
> Punctuated with stately processions of an earthy but uncanny beauty and invigorating tribal dances and blessed with a 66-member cast whose clarity of gesture and expression makes the supertitles nearly superfluous, the show is above all an entertainment that glories in its own energy and visual spectacle. It moves through its scenes of political plotting, martial mayhem, and ribald comedy at a speedy clip that nonetheless allows individual characters to emerge with vivid precision.

Undoubtedly one of the most well-known musicals from South Africa that received five Grammy nominations and enjoyed international acclaim is *Sarafina!* Based on the 1976 Soweto uprising, this production was the brainchild of Mbogeni Ngema, who had honed his craft under Gibson Kente's tutelage. Ngema had already established himself as an internationally successful playwright with the success of the political satire *Woza Albert* (meaning

"Come, Albert") that he had cowritten with Barney Simon and Percy Mtwa. It premiered at the Market Theater in Johannesburg, South Africa, in 1981. *Sarafina!* was conceived and directed by Mbongeni Ngema, who wrote the play and composed the music and the lyrics for the songs. This musical's first performance was also at the Market Theater in June 1987, with Leleti Khumalo in the title role.

It was a theater experience beyond compare for me to attend one of the performances of *Sarafina!* at that time. The play was riveting; the music was intense; the actors were believable, and it was a source of great pride to share this artistic expression of a profoundly emotional experience with fellow South Africans. As a child of color who had engaged in sit-ins and boycotts on my school grounds in solidarity with the African children in Soweto and other parts of the country, this was a poignant moment where real-life inter-sected with theater. *Sarafina!* premiered on Broadway on January 28, 1988, at the Cort Theatre, with a run that only ended on July 2, 1989, after almost six hundred performances and eleven previews. This story of South African chil-dren protesting the apartheid system, and paying for the liberation struggle with their lives, was adapted into a film in 1992 with Whoopi Goldberg and Leleti Khumalo.

This overview of traveling musical tours is far from complete. Still, it high-lights musicians, playwrights, and performers who helped mobilize a broader audience at home in South Africa and abroad in opposition to apartheid. The release of Nelson Mandela from Robben Island in 1990, with the first demo-cratic elections imminent in1994, was a turning point for South Africans. They had been craving these steps to democracy.

Formation of The Peace Train

It was no surprise that the path to democracy would have its challenges. The Peace Train was created to bridge the deep chasms created by the forced segregation of South Africans through apartheid. Its purpose was to rally the support and goodwill of all people across the country through music, song, and dance. Nowhere was the call to action more explicit than in the words of Nelson Mandela on the day of his release, February 11, 1990, as he addressed the people in Cape Town:

> In conclusion, I wish to quote my own words during my trial in 1964. They are true today as they were then: "I have fought against White domination, and I have fought against Black domination. I have cherished the ideal of a demo-cratic and free society in which all persons live together in harmony and with equal opportunities. It is an ideal which I hope to live for and to achieve. But if needs be, it is an ideal for which I am prepared to die."[16]

These words resonated with activists from South Africa. President Mandela motivated and inspired activists like Sharon Katz. She was determined to help realize this ideal of a free society. The cover photo (taken by Marilyn Cohen) captures Katz's meeting with Nelson Mandela on his seventy-fifth birthday celebration in 1992. Katz went on to become a cultural ambassador for the post-apartheid government. (Katz, personal communication, May 14, 2015).

In 1992, Katz disrupted the entrenched racial segregation among communities in South Africa when she formed a 500-member choir that performed both multicultural and multilingual songs in a staged production called *When Voices Meet*. This production, which incorporated music, songs, and dance, was intended to promote a peaceful transition to democracy in South Africa. Katz (2011) describes the rationale of the initiative as follows:

> I conceived of forming a 500-voice multi-cultural and multi-racial youth choir to teach youth to sing in each other's languages, to dance each other's cultural dances, and to perform together before a multi-cultural and multi-racial audience—something very unusual for South Africa at that time. [It was] a project which would use the therapeutic power of music to bring youth together of the previously separated races and cultural groups in South Africa in a shared experience . . . which dealt with the potential for a more normalized future in the country. (p. 1)

Katz's education and training as a music therapist played a pivotal role in her decision to mobilize children from segregated schools to create a multi-racial musical experience through rehearsals and a concert for a massed choir event. It was this ground-breaking concert that served as the springboard for the creation of The Peace Train. Katz's efforts were a significant step toward creating an atmosphere conducive to healing the souls of hurting South Africans ravaged by the dehumanizing effects of apartheid. Although Katz must be credited for defying the odds in her quest to unite children through song in the modern-day context of the 1990s, it is essential to note that South Africa's long and deep history of indigenous healing practices includes music and dance.

Several scholars such as Mashabela (2017), Mugovhani (2015), Nzewi (2003), Gouk (2000), Omibiyi-Obidike (1998), and Merriam (1982) attest to the value of music and dance in traditional African healing practices. In South Africa, traditional healing was banned by the apartheid government through the Suppression of Witchcraft Act in 1957. In a recent study by Maluleka (2020), this Act is described as "a piece of colonial legislation, which declared divination including traditional healing to be illegal, thereby theoretically making the work of traditional healers impossible. Traditional healing was associated with witchcraft, and that stigma continues to shadow traditional healing even today" (p. 1). This legislation did not eradicate traditional African beliefs, as many healers practiced covertly. However, the attempts at subversion were ongoing. Maluleka cites the influence of missionaries from the Congregational, Methodist, Anglican, Lutheran, and Catholic churches. They were vehemently opposed to African healers who, from their perspective, were "barbaric and superstitious." The impact of this bias against traditional healers was most keenly felt by people born during and after apartheid since this was when the South African government was undermining African cultures and traditional practices (ibid., 2020, pp. 1–2).

Other studies by Idang (2015), Davhula (2008), and Etuk (2002) explore the intersection of culture, music, and identity that is pertinent for the musical activism of Sharon Katz & The Peace Train. Davhula (2008) argues that "there is something else about the way music functions in our culture that is noteworthy [. . .] our songs may be the most effective means we have of defining ourselves as a group, of refining our emotions and perhaps of helping us to clarify even our thoughts" (p. 129). Etuk (2002) corroborates this view in stating that "an entire way of life would embody, among other things, what the people think of themselves and the universe in which they live—their world view—in other words, how they organize their lives in order to ensure their survival" (p. 13). As an activist and a music therapist, Katz opened the door to communal group singing to raise societal awareness and empower its participants to survive the effects of political and social injustices: from apartheid in South Africa to racial unrest in the United States, to the refugee crisis in Mexico. This form of musical activism is connected to Community Music Therapy referenced in Chapter 3. While the therapeutic aspects of Katz's initiatives are an integral part of her process, it is the staged performances that receive the most public and media attention.

A direct result of the success of the concerts *When Voices Meet* was Katz securing sponsorships. She had the funding to hire a train, "The Peace Train," which transported 130 performers from city to city. These events came to the entire nation through television and radio crews who rode aboard the train. The performers' ostensible mission on this journey was to create an environment of trust, joy, and sharing through music while breaking down the artificially imposed barriers of a racially segregated society. At each stop along the route, the performers encouraged people of all races, cultures, ages, and political affiliations to embrace the demise of apartheid, end hostilities, and prepare for South Africa's transition to a peaceful democracy. Through their numerous performances, the name of the performing group solidified as The Peace Train.

The Significance of the Train

More than a century before the formation of The Peace Train, Mohandas Karamchand Gandhi, an Indian lawyer in South Africa, was forcibly removed on June 7, 1893, from a train in Pietermaritzburg because he sat in a coach designated for Whites only. Long before the Nationalist Party came into power in 1948, laws segregated people (even the coaches on a train) according to race. Mohandas Gandhi, born in India and studied in London, was deeply affected by this demeaning act on a South African train. It is one of the incidents that influenced the political activism of this young lawyer. He went on to protest policies of segregation in the early 1900s in South Africa. He created a movement of passive resistance, called Satyagraha, meaning "force which is born of truth and love or non-violence." Today, Gandhi has a long legacy, fondly known as "The Mahatma" or "Great Soul."[17]

While this experience of Gandhi speaks to some of the indignities suffered by Indians in South Africa, nowhere was this shoddy treatment more apparent than the train to transport African migrant laborers. They provided "black gold"[18] for the critical gold-mining industry that was the South African economy's lifeblood from the 1880s into the twentieth century. The conditions of the trains were deplorable. The mining companies—to protect their own interests—negotiated cheap tickets for the miners, and the train accommodation was tailored accordingly.[19] The families of African migrant laborers were collateral damage. Fathers, brothers, and sons were absent from their families for as long as nine months at a time. The disintegration of African families was the heavy price paid to serve the broader political economy that benefited the White population predominantly.

Despite this tragic history, the 1990s signified a change in the narrative when Sharon Katz took a multiracial group of jubilant performers from city to city by train, bringing a message of hope and peace. This experience came with its own challenges since Katz had to seek special permission to realize this racially and culturally integrated journey. Remember, segregation affected all aspects of life for South Africans at that time. In organizing this journey, Katz knew that the train would be ideal for creating cohorts of integrated coaches where children and youth could enjoy the scenery, play board games, and develop friendships in a relaxed environment through conversations and songs. Each town on their itinerary was also easily accessible by train.

From a historical perspective, it is critical to research and document the contributions of social and cultural ambassadors such as Sharon Katz. She has, to some extent, helped shape the political and social evolution of a society. In a 2011 article, Katz describes her ongoing involvement in The Peace Train project, focusing on humanitarian efforts. The nonprofit organization,

Friends of The Peace Train, formed in 2004, raises money to implement pro-grams that respond to essential needs in South Africa, such as HIV and AIDS prevention, as well as the general education and schooling of children and youth in rural areas (Katz 2011, 3).

As a grassroots musical activist, Katz is not a commercial sensation. However, she drew the attention of an international audience unusually. The first time that worldwide audiences saw Katz perform was on the American television station CNN in April 1994. With South Africa's first democratic election scheduled, the Independent Electoral Commission wanted to educate people in South Africa, who were the previously disenfranchised majority, about the process of voting, primarily African (Black) communities in the rural areas. Africans had never been allowed to vote during the apartheid era. Sharon Katz was commissioned to write songs in some of South Africa's African languages as a tool to teach people to vote for the very first time in their lives. CNN captured Katz emerging from a helicopter to perform songs in remote and rural parts of KwaZulu-Natal because Chief Buthelezi[20] had agreed to let his people vote.[21]

This CNN coverage garnered international enthusiasm. Sharon Katz & The Peace Train have recorded for CD compilations alongside international artists such as Sting, Tina Turner, Madonna, Paul Simon, and Pete Seeger. Among this esteemed group of musicians, Katz only met Pete Seeger. However, she felt that appearing on a CD in the company of such highly respected musicians was "an honor and a privilege" (Katz, personal communication, October 15, 2016). Katz went on to share a stage with Pete Seeger in later years in New York City (see Figure 1.2). In an article entitled "Joe's Pub Remembers Pete

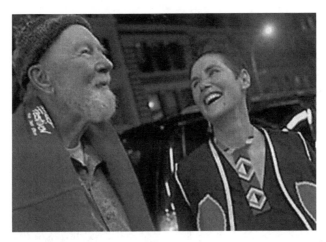

Figure 1.2   Pete Seeger and Sharon Katz Performed at *Joe's Pub* in New York City in 2009. Courtesy of Sharon Katz. Used with permission.

Seeger" published by *Broadway World*, a week after Seeger's death in 2014, Katz declared:

> Pete's politics and generosity are an inspiration to us all. He performed with me at Joe's Pub and helped me build a school in South Africa, and encouraged me to continue using my music to benefit humankind. I'm sure he and Mandela are singing together and watching over us.

Katz has also felt privileged to share the stage with fellow South African musicians such as Abigail Kubeka, a former member of Miriam Makeba's "Skylarks." Kubeka toured with Sharon Katz across the United States, sharing South Africa's music with audiences far and wide. The musical collaborations and activism of Sharon Katz are both prolific and varied with the Peace Train initiative, building on the rich history of South Africa.

Guiding Questions

This study focused on three broad research questions:

1. In what ways can Sharon Katz's various initiatives be understood within a framework of political and social activism?
2. How has Sharon Katz advocated social change through musical activities?
3. Which strategies of cultural activism have Sharon Katz employed in these initiatives?

Besides, the following sub-questions guide this discussion:

1. How did Sharon Katz arrive at a repertoire of music for the Peace Train project that would be accessible to all participants across different social and cultural backgrounds of performers?
2. To what extent do race, gender, or other factors influence Sharon Katz's activism?
3. What are the political implications of Sharon Katz's projects?
4. How do Sharon Katz's initiatives transform or renegotiate the participants' sense of identity and belonging?
5. Did participants forge long-term connections during their experiences in each endeavor, or did the music-making activity simply bind them at the time?
6. How does The Peace Train sustain its relevance twenty years after its formation in post-apartheid South Africa and other countries?
7. What were the motivating factors that led to the formation of the non-profit Friends of The Peace Train?

NOTES

1. Historical information accessed April 10, 2020, at https://www.caffelena.org/about/.

2. The terms "emic" and "etic" refer to two different anthropological study approaches. The emic perspective strives to understand humans from an insider point-of-view, while the etic takes an objective outsider's point-of-view. Available at https://www.reference.com/world-view/difference-between-emic-etic-5e5b10004caaeb20. This research incorporates both approaches as the author (a person of color) was born into the system of apartheid. During the course of fieldwork in South Africa, there were some situations that were familiar to her that lent itself to an emic perspective. However, the fieldwork in a rural African township, and the work in the United States presented situations that were novel, lending itself to an etic approach.

3. PAC refers to the Pan-African Congress founded in 1959.

4. South Africa was first colonized by the Dutch in 1652. Under the leadership of Jan van Riebeeck, an official of the Dutch East India Company, created a fortified base in the Cape as a refreshing post for Dutch ships on their way to their eastern empire in Batavia, Java, that was rich in spices and crops unavailable in Europe. In 1795, the Cape Colony came under British control, but the British returned the colony to the Dutch under the terms of the Treaty of Amiens in 1803.In January 1806, the British regained control of the Cape. The Cape Peninsula was seen as an important part of the sea-route to Asia. The arrival of British settlers in 1820 changed the Cape Colony and the future of South Africa forever. See Leonard Thompson's *A History of South Africa* (2001).

5. "Colored" is a race classification in South Africa meaning of "mixed" race.

6. "Blackface" refers to the wearing of dark makeup by a performer, such as the minstrel shows that started in the United States in the 1830s. It is a caricature of the appearance of a Black person. It is considered deeply offensive today.

7. William Edward Burghardt Du Bois (1868–1963) was an American sociologist, socialist, historian, civil rights activist, Pan-Africanist, author, writer, and editor. Du Bois was one of the founders of the National Association for the Advancement of Colored People (NAACP) in 1909.

8. The laws of South Africa under apartheid prohibited Africans from entering pubs or bars. This was reserved for Whites only. Consequently, Black people in the townships created shebeens that were alternatives to pubs and bars. Shebeens were operated illegally by women who were called Shebeen Queens. This designation harks back to the traditional role of women in Africa as the brewers of alcohol.

9. Accessed April 20, 2020, https://www.sahistory.org.za/article/development-music-south-africa-timeline-1600-2004; https://www.sahistory.org.za/article/king-kong-musical-1959-1961.

10. The Treason Trial commenced in December 1956, after 156 individuals were arrested on charges of treason as they were believed to oppose the ruling National Party and its Apartheid regime. Of the 156 individuals, 105 were Africans, 21 were Indians, 23 were Whites, and seven were Colored. Of the 156, only 10 were women.

The individuals arrested included the likes of Ruth First, Yusuf Dadoo, Ahmed Kathrada, Chief Luthuli, Nelson Mandela, Walter Sisulu, Joe Slovo, and Oliver Tambo. It ended in March 1961. The accused were found not guilty. Accessed May 4, 2020, https://roodepoortnorthsider.co.za/271755/today-in-history-the-1956-treason-trial-came-to-an-end-in-1961-reliving-the-trials-key-moments-web/.

11. Accessed April 30, 2020, https://warrenludskimusicscene.com/interviews-3/touring-dixies-paved-way-60-years-ago-and-some-never-came-back/.

12. The Boers were also called the Afrikaners because they spoke the Afrikaans language in South Africa. These were people of Dutch descent who were among the early settlers in South Africa.

13. *kak* is the Afrikaans word for excrement.

14. In South African slang "bra" is a male friend that may be compared with the American English "dude" or "buddy."

15. Accessed April 30, 2020, https://www.sahistory.org.za/people/gibson-kente.

16. "Nelson Mandela's five most memorable speeches" in *Firstpost*. Accessed January 23, 2016, at http://www.firstpost.com/world/nelson-mandelas-five-most-memorable-speeches-1270759.html.

17. Accessed April 16, 2020, at https://www.sahistory.org.za/dated-event/mk-gandhi-forcibly-removed-whites-only-train-carriage.

18. "Black-gold" in this instance refers to the Black men, the migrant laborers, upon whose backs great wealth was created for the White owners of gold mines. The Black men were the real "gold" of the country for wealth could not be attained without their labor.

19. G. H. Pirie, "Brutish Bombelas: Trains for migrant gold miners in South Africa, c. 1900–1925," *Sage Journals*, 18, no. 1 (March 1997): 31–44, https://doi.org/10.1177%2F002252669701800104.

20. Mangosuthu Buthelezi is a South African politician and Zulu tribal leader who founded the Inkatha Freedom Party in 1975 and was Chief Minister of the KwaZulu Bantustan until 1994.

21. Accessed January 30, 2014, https://sharonkatz.com/bio/

Chapter 2

Creating a Platform for Musical Activism

My activism always existed. My art gave me the platform to do something about the activism.

—Harry Belafonte

ACTIVISM IN CONTEXT

Long before Europeans came to South Africa's shores, music was woven intrinsically into the fabric of culture in traditional African societies. Music was not only educational but it also provided entertainment during leisure hours. It relieved the drudgery of repetitive work through work songs. There were songs of war, hunting songs and funeral dirges, rites of passage songs, wedding songs, fertility songs, songs for birth, ritual chants, children's songs, rain songs during droughts, and many more. The range of music was boundless—each inspiring and supporting the many activities within societies.

Music accompanies some of the activities described even today. However, in modern and postmodern societies throughout the world, music has long been used as a tool to highlight social injustices and to promote activism among communities. The term "activism" conjures up varying contexts for social and political change. The Oxford Dictionary defines activism as the "policy or action of using vigorous campaigning to bring about political or social change." Kuntz (2015) describes activism as a "way to work for social change" (p. 28). Besides, he contends that "activism involves the determined intervention into the normative processes and practices that govern the world in which we live. [. . .] Through activism, one might seek to generate new meanings, new ways of considering and engaging with the world" (ibid.).

This study of Sharon Katz & The Peace Train examines how she negotiates her musical activism in different communities. Katz's projects appear to align more closely with the notion of catalysts for change rather than the kind of "vigorous campaigning" described in the Oxford definition. As this book will demonstrate, the music of Sharon Katz & The Peace Train lends itself to conciliatory, therapeutic, and collaborative experiences rather than offering a provocative call to action.

The intersection of music and activism creates a complex entity comprising several layers. These include the aesthetic function, the historical background, the psychological effects, and the symbolic aspects of music. Closer analyses of these components of music are vital to a comprehensive understanding of music within society. Hess (2019), in her study of activist-musicians, describes the social impact of music projects:

> Activist-musicians viewed engagement with music as profoundly connective, underscoring the nature of music as a human practice and a social phenomenon. Musicking [. . .] allows participants to create community and build relationships. Musical engagement also potentially connects us to people outside our immediate communities. We may draw upon music to connect our personal experiences to larger narratives, as well as to histories and past struggles. (Kindle location 1178 of 5965)

Eyerman and Jamison also describe connections between protest music and long-standing cultural traditions, including how music embodies and reinterprets traditions "through the ritual of performance" (Eyerman and Jamison 1998, 35) as well as the collective use of music to "mobilize protest and create group solidarity" (p. 45). The ultimate outcome of such practices is the formulation of "collective memory" as cognitive codes, aesthetic principles, and "living sources of collective identity" (p. 47). These uses of music for social change, combined with the goals of promoting hope and healing, are examined within this study of Sharon Katz & The Peace Train.

Biographical Details: An Interview with Sharon Katz

In an interview with Sharon Katz at her home on October 15, 2016, in Philadelphia, Pennsylvania, the singer, songwriter, music therapist, educator, and performer shared the details of her childhood that shaped her understanding of the world. She spoke of the many people who impacted her thinking and the path of activism that she subsequently followed. The discussion of this in-depth interview with the primary subject of this research, Sharon Katz, follows.

It was a warm afternoon in the Fall when I arrived at the home of Sharon Katz and Marilyn Cohen. From the moment I entered, I felt the history of this cozy place nestled in the heart of Philadelphia. It was not ostentatious or glamorous but rather a modest abode filled with memorabilia, instruments, and music, much of which was reminiscent of South Africa. Over a cup of tea, Katz shared her early feelings of growing up as a Jewish South African in a "White"[1] suburb of Port Elizabeth, now known as Nelson Mandela Bay. As a child of the 1950s, Sharon Katz was growing up when the apartheid system was well on its way to becoming entrenched in South Africa. She did recognize from early on that she was more privileged than the Black people who worked in her neighborhood as maids and "garden boys."[2] This realization became even more evident when her family took holidays. They drove through the Transkei area,[3] where she witnessed the abject poverty of Black people living in this rural area. Katz (2016) describes her feelings of anger and angst that she felt from the time she was ten or eleven years old:

> We were White privileged South Africans, but the background and history (of the Jewish people) was the suffering in our community. A considerable part of my upbringing was learning about the holocaust and injustice [. . .] when I saw everything around me, that was a holocaust. (S. Katz, personal communication, October 15, 2016)

Besides her strong Jewish upbringing, Katz was also a member of the [Jewish] Zionist Youth Movement in her community. Zionists expounded socialist ideals, which "fired up" the young activist. The Marxist ideologies "meant a lot to me" (ibid.). An attraction to aspects of Marxist ideologies was not unusual among left-leaning intellectuals in South Africa. One such intellectual is South African musicologist Christopher Ballantine, who helped found the University of Natal's Music Department (now the University of Kwa-Zulu Natal) in the early 1970s. In an interview with Ballantine in 2003, he explains that the "events of [. . .] 1968 as having a central influence on his scholarly work that was a life-changing experience" (Ramanna 2013, 154). Ballantine identified this as a period when he "started to get very seriously interested in Marxism. [He] encountered the Frankfurt school and Adorno and ate and breathed and slept this stuff" (ibid.). While Zionism and Marxism informed Katz's religious and political beliefs, she was simultaneously absorbing a rich repertoire of music from South Africa and abroad.

By the age of eleven, Katz played the guitar with Simon and Garfunkel and Bob Dylan's songs forming the core of her repertoire. Katz describes Dylan's *The Times They Are A-Changin,'* and Seeger's *Where Have All the Flowers Gone?* as songs that resonated with her. She also played Jewish Israeli folk songs and the folk music of Pete Seeger, performing with her band by the time she was twelve. Katz describes this as "my separate White Jewish life" (Katz 2016). Understanding Katz's "Jewish life" may be better appreciated through the social and political lens of the apartheid era.

The Jewish People in Apartheid South Africa

The history of the Jewish people is an extensive study, the breadth of which is beyond the scope of my research. However, a snapshot of this period of Jewish life in South Africa will place Sharon Katz's experiences in context. The earliest emigration of Jews from Europe and Great Britain began in the nineteenth century. Between 1880 and 1910, approximately 40,000 Jewish immigrants entered South Africa. By 1948, another 30,000 immigrants arrived. This number included 3,600 German Jewish refugees who fled Nazi Germany[4] (Shimoni 2003, 2). The most significant advantage that Jewish immigrants enjoyed was that they were classified as Europeans, meaning Whites. This afforded Jews the socioeconomic and political benefits of White governance in South Africa.

However, Jews in South Africa found themselves in an uncomfortable situation during the apartheid era. While the system propagated by the White nationalist government welcomed Jews as members of the "White" race, the oppression of Black people and all other people of color was hauntingly familiar to Jewish families descended from European refugees. When six Jews and seven Blacks were arrested in a South African police raid in Rivonia (a suburb in Johannesburg) in 1963, the responses were mixed. This incursion on an African National Congress hideout eventually landed Nelson Mandela in prison for more than twenty-five years.

When the Jewish people's loyalty was questioned, the South African Jewish Board of Deputies responded that "No part of the community can or should be asked to accept responsibility for the actions of a few." They distanced themselves from any political activism associated with Mandela. The Jewish Board of Deputies (SAJBD), established in 1912 in South Africa, was based on a London organization of the same name. This body sees itself as a civil rights organization and continues to fiercely protect the Jewish people's interests and aspirations in South Africa. Besides monitoring levels of antisemitism in South Africa, they also promote good relations with the government and meet with political leaders from across the spectrum (ibid.).

It is striking, though unsurprising that most South African Jews followed the Board of Deputies' conservative position. In the wake of their loss of Jewish existence in Europe inspired by the antisemitism of the Nazi regime, Jews in South Africa were negotiating their place within the political system of the Nationalist government. Although most Jews were supportive of the Zionist cause, they wanted to secure their safety and security, post-holocaust, within a system that was unusually partial to them. Yet, the majority of White South Africans involved in "the struggle" were Jewish. Many Jews identified as Communists. Many were in legal professions. Despite the benefits they enjoyed, many Jews experienced a "double marginality" of knowing that they were not entirely accepted as White while also feeling isolated from an organized Jewish community pandering to the White Nationalist government.

In his autobiography *Long Walk to Freedom,* Nelson Mandela reflects, "I have found Jews to be more broad-minded than most Whites on the issues of race and politics, perhaps because they themselves have historically been victims of prejudice."[5] Mandela's association with Jewish activists began at Johannesburg's University of the Witwatersrand (also known as Wits University), where he first enrolled as a part-time law student in 1943. Mandela's early encounters were with Harold Wolpe, Ruth First, and Joe Slovo, with whom he became firm friends and later hardcore activists in the struggle for freedom from apartheid. Although Wits University and the University of Cape Town were the only "open" universities admitting students of all race groups, students of color were excluded from all formal social events such as dances. "Non-White" students were also not allowed to join Sports Clubs or use the university's swimming pool.[6] In the same year, after completing his Bachelor of Arts degree by correspondence through the University of South Africa, Mandela served as an articled clerk at the Jewish law firm Witkin, Sidelskey, and Eidelman. This hire is significant as a limited number of White firms would consider employing Black people at that time.

Adler (2000) notes that among Whites, it was Jews who offered Mandela enormous support and encouragement. There were "those who hid him when he was forced to go underground; those who, as lawyers, defended him at trial; those who, as journalists, supported the anti-apartheid cause; and those politicians, like Helen Suzman, who made it their mission to see that Mandela and other political prisoners received the best treatment possible from a legal and penal system structured to humiliate and degrade Black prisoners."[7] Adler highlights the efforts of the South African Jewish writer, Nadine Gordimer, who covertly edited the now-famous speech that Mandela delivered in his defense at the Rivonia trial. Gordimer also "donated all the prize money from her 1991 Nobel Prize for Literature to the Congress of South African Writers, an organization aligned with the ANC" (ibid.).

Several Jews compromised the material comforts of their own lives of privilege to actively join forces with Mandela and the African National Congress (ANC) in this fight for human rights and social justice. Joe Slovo was the primary link between the Communist Party and ANC in the late 1950s. He collaborated with Mandela in shaping the military wing of the African National Congress known as UMkhonto we Sizwe.[8] In the film *Mandela: Long Walk to Freedom,* released in 2013, the actor Idris Elba recounts Mandela's long struggle, highlighting many Jews in South Africa who stood with him and marched with him, a testament to their understanding of oppression through their history in Europe. Adler (2000) asserts that Jews in the struggle against apartheid were also assassinated, tortured, mutilated, and imprisoned along-side their counterparts who were not White. Among them was Ruth First (a Jewish activist married to Joe Slovo), killed by a bomb planted by the South African security forces. The same state agents targeted Albie Sachs. Rowley Arenstein was banned for thirty-three years, longer than any other South African during apartheid (ibid.). Other Jews described in Mandela's autobiography *Long Walk to Freedom* include Arthur Goldreich (the décor and costume designer of *King Kong*), whose debonair persona and extravagant lifestyle provided the perfect cover for military operations of the ANC. Goldreich's farm called Lilieslief served as a hideout for Mandela (posing as a gardener) from 1961 until his arrest in the 1963 raid.

The Jewish community was divided in its response to apartheid. However, the active engagement of several Jews during the struggle became a source of pride when Mandela, heralded a hero, was finally released on February 11, 1990. The impact of the Jewish people on the political and social landscape of South Africa finds its parallel in the musical scene of South Africa and other countries during these tumultuous times of the apartheid era.

Jewish Influence on Music in South Africa and Abroad

The ensuing discussion of a few significant musicians in South Africa and abroad is not an assessment of each artist's "Jewishness." Instead, it is a commentary on the Jewish heritage of musicians who have impacted the musical landscape during the apartheid era. This connection demonstrates the broad swathe of Jewish musicians' experiences in different countries in the years leading up to the formation of The Peace Train. Among some of the most well-known Jewish women singers in pop culture are Barbra Streisand, Bette Midler, Diane Warren, Pink, Lisa Loeb, Regina Spektor (Russian-Jewish), and Carly Simon. Billy Joel, Adam Levine (lead singer of *Maroon 5*), Gene Simmons (Israeli American), Neil Diamond, David Lee Roth (lead singer of the hard rock band *Van Halen*), Paul Simon, and Art Garfunkel are easily recognizable performers having Jewish ancestry.

The dilemma of Jewish musicians discussed in Bernarde's *Stars of David: Rock 'n Roll's Jewish Stories* deals with a history of people in diasporas globally wanting to "fit in." Judah Cohen in McCollum and Hebert ((2014) expands the discussion of diasporas by addressing the "dialogue between the two populations that have historically represented classic paradigms for diaspora theory: Jews [. . .] and the African diaspora" (p. 152). This approach differs from many other studies that have looked at diasporas as a broader phenomenon or research of individual case studies. All the methodologies mentioned above are relevant in studies of diasporas. The glimpse offered here of Jewish musicians in diasporas is intended to touch on the instinct for survival in music where Jewish musicians are in the minority.

Jewish performers changed their names in an unprecedented manner even before the 1950s. Carole Klein became Carole King, British blues guitarist Peter Greenbaum dropped "baum" to become Peter Green before cofounding Fleetwood Mac in 1967, and writing "Black Magic Woman" that went on to become a sensational hit for Santana in 1970. The South African keyboard player and arranger Manfred Mann was instrumental in taking Bob Dylan and Bruce Springsteen to the top of the music charts with the songs "Mighty Quinn" and "Blinded by the Light." Manfred Mann may not have enjoyed such success as Manfred Lubowitz. The South African musician and composer, Trevor Rabin, is a contemporary of Sharon Katz. He enjoyed significant musical success in South Africa as a singer and guitarist for the rock band *Rabbitt*. Rabin moved to London in the late 1970s working as a solo artist and a producer. He finally relocated to Los Angeles, where he performed as a guitarist for the progressive rock band *Yes*. He also became a prolific composer of movie scores in the United States. Rabin's grandfather was a Lithuanian Jew, Gershon Rabinowitz, who arrived in South Africa toward the end of the nineteenth century. As with many Jewish families in diasporas, leaving out the last syllable/s of their names helped the Jewish people blend into the mainstream American culture and the Christian British and European cultures of countries like South Africa that were still under colonial rule.

Bernarde (2003) asserts that another reason that Jewish musicians "kept their pedigree quiet" was a fear of antisemitism and the possibility of losing work and their fans. However, the record producer Brooks Arthur (born Arnold Brodsky) observed that by the 1980s and the 1990s, "your [Jewish] pride was more covert back then, and now it's overt" (ibid., p. 4). Arthur had established his career with several hit singles as a sound engineer for Neil Diamond, whose parents were Jewish immigrants from Poland. Arthur also produced Adam Sandler's "Chanukah Song," which sold over a million copies. This turnaround for Jewish singers where their religious identity is no longer an impediment to commercial success is evident in the popularity of Matthew Paul Miller (born June 30, 1979). He is a rapper, reggae singer, beatboxer, and alternative rock musician, better known by his Hebrew name, Matisyahu. Bands such as the Beastie Boys, founded in 1981, comprised four young Jewish musicians from New York. They started as a hardcore punk quartet that evolved into a trio by 1983, touring with Madonna in 1985. Despite the media attention with Madonna, it was only after their collaborations with Black rappers that the Beastie Boys gained credibility with rap audiences. Their musical styles evolved over the decades, keeping the Beastie Boys relevant.

Paul Simon, a Jewish New Yorker, had a consequential impact on South African musicians' lives with whom he collaborated in the mid-1980s on his *Graceland* album (discussed in chapter 4). Simon's controversial visit to South Africa occurred after listening to a bootleg cassette recording of a song called "Gumboota" by a group called Boyoyo Boys. He was captivated by this township music. Simon recorded the song, retitled "Gumboots," with the popular Boyoyo Boys, adding new lyrics and melody while maintaining the fast-paced accordion-driven tempo reminiscent of the polka. Simon's time in a South African recording studio became a fruitful artistic endeavor with musicians such as the guitarist Ray Phiri among other African artists. The South African a capella choral group Ladysmith Black Mambazo founded by Joseph Shabalala, feature in two songs, cowritten by Simon and Shabalala, "Diamonds On the Soles of Her Shoes" and "Homeless" (with Zulu lyrics). Graceland won the 1987 Grammy Award for Album of the Year that brought international attention to the South African group. In 1993 (through fortunate circumstances), Ladysmith Black Mambazo went on tour with the Jewish musical activist Sharon Katz & The Peace Train. Bernarde (2003) describes Katz as "the daughter of Zionists, who moved to Israel while she stayed [in South Africa] to pursue her love of *mbaqanga*, *kwela*, and reggae music" (p. 3). The author describes Katz's songs as "beacons of unity and social justice [and that] her first U.S. release, *Imbizo*, in 2002 was filled with optimism and hope" (ibid.).

Johnny Clegg was a contemporary of Katz, born just two years earlier in 1953. He was a noteworthy South African artist whose mother was Jewish. Johnny Clegg (discussed later in this chapter) of *Juluka* and *Savuka* fame—created both interracial bands during the apartheid era. Clegg's maternal grandparents were Jewish Lithuanian immigrants. Since the seventies, audiences were familiar with Clegg's spectacular and energetic concerts featuring Zulu dances and songs that included Zulu and Swahili. An anthropologist and a musician, Johnny Clegg's crossover music embraced a blend of folk, rock, and *maskandi* guitar. He was lauded for his anti-apartheid messaging. Although Clegg resisted his Jewish roots growing up, he acknowledged and embraced his Jewish heritage during his later career with songs like "Jericho," "Jerusalem," and "Warsaw 1943." Sharon Katz and Johnny Clegg not only share their Jewish ancestry but also started their careers in academic fields and share a condemnation of racism and social injustices. Unlike Sharon Katz, whose focus has been grassroots efforts through music within communities in South Africa and abroad, Clegg became a commercially successful artist in South Africa and other countries. He died in 2019 at age 66.

There have always been tensions and taboos that have prevailed among Jewish people. Clegg's rebellion against Judaism as a young person raises the broader question of Jewish identity, whether this applies to Clegg specifically or not. Benarde (2003) describes a 1995 event when Katz's childhood American idol, Bob "Robert Allen Zimmerman" Dylan, walked into Temple Beth El and attended Yom Kippur Services in West Palm Beach while on tour in Florida. Dylan's appearance was a moment of great pride for the local Jewish community since Dylan had revealed that he was a born-again Christian in the late seventies. This simple act of going to the temple seems analogous to the prodigal son's return to the Jewish people. Scott Marshall (2017), a Dylan biographer, speaks of Dylan's spirituality in an interview as follows:

> Christianity can mean different things to different people; for Dylan, it seems it's more about the figure of Jesus than the following of an organized religion. Dylan's own Jewish roots cannot be denied, whether it's the revolutionary figure of Jesus in the first century or Dylan's childhood in Minnesota in the 1940s and 1950s, or his naturally slipping into synagogues as an adult. Dylan appears to be a child of God, not tethered to any religion for religion's sake, but trying to pursue the truth, clay feet, and all. I'm sure it hasn't been an easy trip.[9]

Dylan's pursuit of the truth and spirituality are an integral part of his craft as a musician. His output's highest recognition was best explained when he was awarded the Nobel Prize for literature in 2016. The Academy succinctly stated that he deserved the honor "for having created new poetic expressions within the great American song tradition."

The poetic sensibility lauded in Dylan's songs is also apparent in the lyrics of another legendary Jewish musician, Leonard Cohen. He was born into a middle-class Jewish family from Canada. His song, "Hallelujah," composed in the 1980s, is reportedly the most covered song of the twenty-first century.[10] Cohen's search in this song begins with the indefinable King David, the author of a book of psalms that forms the basis of worship for both Jews and Christians. These psalms provide insights into David as a poet and a musician that Cohen references in the lines, "I heard there was a secret chord/That David played, and it pleased the Lord." The divine expression of these lines contrasts with, "Your faith was strong, but you needed proof/You saw her bathing on the roof" as Cohen grapples with the more human transgressions of King David based on Psalm 51. "Her beauty and the moonlight overthrew you" speak to King David's succumbing to mortal temptation. Cohen's knowledge of these psalms is not a coincidence. At a press availability in London in 2014, upon the release of his album *Popular Problems*, Cohen describes his connection to Judaism:

Well, I grew up in a very conservative, observant family, so it's not something that I ever felt any distance from, so it's not something I have to publicize or display, but it is essential to my own survival. Those values that my family gave me—Torah values—are the ones that inform my life. So, I never strayed very far from those influences.[11]

The influence of Jewish musicians is prevalent among all genres of Western music. The music of the unapologetic American composer George Gershwin from Brooklyn, New York, whose parents' ancestry were Russian-Jewish and Lithuanian-Jewish. The breadth of his output is remarkable. On the one hand, he challenges scripture in "It Ain't Necessarily So" from his dramatic folk opera, *Porgy and Bess*, spawns the hit "Summertime," and then creates "I've Got Rhythm" that goes on to become a jazz standard. From Gershwin in New York to Schoenberg in Los Angeles (L.A.), there have always been notable Jews in music. From a Jewish family in Vienna, Arnold Schoenberg freed himself from the shackles of German music through serialism and atonality. He found personal freedom for himself and his family during the Nazi regime by moving to the United States. Schoenberg reflects poignantly on his cultural heritage with the last words on a sheet of music paper that says, "*Ich bin ein kleiner Judenbub*" (I am a little Jewish boy).

Katz's Awakening

Born in 1955 during the apartheid era of turmoil and angst, Sharon Katz grew up in a Jewish neighborhood of Port Elizabeth (now known as Nelson Mandela Bay) in Cape Province. At the age of fifteen, Katz was going to the townships with her friend, actor, and activist, John Kani.[12] Katz had met Kani by chance at a closed audience play performance of Athol Fugard's *The Just Assassins* hosted by the Progressive Party[13](a liberal political party against the White apartheid Nationalist Party in South Africa) in a church's basement. The powerful ending of that play with the killing of an innocent child during a Russian revolution and the singing of "Nkosi Sikelele iAfrica" was an intense experience for Katz. She describes being "riveted," stating that she was "moved to tears . . . it was my awakening" (Sharon Katz, documentary film *When Voices Meet*, 2015). Through her friendship with Kani (see Figure 2.1) and other Black actors, Katz became familiar with the workshops and plays of Athol Fugard at the Livingston Hospital. Rehearsals were held there at that time. Katz felt a deep ambivalence about her life since her father owned a factory in the mudflats area on the outskirts of Port Elizabeth, the setting of Fugard's play *Boesman and Lena*. This work focused on the lives of oppressed people of color in apartheid South Africa. She could not reconcile the hypocrisy of being taught about the holocaust by her parents when they were also perpetuating the oppressive system of government in their day to day lives. She describes her angst as being "completely untenable." Katz says that "the thing that saved me was my music" (Katz, personal communication, October 15, 2016). In the documentary *When Voices Meet* (discussed in chapter 4), John Kani speaks fondly of his relationship with Sharon Katz:

> Somehow, sometime life does it. It puts you in front of another kindred spirit—you connect—you never lose that connection [. . .] my friendship with Sharon. She's just a good spirit [. . .] to make this a better place for all. I was fifty-one when I voted for the first time in my life [. . .]; therefore, I remember 51 years of apartheid. We could see that the apartheid state was mounted on feet of clay, and all it needed was all of us to push at the same time, and it would crumble. I couldn't push from the Black side only; I needed Sharon to push from the other side. (Kani, *When Voices Meet*, 2015)

In the film, John Kani describes himself and his fellow actors as hardcore revolutionaries who were also members of the underground movement. He recalls his younger brother's concern about Kani bringing Katz to the township when she was as young as fifteen years old. Katz describes being hidden under a blanket in a vehicle to get into the Black townships, often in the company of her friend and fellow activist, John Kani (Katz, personal communication, October 15, 2016). Kani's brother's concern was with the growing list of White people they could not kill when the revolution came—among that list

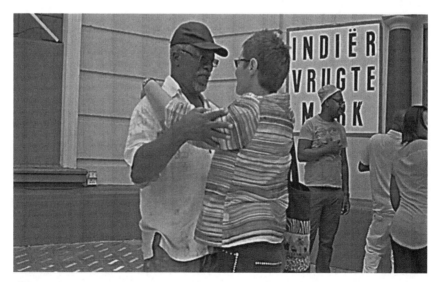

Figure 2.1   John Kani and Sharon Katz—Old Friends Greet Each Other at the Market Theatre in Johannesburg. Photo frame from the documentary DVD, *When Voices Meet*, 2015. Courtesy of Sharon Katz. Used with permission.

were Athol Fugard, the South African writer and activist, and Sharon Katz. Kani says, "She was a kid . . . she did not understand that we were terrorists. She thought we were good guys [. . .], so we protected her first from the truth of who we were; then, we protected her every time she crossed the line and came into the Black townships" (ibid.).

Katz has an extensive body of work as a musician and performer, engaging with many different communities over the years. She shared her substantial list of academic experiences with me, ranging from classroom to university teaching to her presentations at conferences and speaking engagements at several events.

International Presentations:

Cape Town Music Therapy Conference 1994
South African Music Educators Society Conference 1995, 1996
University of Ghana Panafest Symposium on Music and Healing 1998
Ethnomusicology Conference, Bloomington Indiana 1999
World Congress on Music Therapy, Washington DC 1999
Lesley University, Natanya, Israel 2007 & 2008
Lesley University Boston/Empower Peace: Women to Women Conference
    2008
Lesley University Boston, Arts in Healing Conference, 2015
Abraham Hospital, New York City, Music Therapy and Mass Trauma
Canadian Music Therapy Association, Halifax 2010 Keynote
Nova Scotia Music Educators Association Conference, Halifax 2013—Keynote
Acadia Association of Music Therapy Conference, Wolfville, NS
    2013—Keynote
California State University, San Francisco, Arts in Medicine Conference,
    2014
U.S. Peace Institute, Washington DC, 2016

Teaching Experiences with Courses Listed:

University of Durban-Westville, South Africa 1993–1997
Music Improvisation; Introduction to Music Therapy; Music Therapy and
    Community Development in the South African context.
Training the Trainer; The Peace Train as an African Model for Music Therapy
South African Teacher Training Colleges 1992–1998
Introduction to Music Therapy; The Role of The Peace Train in facilitating
    conflict resolution.
University of Ghana 1998–2000
Introduction to Music Therapy; The Role of The Peace Train as a musical
    movement for change in South Africa; South African Music and Songs of
    The Peace Train

Michigan State University 2008

Ending Apartheid with Music Therapy and The Peace Train: Towards an African Model of Music Therapy

University of the Arts, Philadelphia 2001–2005

The history of apartheid through music and the role of The Peace Train in facilitating social change

Philadelphia Teacher Training Institute 2006–2008

Music Therapy and Conflict Resolution; Converting gang members to Band members; The Peace Train model of Music Therapy

Lesley University, Israel 2008, 2009

Music Therapy, The Peace Train and Conflict Resolution; Facilitating peaceful coexistence in Israel/Palestine using the model of the Peace Train in South Africa; Building A Future with the youth of Israel/Palestine

Fredonia University 2009

Berkeley College of Music 2007, 2011, 2012, 2014

International Music Therapy Lectures: The role of The Peace Train as a musical movement for change in South Africa.

Wheelock College w Abigail Kubeka 2011

Introduction to Music Therapy; A musical history of South Africa and the ending of apartheid.

Wheaton College 2011

Introduction to Music Therapy; A musical history of South Africa and the ending of apartheid

Wheelock College in Music Dept. 2012

Introduction to Music Therapy; The role of The Peace Train as a change agent in the New South Africa; Peaceful conflict resolution through music therapy; Converting Gang Members to Band Members.

Acadia University, Nova Scotia 2013

The role of The Peace Train as a musical movement for change in South Africa at the ending of apartheid.

The impact of The Peace Train project on the lives of its participants twenty years later.

Music Therapy Symposium, City of Knowledge, Panama City 2013

Music Therapy and Apartheid; Music Therapy and The Peace Train; Improvisation techniques; South African Songs of Struggle, Change, and Liberation; The impact of The Peace Train project on the lives of its participants twenty years later.

California Institute of Integral Studies, Professor Expressive Arts Therapy, San Francisco 2014–2016

Advanced Seminars in the use of Music Therapy in Practicum Experience, South African Music & Dance; and The Peace Train as a model for Arts in Therapy for Social Justice and Conflict Resolution

Political and Social Change through Music

The multiple case studies of Sharon Katz elucidated in chapters 3–5, and her varied experiences demonstrate how music is created, experienced, and used in different and specific settings. The goal is positive outcomes for its participants, using music as an instrument for societal change. Katz sees her work as an effort to raise social consciousness and awareness of social justice through systematic musical engagement. Her activities include performances (small and large group), music workshops, and group therapy using music. More recently, Katz has reached diverse audiences through the screenings of a documentary that reveals video footage of her work since the 1990s (S. Katz, personal communication, October 15, 2016).

The anti-apartheid movements that emerged during this time are the backdrop against which the activism of Sharon Katz & The Peace Train emerged. The South African movements bore some resemblance to the protest movements that arose in the West during the 1960s. However, an understanding of the varied character of communities within the South African context in the late 1980s and early 1990s is necessary to unpack the complex nature of these movements fully. One such movement initiated by a group of White Afrikaner[14] musicians was known as "Voëlvry." Grundlingh (2004) describes their music as a "rock and roll style, with an overlay of punk[15] and hard-hitting lyrics (that) satirized the state, Afrikaans-speaking political leaders, the South African Defence Force, the apartheid system, and White middle-class values" (p. 485).

The "Voëlvry" musicians included Ralph Rabie (the composer/singer behind the pseudonym Johannes Kerkorrel—meaning Johannes Church Organ) and the *Gereformeerde*

[Reformed] Blues Band, André le Roux du Toit, also known as André Letoit (the singer/songwriter and writer behind the pseudonym Koos Kombuis—meaning Koos Kitchen), and James Phillips (the composer/performer behind the pseudonym Bernoldus Niemand—meaning Bernoldus Nobody). These musicians set off on the Voëlvry tour in 1989, visiting major Afrikaans universities in South Africa (Jury 1996, 103–106). Although there may be some speculation as to the selection of pseudonyms of musicians on the Voëlvry tour, the satirical innuendo of their surnames draws attention to several social issues of the time. The selection of "Kerkorrel—Church Organ" speaks to the core of the upbringing of many of these middle-class musicians whose aim was to free themselves from the shackles of a church, the Dutch Reformed Church, that endorsed the policy of apartheid. The choice of this name was taking on one of the pillars of Afrikaner nationalism. The choice of "Kombuis—Kitchen" highlights the perpetuated stereotype of the woman's place being in the kitchen and the home, thus relegating women

to a more subservient position in society. "Kombuis" may also allude to "Kitchen Dutch," a reference to the Afrikaans language as a "kombuis taal" or "kitchen language."

Jani Allan (2016) recalls an interview originally published in a *Sunday Times* column on July 9, 1989. In this interview, Kerkorrel expresses his disdain for the South African Broadcasting Corporation and his assessment of Afrikaans as a language when he says, "'Kyk na daai mense wat by die SAUK werk. And they are controlling the taal [. . .]. It's a kombuis taal. They've tried to turn Afrikaans into English." Letoit adds during that interview, "The right word to use is *ons wil die Afrikaner demitologiseer—* demythologise the Afrikaner. Afrikaners are also people."[16] This quote places into perspective their pride in their Afrikaner identity. As White South Africans and as Afrikaners, they rejected the policies of apartheid, wanting to change the dynamics of an unjust society through their music. "Niemand— Nobody" is the paradoxical choice of being an insignificant person and yet representing everyone who shared his beliefs. The musical style and attitude of the "voëlvryers" were overtly aggressive toward the state. This dark and hard-hitting attitude stands in stark contrast to the more conciliatory and all-embracing stance of Sharon Katz & The Peace Train.

Further, the band's name, "Voëlvry" (made up of two Afrikaans words, "voël" [bird] and "vry" [free], meaning "outcast" or "as free as a bird") was a satirical wordplay on the Dutch Reformed Church (Nederduitse Gereformeerde Kerk [NGK] in Afrikaans). This church supported the government's policy of apartheid.[17] Voëlvry, a band of Afrikaner musicians, with their explicit anti-apartheid message, rock and roll style, and "biting social commentary," unleashed an enthusiasm referred to as "Boer Beatlemania." They enjoyed media attention, the impact of which was to highlight the fact that there were Afrikaners who disagreed with the Nationalist establishment. Voëlvry tried to articulate, through their music, their objection to the idea of South Africa being the God-given right of the Afrikaner *volk*.[18] They saw South Africa as a country that belonged to all its people irrespective of race, color, or creed.

In Figure 2.2 the lyrics of the song, *Swart September* (Black September), written by André Letoit, highlight the political and social climate of South Africa following the Vaal Uprisings that began September 3, 1984. This series of uprisings began in the Transvaal and marked the start of "the longest and most widespread period of Black resistance to White rule. By the end of 1984, approximately 150 people died in political violence. The number of deaths increased to 600 by September 1985 as the revolts spread across the country. The government declared a State of Emergency."[19] *Swart September* encapsulates the social and political chaos and complexity of South African society at that moment. It is a poignant song that expresses the tragic aspects of lives—for people of color—as they navigated the effects of the apartheid policies. There are also the subversive endings of lines of the last two verses, where parodied words of the national anthem reflect the social reality of the apartheid era.

With its simple piano and guitar folk-rock style reminiscent of Bob Dylan, *Swart September's* darkness conveys several thought-provoking references and themes. Omitted are additional verses with some repeats. The last two verses from *Swart September* parody "Die Stem" (the National Anthem of South Africa during apartheid) where, for example, the words "Uit die blou van onse hemel" have been rewritten as "Uit die blou van ons twee skole."

Swart September	Black September
Plant vir my 'n Namibsroos	*Plant for me a Namib rose*
Verafgeleë Welwitschia	*A distant Welwitschia*
Hervestig hom in Hillbrow	*Transplant it to Hillbrow*
En doop hom Khayelitsha	*And christen it Khayelitsha*
September is die mooiste, mooiste maand	*September is the fairest, most beautiful month*
Viooltjies in die voorhuis	*Violets in the parlor*
En riots oral in die land	*And riots throughout the land*
Die aand was vrolik om die vure	*This evening it was merry around the fires*
Gatiep was olik by die bure	*Gatiep was not well at the neighbors*
Die tyres het gebrand	*The tires were on fire*
Daar aan Mannenberg se kant	*Over in Mannenberg*
Al die volk was hoenderkop	*All the people were as drunk as headless chickens*
Die Casspirs was vol guns gestop	*The Casspirs were packed full of guns*
En die vroue by die draad	*And the women at the fence*
Het eerste die gedruis gehoor	*Were first to hear the rumble*
Tjank maar Ragel, oor jou kind	*Weep, Rachel, for your child*
Die boere het hom doodgemoer	*The boers have beaten him to death*
Groot masjiene oor die land,	*Great machines across the land,*
September '84	*September '84*
Die seisoen wat brand en aanhou brand,	*The season that burns on and on*
'n Lente bleek en dor	*A spring both bleak and dry*
Waar swartes sonder pas	*Where blacks without passbooks*
Nog skuifel langs die mure	*Still shuffle along the walls*
En Niemandsland se as nog waai	*And no-mans-land's ash still blows*
Oor Niemandsland se vure	*Over no-mans-land's fires*
Die swarte sonder pas	*The blacks without passes*
Ja die swarte sonder pas	*Yes, the blacks without passes*
Skuifel langs die mure	*Shuffle alongside the walls*
Verlustig hom in derde klas	*Feeling deprived in third class*
[...]	*[...]*
Uit die blou van ons twee skole	*Out of the blue of our two ideologies*
Uit die diepte van ons heimwee	*Out of the depths of our nostalgia*
Uit ons ver-verlate homelands	*From our long-forgotten homelands*
Waar die tsotsies antwoorde gee	*Where the tsotsies give the answers*
Oor ons afgebrande skole	*Over our burned-out schools*
Met die kreun van honger kinders	*With the whimper of hungry children*
Ruis die stem van all die squatters	*Rises the call of all the squatters*
Van ons land, Azania	*Of our land, Azania*
Ons sal traangas, ons sal Treurnicht	*We'll be teargassed, but we won't cry*
Ons sal klip gooi as jy vra	*We'll throw stones if you just ask*
Ons sal dobbel in Sun City	*We'll gamble in Sun City*
Ons vir you, Suid Afrika	*Just for you, South Africa.*

Figure 2.2 Lyrics of a Song from the Album, *Niemandsland,* **Released May 31, 1985.**
Transcriptions of the recording and Afrikaans translations by the author.

In the song's opening lines, Letoit refers to the Namib rose noted for its hardiness in desert conditions. Transplanting this desert rose to Hillbrow, a bustling urban setting, draws a parallel with the forcible relocation of Black people to Khayelitsha (a Xhosa word meaning "our new home"), a suburb on the outskirts of Cape Town. Letoit then juxtaposes the image of violets in the parlor (of presumably White homes) with the violence of riots (in Black neighborhoods). There is a constant contrast of ideas in Letoit's lyrics. He shines a lens on the more everyday joys of human beings, such as standing around a fire and becoming inebriated. Letoit contrasts this with the violent act of burning tires and tire "necklacing," which refers to the unrest of the 1980s when tires were set alight as roadblocks or to kill individuals where a gas-filled tire around a victim's neck would be set ablaze. Mannenberg was a "Colored" area where violence erupted often, and the Casspirs[20] created a threatening presence with their guns.

The last two verses of this song are most striking. In a direct reappropriation of the Afrikaner national anthem, Letoit refers to South Africa as "Azania." The choice of "Azania" was a direct assault on Afrikaner nationalism as pan-Africanists selected the term as the new name for South Africa. According to Hopkins (2006), Letoit was banned from Rand Afrikaans University after he performed *Swart September* there in 1988 (p. 132). Letoit captures images of a socially and politically dysfunctional society: a society of poverty (hungry children); a society of homeless people (squatters); a society deprived of education (burned-out schools); a society run by hooligans (tsotsi); a society of hypocrisy (the gambling and indulgences of Sun City enjoyed by the rich and privileged in a homeland created for the disenfranchised).[21] As the ultimate wordsmith, Letoit employs the Dutch Afrikaner surname, Treurnicht,[22] which means "not to cry," highlighting the futility of an Afrikaner stance and apartheid policy that was not sustainable. Kerkorrel sums up the course of the future in South Africa in the Allan (2016) interview when he says, "It's the dawning of a new age. It's up to this generation to come to an agreement with Blacks. It's pragmatic." Despite the enthusiasm surrounding Voëlvry, Grundlingh's assessment of this mainly "White" anti-apartheid initiative asserts:

Voëlvry did rock the boat, but more gently than has often been assumed. It was mainly a White middle-class movement that sought to redefine elements of Afrikaner ethnicity in the eighties without fully rejecting it. Although the movement was largely restricted to the White community and its proselytizing effects were uneven, it was a brave stand to take at the time. As a social movement, it was overtaken by events from 1990 onwards, and predictably, it lost its impetus; the boat did not sink. The Voëlvry stance taken in the eighties still resonated sixteen years later to help manufacture an anti-apartheid past for a younger generation of Afrikaners grappling with a sense of identity in quite a different context. (2004, 510)

Although there are differing views on the impact of White musicians in the anti-apartheid struggle, what is clear is that the White voices of dissension created a fissure among the ranks of the White privileged class of South Africa between the ruling White minority and the "nonWhite" majority. Many layers of protest exerted anti-apartheid pressure from Blacks and Whites. Both nationally and internationally, all efforts, whether conciliatory or confrontational, contributed toward the eventual dismantling of apartheid. This system of forced segregation was not sustainable.

The musical climate leading up to the dismantling of apartheid boasts crossover (see Glossary) bands—Juluka, Savuka, Mango Groove, Bright Blue, and Zia—all-important precedents to the musical intervention of Sharon Katz. Some White musicians integrated rock and *boeremusiek* (Afrikaans for country dance music) as a vehicle for their "protest" music. At the same time, others also incorporated "Black" idioms such as *marabi*, *kwela*, township jazz, or *maskanda* (see Glossary), among others, into their compositions of favorite music. Johnny Clegg, a singer and guitarist, achieved national and international success since the 1970s with his combination of western musical styles with *maskanda*. Clegg learned the Zulu language and traditional Zulu music and dance styles through his friendship with Sipho Mchunu (a migrant worker and street musician in Johannesburg). Mchunu and Clegg performed as a duo at first but later assembled a band called Juluka (Zulu word meaning "Sweat").

Johnny Clegg, with Juluka, avoided confrontations with the apartheid government by playing church halls and township venues. Baines (2008) describes Juluka's resistance to the South African regime as being coded from how band members dressed, how they moved, and the lyrics that they sang. Clegg's "adoption of traditional Zulu attire in combination with Western dress, and the appropriation of Zulu dance routines amounted to a politicized cross-cultural collaboration" (p. 107). Baines asserts that "Clegg's performances suggest that Whiteness (and also Zuluness) is a matter less of race than of style, and that style itself is a cross-cultural phenomenon, working against the grain of racial essentialism"[23] (p. 108).

Sharon Katz, working as a grassroots activist rather than a commercial band in the 1990s, did not deal with censorship issues as Juluka had done with their first debut single, *Woza Friday*,[24] released in 1976. However, the struggle for democracy was very much alive, and the apartheid policies were still in place. Like Clegg, Katz embraced Zulu as well as other African languages such as Xhosa and Sotho. Katz's style also reflects her adoption of traditional African dress in combination with Western dress. Another similarity is the appropriation of African dance routines in her performances. Clegg's training as an anthropologist informed his rejection of the essentialist notion of ethnic identity. Katz trained as a music therapist, and she shared her personal belief that race is a social construct[25] (Katz, personal interview, October 15, 2016). Both musicians renegotiated their identities based on their own experiences. These different experiences demonstrate how "explorative, shifting, and malleable White identities during the apartheid era were at times . . . although the regime invested much in racialized identities" (Baines 2008, 111).

Juluka's first album, *Universal Men*, released in 1979, highlighted the plight of the migrant workers whose work in the cities forced their separation from their families (Gorlinski, n.d.).[26] Ballantine (2004) argues that:

> At a time when the inhumanity and the contradictions of the apartheid system were reaching a breaking point, Juluka [. . .] embodied a number of potent cultural transgressions [. . .] they offered hope: an often-euphoric promise that the final struggle against apartheid could be won. Yet from the start, the band's musical integrations were awkwardly worked. Certain symbols for "White" and "Black" met in the songs' own interiors—but typically as binary, and often unequal oppositions: "White" represented largely by an English folk-rock style derived from the 1960s, which carried the song's narrative, and "Black" virtually relegated to the choruses. The lyrics addressed topics relevant to the anti-apartheid struggle, but commonly in two languages (English and Zulu) split along the same lines (109–110).

Ballantine adds that despite the awkward integration of "Black" and "White," it was a "winning formula." Mchunu from the band Juluka went back to farming in the mid-1980s, and the band (renamed Savuka), found international fame with the 1982 hit "Scatterlings of Africa" (reissued on Clegg 1999), reaching the top fifty in the United Kingdom and number one in France and elsewhere (ibid.). The "protest" element in popular music among White musicians that included collaborations with Black musicians and a blending of musical styles foreshadowed the post-apartheid integration in popular music. While not commercialized like Johnny Clegg, Sharon Katz's music also combines "Black" and "White" musical styles. At one level, her music appeals to a racially diverse audience and, at another level, offers hope with the "euphoric promise that the final struggle against apartheid could be won" (ibid.). Sharon Katz & The Peace Train emerged at a time that was a "rainbow" moment musically in which several musicians were working across traditional musical boundaries to create new music. While this moment lasted into the twenty-first century, it certainly had its roots in this time.

Musical activism does not enjoy a prolific range of scholarly articles or studies. As historian Grant Olwage (2008) has observed:

> There has been little investigation of how music was used by political movements, either within the country or in exile. In addition, little detailed research has been conducted on freedom songs, the ubiquitous but largely informal and un-professionalized genre that was probably the dominant musical medium of popular political expression. (p. 157)

Researchers in different areas of study have, to some extent, explored the intersection of music, politics, culture, and social change. Some scholars such as Nettl (2005) emphasize the significance of early researchers such as Merriam and Seeger. In his ethnographic study of Flathead music, Merriam (1967) highlights the interdisciplinary nature of music research in culture. He states that "All people, in no matter what culture, must be able to place their music firmly in the totality of their beliefs, experiences, and activities, for without such ties, music cannot exist" (p. 3).

Seeger (1977), whose thoughts on musicology continue to inform the field, states that the ultimate purposes of musicology are "the advancement of knowledge of and about music [and] of the place and function of music in human culture" (p. 217). Katz's music speaks to the political and social change that she hopes to impact while appealing to participants' cultural and musical ties when performing the songs. For Americans performing South African music, the connection is the message: the singing of hope, optimism, and unity when the oppressive forces within a society threaten to crush the dignity and spirit of its people. This response is the healing through music to which Katz subscribes. Besides, the melodies and the lyrics of songs are easily accessible to both children and adults alike. Katz adapts the complexity of her music to include as many participants as possible. Therein lies its value.

In the concluding paragraph of his book, *How Musical is Man?* John Blacking (1973, 116) maintains that:

> In a world such as ours [. . .] it is necessary to understand why a madrigal by Gesualdo or a Bach passion, a sitar melody from India, or a song from Africa [. . .] a Cantonese opera, or a symphony by Mozart, Beethoven or Mahler, may be profoundly necessary for human survival. . . . It is also necessary to explain why, under certain circumstances, a "simple" "folk" song may have more human value than a "complex" symphony.

Nettl (2005) describes Merriam, Seeger, and Blacking as "giants [who all] express the same principle: for understanding music, the significance of its relationship to the rest of culture is paramount" (p. 215). The music of

Katz, whether it is an Afro-pop arrangement of a traditional Xhosa song like *Sanalwami* or a wistful ballad such as *Rocking Chair*—all her songs reflect South African experiences that resonate among people from varying back-grounds and different cultures. Her eclectic musical style in a western idiom with African elements transcends cultural boundaries in Africa and the West. Her lyrics speak to human experiences not confined to South Africans alone. Moreover, Katz has maintained her relevance by updating and adding new music and musical styles into her repertoire since the first Peace Train Tour of 1993. Although her message has remained constant, her music has evolved to keep abreast of current trends.

The Role of "Freedom Songs" and "Peace Songs" in Social Transformation

Peace songs and freedom songs provide another point of entry to the study of musical activism. The popularity of peace songs in the United States, for example, is demonstrated in opposition to the Vietnam War (1959–1975). As the voices of dissent grew within the country, Americans saw a parallel rise in the popularity of peace songs, which peaked in the late 1960s. Singers such as Pete Seeger (1919–2014), Joan Baez, and Bob Dylan (both born in 1941), the group Peter, Paul, and Mary, and many other performers placed the spotlight on social and political issues through their music, serving as a commentary of the times. During my interview with Sharon Katz in October 2016, she spoke of these singers' influence mainly on her musical journey as a child. Whether writers, activists, or the media have used the terms "Songs of Resistance" or "Songs of Liberation" or "Peace Songs," the opposition to political and social havoc and a need for peace was articulated through song.

When it seemed that the Vietnam War was never going to end, the Americans vented their ongoing frustrations through their output of songs. Among "Songs of Resistance" are many songwriters who boast prolific works. *The Times They Are A-Changin'* (identified by Katz as having a profound influence on her music) penned by the folk artist Bob Dylan in 1963 sums up the opposition to the Vietnam War and the angst of the Civil Rights Movement in America. In the first verse of this poetic political ballad, Dylan's ability to speak truth to power is on display. He urges all people to observe and understand the social and political landscape in the first verse. He says, "*Come gather 'round people wherever you roam: And admit that the waters around you have grown.*" Dylan follows this call with the cer-tainty of consequences that will follow when he says, "*And accept it that soon, you'll be drenched to the bone.*" This dire warning is followed by a call to action through the words, "*If your time to you is worth savin,' then you better start swimmin' or you'll sink like a stone.*" He concludes this verse with the memorable title line, *"For the times they are a-changin'."*[27] Dylan's creative output earned him, not without controversy, the 2016 Nobel Prize in Literature.

The interaction among artists provides insights into their sensibilities that influence historical perceptions. Nyairo (2016) describes a moving encounter between Bob Dylan and Joan Baez that took place on August 28, 1963:

> Dylan attended the civil rights "March on Washington for Jobs and Freedom." Not long before that, he had experienced discrimination first-hand when he was denied a hotel room on account of his appearance and his obscurity. Joan Baez, who had by that time achieved national success as a folk singer, stepped in and secured a room for Dylan. He spent the rest of that night writing *The Hour When the Ship Comes In.* That was the song that he and Baez performed for the "March on Washington," building up the crowd's demand for change. The chorus had the same protest message as *Blowin' in the Wind.* Dylan never attended another civil rights march. But by that time, in Baez's view, Dylan had "provided the biggest song in our anti-war, civil rights arsenal."

The opposition to the Vietnam War and the civil rights movement in the United States occurred at a time that paralleled the intensity of the liberation struggle in South Africa with the imprisonment of Nelson Mandela and many other South African political activists. There was a resonance between the political and social climates in both countries. The 1969 Woodstock Festival held in Bethel, New York, captured the imagination of people all over the world. Billed as "An Aquarian Exposition: 3 Days of Peace and Music," it featured famous musicians such as Ravi Shankar, Joni Mitchell, Joan Baez, the folk-rock group, Crosby, Stills, Nash & Young, Santana, and Jimi Hendrix. His song *Machine Gun* demonstrates his protest of the Vietnam War in a stark and jarring manner. Through his virtuosity on guitar, Hendrix simulates the sounds of war, most notably the imitation of machine guns. Other sounds include those of bombs and explosions, as well as the plaintive sounds of wounded soldiers or people crying. Not to be silenced, Hendrix's lyrics reveal his criticism against the death and suffering caused by the Vietnam War. These lines could easily have applied to the violent destruction of South African society. *"Tearing my body all apart/Evil man make you kill me."* He describes the tragic nature of war since we are all connected through our humanity *"Evil man make me kill you/Even though we're only families apart."* The violent horror of war is emphasized in, *"Yeah, machine gun/ Tearing my family apart."*

In contrast to Hendrix, some "Peace Songs," more closely aligned with Katz's message, have sustained popularity over several decades. One of the most memorable songs is John Lennon's *Imagine,* released in 1971. The second verse speaks directly to a call for peace. The lines, *"Imagine there's no countries/It isn't hard to do,"* speak to the physical divisions of countries through borders that lead to discord among people. The words that follow are a reminder that human-made separations and religious fanaticism destroy peace. Lennon says, *"Nothing to kill or die for/and no religion too."* This yearning for a utopian world is reiterated in the line, *"Imagine all the people/ Living life in peace."* Finally, in the chorus, the composer speaks to skeptics when he declares that he is not alone in his thinking. He says, *"You may say I'm a dreamer/but I'm not the only one."* He goes on to implore the listener, *"I hope someday you'll join us / and the world will be as one."* In an analysis of *Imagine* by Bridget Minamore and Peter Aspden in *The Guardian*, dated June 26, 2017, the writers' muse:

> It is an intimate, vulnerable song, an exhortation to love and peace that sounds exhausted from beginning to end. There is a Sisyphean tension in that delicate four-note motif that introduces each line of the verse. [. . .] Too introspective to be anthemic, not pompous enough to make a stirring hymn, Imagine is the tentative vision of a secular skeptic, who knows that imagination will never be enough. And that is what makes it so moving. The evanescence of hope is Lennon's theme; never has the utopian dream sounded so fragile.

The evanescence of hope described in Lennon's *Imagine* (1971) is ever-present in Katz's work with The Peace Train. Her activism projects a resilience and stoicism that the power of social interaction and cultural exchange through music will achieve hope and healing. It was not only the music of the United States that had a lasting impact on Katz. Across the Atlantic Ocean in Jamaica, Bob Marley's *One Love* was written in 1976 amid the Jamaican elections' turmoil and violence. Marley wanted to provide safety, peace, and shelter for all who needed it. The reggae musical style of *One Love* stands in sharp contrast to the balladic quality of *Imagine*. However, Marley expressed a similar sentiment to Lennon's *Imagine* (1971) call for peace, explicit in the lines: *"One love, one heart; Let's get together and feel all right."* Again, this harks back to conciliatory and therapeutic aspects of activism described in the definition.

Many social and political events sparked this dissatisfaction expressed through song. On May 4, 1970, the National Guardsmen in the United States attacked anti-war demonstrators on the campus of Ohio's Kent State University. Student protests were sparked by President Richard Nixon's announcement on April 30, 1970, that U.S. troops would invade Cambodia, intensifying the already unpopular war in Vietnam. The attack on unarmed students in Ohio became known as the Kent State Massacre. Penned as one of rock's most remembered protest songs, *Ohio,* written by Neil Young of

Crosby, Stills, Nash & Young fame, served as a poignant reminder of this tragedy. Young's opening lyrics, "*Tin soldiers and Nixon's coming*," are explicit. These lines evoke the image of toy soldiers being manipulated through Nixon's orders. "*Soldiers are gunning us down/Four dead in Ohio*" speaks of the lack of trust in the National Guard and the horror of soldiers killing their own people. The lyrics of this song revealed anti-war and anti-Nixon sentiments. As a result, the song was banned on some mainstream radio stations in America.[28] Despite some of the adverse reaction to the music, Crosby wrote in the liner notes of the *CSN* collection, "For me, *Ohio* was a high point of the band, a major point of validity." He explained, "There we were, reacting to reality, dealing with it on the highest level we could—relevant, immediate. It named names and pointed the finger."[29]

The protest consciousness of the 1960s and 1970s motivated by social and political events was propelled in part by the music of those decades. In South Africa, the 1960s and 1970s political climate was no less intense than in America. On March 21, 1960, police opened fire on an unarmed crowd demonstrating against pass laws outside a police station the pass laws in the township of Sharpeville in Transvaal—today a part of Gauteng (Province). Sixty-nine people died, and according to the official inquest, 180 suffered injuries in the Sharpeville Massacre. The aftermath of this devastation resulted in the banning of the African National Congress and the Pan Africanist Congress. Both these South African political organizations continued their work in exile, inspiring the formation of anti-apartheid movements in several countries, including Britain, Holland, and Sweden.

Protests from the international community and later boycotts placed pressure on the South African government to dismantle their policy of apartheid. However, the atrocities continued with the imprisonment of Nelson Mandela on June 12, 1964. In a poignant folksong, *Ballad of Sharpeville*, by Ewan MacColl and Peggy Seeger (sister of Pete Seeger) released in 1978 by Smithsonian Folkways Recordings, this husband-and-wife duo lay out the events of that tragic day in South Africa. It is symbolic that upon the dismantling of apartheid, President Nelson Mandela chose Sharpeville as the site at which, on December 10, 1996, he signed into law the country's new constitution.

Among the many notorious instances of brutality during the apartheid era is the Soweto uprising of June 16, 1976. These riots were precipitated by a government decree that imposed the Afrikaans language as the medium of instruction in half the subjects in higher primary (middle school) and secondary school (high school). This protest against education—in what many Blacks considered "the language of the oppressor"— resulted in two students' deaths, Hastings Ndlovu and Hector Pieterson. They were both killed by police. Hundreds of more students sustained injuries during the chaos that followed.[30] Then in 1977, the death of Steve Biko while in detention drew attention not only to the systematic killing of Black people but also the "immorality of the apartheid government" (Malisa and Malange in Friedman (ed.) 2013, 314).

Musicians from South Africa and abroad penned anti-apartheid songs that shone a light on the human rights violations of the apartheid government. In his song *Biko*, Peter Gabriel, an English musician, laments a heart-breaking event in South Africa. He sings of "*September '77—Port Elizabeth weather fine*," beginning with a mundane description of an ordinary day. The lines that follow are an ominous revelation that "*It was business as usual—In police room 619.*" The chilling reality of the brutality of the apartheid system is described. The beauty of the weather outside stands in stark contrast to the callous and routine murders of political prisoners by the South African apartheid police force. The lamentation that follows is filled with angst: "*Oh Biko, Biko, because Biko; Oh Biko, Biko, because Biko.*" The song's opening in the Xhosa funeral song's style with the Xhosa words "Yihla Moja," meaning "Come Spirit," acknowledges Biko's death. There is a sense of finality in the blunt statement that "*The man is dead. The man is dead.*" The words that follow, "*When I try to sleep at night, I can only dream in red,*" may allude to the socialism with which the South African anti-apartheid movements identified. This song gives one of the many victims of apartheid a name and a face. International outrage is reflected in "*the eyes of the world are watching now, watching now.*"[31]

Among South African musicians, the "nature and spirit of ubuntu"[32] is clearly expressed "by blending the collective with the personal" (Malisa and Malange in Friedman (ed.) 2013, 314). Hugh Masekela's song *Bring Him Back Home* illustrates South African musicians' profound insights into the societal dysfunction created through apartheid. Gans (2014) describes the inspiration for this song in an article written for the celebration of Masekela's seventy-fifth birthday with his long-time friends Paul Simon and Harry Belafonte at the Lincoln Centre in New York City:

> He then performed his song *Bring Him Back Home* (Nelson Mandela), inspired by a letter from Mandela smuggled out of prison in April 1985 wishing the trumpeter a happy 46th birthday. The song, which became an anthem of the anti-apartheid movement, anticipated the day Mandela would walk freely down the streets of Soweto.

Matthew Greenwald (2017) describes the music as a testament to Mandela and Masekela's relationship in his review. Greenwald asserts that Nelson Mandela is the most famous modern-day political prisoner and one of the biggest fans of Hugh Masekela. Musically speaking, he describes the melody of *Bring Him Home* as "a buoyant, anthemic, and grand series of chords and trumpet riffs, filled with the sense of camaraderie and celebration that are referred to in the lyrics." He adds that "the vocal choir during the joyous chorus is extremely moving and life-affirming."[33] Not only does Masekela create a celebratory instrumental musical background in his song, but he also addresses through his lyrics a more profound expectation of the release of Mandela. The freedom of Mandela symbolizes the political liberty of a nation. In referring to Mandela reuniting with Winnie Mandela (his wife while imprisoned) and going home to Soweto and the people of South Africa, Masekela (in a musical style much different from Hendrix) also draws attention to the disruption of families—in this instance—through the senseless imprisonment of political leaders. The apartheid government's actions exacerbated an already abnormal society's chaos in a state of constant conflict.

One of the enduring messages of musicians as activists is evident in Joan Baez's words in her April 7, 2017, plea for social justice in her Rock and Roll Hall of Fame speech at Brooklyn's Barclay Centre in New York, reported in *Rolling Stone*. Early in her remarks, Baez describes the influences of Pete Seeger and Harry Belafonte in her life during the 1960s and 1970s:

> When I was 16, my aunt took me to a Pete Seeger concert. And my mom brought home a Harry Belafonte album. Though Pete was not in any way gorgeous like Harry, he was already committed to making social change. He paid a high price for holding fast to his principles. I learned the meaning of "taking a risk" from Pete. The Cold War was getting a foothold and ushered in a shameful period in this country [America].[34]

Although Katz met Pete Seeger and the Belafonte family several decades later, elucidated in chapters 4 and 5, these overlapping musical influences among musicians determined to make a difference to the social and political landscape through musical endeavors are striking. Musicians such as Baez, Seeger, Mitchell, Belafonte, and Dylan have been significant sources of inspiration for Katz because of her shared belief in the many causes of activism they represent through music (S. Katz, personal communication, October 15, 2016).

The world's circumstances had evolved since the 1960s and 1970s when many Americans expressed their disagreement with the Vietnam War. Still, the message of Baez at her induction in 2017 reveals a steadfast belief in social justice. Baez stated that since I was sixteen, she became a student and practitioner of nonviolence, both in her personal life and as a way of fighting for social change. She believes that using her voice in the battle against injustice has given her life deep meaning and eternal pleasure. Baez touched on the quality of empathy when she says that she has met and "tried to walk in the shoes of those who are hungry, thirsty, cold and cast out, people imprisoned for their beliefs, people of color, the old, the ill, the physically challenged, [and] the LGBTQ community." Baez concluded her speech with the sincere hope that people would replace brutality with compassion as she believes that people are the only ones who can create change.[35]

Katz had written the song *We Are the Children of South Africa* in 1993. Still, the overlap of messaging between Baez and Katz is apparent in the following lines from the song, discussed in greater detail in chapter 5 when she says, "*We're hoping for change and at last we can see, Without color blinding our vision of peace.*" The final comments of Baez's speech make the powerful connection between activism and music. She states, "When all of these things are accompanied by music, the music of every genre, the fight for a better world, one brave step at a time, becomes not just bearable, but possible, and beautiful" (ibid.).

On April 5, 2017, David Browne of *Rolling Stone* described Baez's importance as more than just musical. He refers to her as "the moral center of the anti-war and social-justice movements that arose in the Sixties." Among Baez's many acts of activism, Browne cites her: singing at the 1963 March on Washington; creating the Institute for the Study of Nonviolence in Northern California; visiting Vietnam during the war, and going to jail for eleven days for participating in a sit-in at a military induction center.[36] Baez, who performed with other iconic musicians at the Woodstock Festival, created an American history event that became a cultural touchstone. There are some overlaps between American protest songs that focus on civil rights, labor movements, and anti-war sentiments.

Joni Mitchell's song *Woodstock* describes the sense of wonder and empowerment derived from the experience. In verse three, she sings: "*By the time we got to Woodstock, We were half a million strong*," describing the momentum that the festival had acquired. This sense of euphoria is captured in, "*And everywhere there was song and celebration.*" This joy contrasts with the ominous sight of "*bombers riding shotgun in the sky.*" Mitchell cleverly counters this image with optimism and hope for a world without war when she says, "*they were turning into butterflies above our nation.*"[37] In a most unforeseen way, Sharon Katz, with her young singers from South Africa in tow, crossed paths with her "childhood idol, Joni Mitchell" (Katz 2016) in New Orleans (described in chapter 4).

The idea of protest through peaceful means was not a unique phenomenon. While the Americans protested the Vietnam War (1955–1975), another strong political outcry emerged across the Atlantic Ocean in South Africa, where the policy of apartheid had become firmly established. The documentary film *Amandla! A Revolution in Four-Part Harmony* (2003), directed by American filmmaker Lee Hirsch, directed a powerful film about music's centrality during the anti-apartheid struggle. He highlights the role of music in the struggle against apartheid from the 1940s to the 1990s. Through interviews, musical performances, and historical film footage, South Africans such as Miriam Makeba, Hugh Masekela, Abdullah Ibrahim, and Vusi Mahlasela, among others, take the viewer on a journey through the apartheid history of South Africa and the role of freedom songs on the social and political landscape.

Byerly (2008) argues that the documentary presents a one-sided view as it focuses only on the Black struggle through music. He asserts that it fails to "recognize the complexity of the revolutionary process, or other players in the arena [and] it fails to recognize the complex yet inevitable 'swings' between both antagonistic and conciliatory strategies" (p. 262). Sharon Katz & The Peace Train represent some of the "other players" in this complex process who adopted a conciliatory strategy.

Several South African songs have unique messages tied to the struggle for racial equality, the release of political prisoners within their own country, and the liberation of a nation from minority rule. Mandela (1994) describes the effect of freedom songs in *Long Walk to Freedom* poignantly during his arrest and detention among other political activists in 1956 when he was accused of treason by the apartheid government:

> Reverend James Calata spoke on African music—and sang in his beautiful tenor voice. Every day, Vuyisile Mini, who years later was hanged by the government for political crimes, led the group in singing freedom songs. One of the most popular was: "Nans' indod' emnyama Strijdom, Bhasobha nans' indod emnyama Strijdom" (Here's the Black man, beware the Black man, Strijdom). We sang at the top of our lungs, and it kept our spirits high. (p. 175)

The fate of political prisoners appeared bleak during the apartheid era, while the Nationalist government retained control. South African artists, as well as every sphere of life, were impacted to some extent. The political turmoil that began in 1948 continued well into the late 1980s and early 1990. During this time, many South African musicians became internationally recognizable and commercially successful pre-apartheid and post-apartheid, such as Miriam Makeba and Hugh Masekela. Washington (2012) emphasizes the responsibility of these artists:

> As South African jazz exiles, Miriam Makeba and Hugh Masekela are certainly better-known names in the music world, and Makeba especially was instrumental in bringing the issue of apartheid to the consciousness of the international community. However, their musical influence in the West, though jazz-tinged, was really strongest in more commercial styles of music. (p. 92)

Compact discs that bear the same title a President Mandela's autobiography (*Long Walk to Freedom,* 2002) deliver a representative sample of three decades of South African music from the 1960s to 1990s, including the music of Makeba, Ladysmith Black Mambazo, and Vicky Sampson, among others.

Shirli Gilbert's chapter on "Singing Against Apartheid: ANC cultural groups and the international anti-apartheid struggle" provides insights into two of the ANC's most significant projects in exile to "explore how culture was actively recruited to promote the anti-apartheid struggle internationally" (2008: p. 156). Gilbert chronicles the work of two groups. The Mayibuye Cultural Ensemble, a highly successful London-based group, incorporated narrative, poetry, and song in their performances. The Amandla Cultural Ensemble, led by trombonist Jonas Gwangwa, became an outspoken voice of the ANC throughout Africa, Europe, South America, and the Soviet Union, among other places. This group was different from Mayibuye in that:

> it offered large-scale, increasingly professionalized performances incorporating choral singing, jazz, theatre, and dance. Its performances were intended not only to raise international awareness about apartheid but also to present an alternative vision of a more dynamic, inclusive South African culture. (Gilbert 2008, 156)

Although Katz brought her brand of South African culture to an international audience much later than Mayibuye or the Amandla Cultural Ensemble, they have all played their part in bringing the anti-apartheid movement to the attention of international audiences. As Gilbert (2008) states of the two groups she documents:

> Though the differences between them on the levels of form, content, approach, and presentation were dramatic, their shared, overriding objective was diplomatic—projecting an image of South Africa that would encourage the international community to lend its political and financial support. (p. 177)

Some artists who remained in South Africa during apartheid were discouraged. Olwage (2004) describes the frustration of some musicians from within South Africa toward those in exile:

> Many Black artists who remained in South Africa throughout the struggle . . . resent the spotlight given to exiles who were away during the height of the struggle, leaving, as singer Dorothy Rathebe pronounced, "us 'inziles' to keep the home fires burning." (p. 263)

Among the "inziles" were also bands like Bayete and Sakhile. There were also folk musicians of the more progressive elite, such as the Lindberg-duo,

Jeremy Taylor, and Roger Lucey (Byerly, 2013). Katz collaborated with Dorothy (Dolly) Rathebe and Abigail Kubeka on her album *Double Take* (2011), demonstrating her willingness to embark on creative ventures with fellow South African musicians. They had all suffered the effects of apartheid in one way or another. Katz is in a unique position straddling both camps as an exile and an "inzile." Although she had left South Africa in the 1970s to study and live in the United States, she returned in the early 1990s to South Africa. Katz believed, in the title of one of her songs, *The Time Is Right Today* (discussed in chapter 5). Many strands of music emerged at this time. A comprehensive record of all artists must include grassroots performers like Sharon Katz. They were "engaging through song" during the days of apartheid within South Africa to forge friendships and unity and initiate change through collaboration in a racially divided society.

All musicians from South Africa against apartheid, irrespective of their direction, belonged to a united group in their disenfranchisement. Washington (2012) addresses this issue with specific reference to jazz musicians:

> One axis describes a trajectory over time (from the late apartheid era to the beginnings of democracy in South Africa) of an evolving aesthetic that moves from protest to celebration. The second axis delineates differences between the possibilities and the formations of jazz music made by some South African jazz musicians who left South Africa during the apartheid era and some of those who remained. (p. 91)

Washington argues that since there are differences between the cultural and practical practice of jazz pre-apartheid and post-apartheid. There are also very different trajectories that were followed by South African jazz musicians depending on whether they emigrated after the Sharpeville Massacre in 1960 or remained in the country. For instance, jazz musicians in exile initially followed the American and European tendencies toward a more avant-garde style. However, they also began to highlight indigenous South African rhythms. Among the many paths followed in South Africa, some jazz musicians managed to update and pay homage to *marabi*, *mbaqanga*, *maskanda*, township jazz, and other home-brewed styles and genres. The expression of indigenous music not only spoke to the historical experience of South Africans. It made a political statement. Washington describes these different trajectories as "the inxile/exile concurrence" (2010, 92). This evolution of jazz into a post-apartheid era finds a parallel in other genres of music.

Musical Activism as a Global Phenomenon

Sharon Katz is a musician and music therapist who has developed a unique model to realize her grassroots activism through music. During my research, I stumbled upon *Sing My Whole Life Long: Jenny Vincent's Life in Folk Music and Activism* by Craig Smith. This book chronicles the life of musical activist Jenny Vincent, an American woman born in Minnesota in 1913 and raised in Chicago. It sheds light on the urban folk song movement in mid-twentieth-century progressive politics and life in New Mexico. With this biography, Smith fills a gap in the history of women's involvement in the mid-twentieth century's political and cultural movements.

There are uncanny parallels between the American-born Jenny Vincent and the subject of my research, Sharon Katz, even though Katz grew up in the 1950s in South Africa. Vincent was educated at a progressive private school and went on to higher education at Vassar College. As a White child in South Africa during the years of apartheid, Sharon Katz enjoyed access to excellent schools and universities. Vincent married and set off with her new husband to trace British author D.H. Lawrence's life in Europe. That trip led them to Taos, New Mexico, and the home of Lawrence's wife, Frieda. Vincent was reportedly "enchanted" with the people and the community of New Mexico. Her introduction to international folk music at an early age influenced her life's work as a cultural activist for Hispano music in New Mexico.

Similarly, Katz felt drawn to African music from an early age. At the age of fifteen, she began sneaking into African (Black) townships with her friend John Kani, whom she met by chance at a Fugard play production described earlier. This association with African people in creative settings and the Black townships was a transformative experience for Katz as a sensitive and artistic teenager coming into her own.

Vincent's interest in working with children parallels that of Katz. Vincent and her husband opened a progressive boarding school on a ranch they purchased at San Cristobal north of Taos. The school recruited students from outside the state and admitted local pupils at no cost to ensure diversity in the student body.

Katz's efforts in South Africa are remarkable. She achieved two goals in creating a 500-voice choir from four separate racial segments of South African society. First, there was cultural diversity among students. Second, recruiting musicians from segregated communities (Black, Indian, Colored, and White) ensured all major race groups' engagement. This inclusion strategy gave credence to her first multiracial concert, *When Voices Meet*, at the Durban City Hall in Kwa-Zulu Natal (one of four major provinces in South Africa). The large-scale production of Katz's concerts with children and young adults differs from Vincent's. The constant desire to take her message through performances from town to town and community to community with The Peace Train in tow sets Katz apart. A significant difference between Vincent and Katz is that Katz, as a trained music therapist, approaches all her music from the standpoint of hope and healing. Vincent's sojourns from town to town in New Mexico were similar to the Hungarian twentieth-century composer Béla Bartók. She recorded local musicians playing and singing old folksongs, often in Spanish.

Vincent began working with the Rocky Mountain Farmers Union (RMFU), becoming the Taos County educational director. Her singing at RMFU events led to other singing opportunities. It was an invitation to sing for a class of public school students that completely shifted her focus from classical piano to folk songs. In that performance, she defied school policy by singing in Spanish, the home language of students. Moments like this would become increasingly typical in Vincent's life—the use of folksong to inspire her listeners and express a political point of view. Throughout her life, Vincent combined her love of music with her commitment to the community.

The accordion was Vincent's instrument of choice to accompany her repertoire of international folk songs, singing at diverse events from a miners' union meeting to a kindergarten classroom visit. She hosted several visitors at her ranch at San Cristobal, many of whom represented the mid-twentieth-century American cultural left: Henry Wallace, Howard Da Silva, Earl Robinson, and Ronnie Gilbert, and other notable guests. Vincent's politics led to the National Folk Festival, in which she had participated frequently, to rescind her invitation to perform. Despite these setbacks, Vincent remained involved with her community and committed to her work in New Mexico. Vincent subscribed to the belief that folk music is the vehicle through which we most meaningfully communicate and find common ground within the global community. Craig Smith's treatment of Jenny Vincent is highly readable though lacking in providing a substantive backdrop of the tumultuous politics and history during that period of history.

Performing with Pete Seeger, Woody Guthrie, Malvina Reynolds, and Earl Robinson, Vincent shared a passion with these social activists. They used music as a voice for world peace, civil liberties, and human rights. Among Katz's musical activism highlights are stage performances for Nelson Mandela and Al Gore, a collaborative recording with Sting, Elton John and Tina Turner, a Grammy-nominated CD "Imbizo," and recordings with South African legends Abigail Kubeka and Dolly Rathebe. Pete Seeger joined Sharon Katz in impressive performances dedicated to her humanitarian work in building a school in South Africa. Concert performances include the New Orleans Jazz & Heritage Festival and the Getty Museum in L.A., Epcot Center in Disney World. Katz has keynoted Music Therapy and Music Education Conferences in Halifax, Nova Scotia, and Panama City. Since Katz composes most of her songs, she has actively recorded several CDs. She has enjoyed much recognition through awards received for her 2015 documentary, *When Voices Meet*, at various film festivals from the Durban International Film Festival in South Africa (July 2015) to the World Music and International Film Festival in Washington DC (August 2015), and to more than ten film festivals in the ensuing year. These are well-documented in my research.

Vincent and her second husband supported such causes as the Salt of the Earth strike, Native American rights, and the rising Chicano movement. Through it all, Vincent raised a family and continued her music. Vincent continued performing well into her 1990s, and in 2006 was honored by the University of New Mexico and the New Mexico State Historic Preservation Division for her many decades as a prominent cultural activist. She died in 2016 at the age of 103. Katz and her partner Marilyn Cohen (manager, producer, and director of The Peace Train) have toured together with The Peace Train since the 1990s in South Africa, the United States, Canada, Cuba, and Mexico. Katz has worn many hats over the years as a musician, a therapist, an activist, and an educator. Katz and the American-born Cohen have an enduring personal and professional partnership spanning over thirty years.

The cultural and musical activism of Katz and Vincent also compares with that of the Argentine-Israeli conductor Daniel Barenboim and the late Palestinian-American academic Edward Said. They founded the West-Eastern Divan Orchestra in 1999. Barenboim's orchestra forms a striking parallel with Sharon Katz's Peace Train Project. In a 2006 BBC Reith Lecture, "Meeting in Music," Barenboim argues:

> In times of totalitarian or autocratic rule, music, indeed culture in general, is often the only avenue of independent thought. It is the only way people can meet as equals, and exchange ideas. Culture then becomes primarily the voice of the oppressed, and it takes over from politics as a driving force for change. Think of how often, in societies suffering from political oppression, or from a vacuum in leadership, culture took a dynamic lead. We have many extraordinary examples of this phenomenon. Some [are] that writings in the former Eastern Bloc, South African poetry and drama under apartheid, and of course Palestinian literature amidst so much conflict.[38]

Barenboim goes on to describe the importance of culture in creating connections and understanding among people. He is very clear about the primary purpose of the West-Eastern Divan project. Barenboim and Edward Said used this orchestra to foster musical collaboration among musicians from Arab countries and Israel. Their idea was validated when they realized that the musicians were like-minded in their commitment to music. Despite the political divide among countries, music is the common denominator creating a convergence of cultures. This orchestra of young musicians came from countries in the Middle East—Egyptian, Israeli, Jordanian, Iranian, Lebanese, Syrian, Palestinian, and Spanish backgrounds. According to Solveig Riiser

(2010, 20–21), "we may well read the orchestra as a project aiming at conflict transformation; it certainly aims at the social transformation of its musicians, and through this transformation encourages reconciliation and mutual understanding on a larger scale."

Rachel Beckles Willson (2009) regards Barenboim's conceptualization of the orchestra as a "utopian republic" but adds that he downplayed its political significance by asserting that its utopian quality was a function of music. Both Said and Barenboim agreed that the orchestra had demolished Arab stereotypes about Israelis and Israeli stereotypes about Arabs. The "utopian republic" became a Middle East model, where the various peoples listened to and understood one another without prejudice (p. 320). This statement bears a striking similarity to Katz's reflections on the formation of The Peace Train, which served a similar purpose of initiating contact among people through a shared cultural experience. The West-Eastern Divan orchestra aimed at bringing together young people from different countries from the Middle East region. The Peace Train sought to bring together people from segregated racial groups and different political affiliations within a single country. A study of The Peace Train also explores possible connections between acts of musical activism and social utopianism.

Elena Cheah (2009) presents a unique perspective of the West-Eastern Divan Orchestra in her book, *An Orchestra Beyond Borders: Voices of the West-Eastern Divan Orchestra*. As a professional musician and assistant to Daniel Barenboim, Cheah presents musicians' stories from the orchestra. Their views, attitudes, and their hopes are shared. They may have opposing voices, but they express their thoughts, never silenced. "Each musician simply opens a window into the soul of the orchestra, which is unimaginable to an outsider" (p. 1). Similarly, The Peace Train participants of July 2016 in the United States provide a window into their private worlds (some of their original work is shared in chapter 5 with their permission)—their struggles and hardships, joys, and sorrows. Through a cathartic evening of prose, poetry, dance, and song the night before their final performance in Washington DC for the Mandela Day Celebrations, participants laid bare their souls.

NOTES

1. The Group Areas Act No. 41 divided urban areas into racially segregated zones "where members of one specific race alone could live and work" (Thompson 1990,194). Group areas were created "for the exclusive ownership and occupation of a designated group" (Christopher 1994,105). It further became "a criminal offence for a member of one racial group to reside on or own land in an area set aside by proclamation for another race" (Dyzenhaus 1991, 71).

2. Often, grown Black men were referred to as "boys" during the apartheid era as a way of reducing Black men to less than equal status as that of White men. It was a derogatory and insulting term. Maids were demeaned in a similar manner, being referred to as "girls" when many were mothers and grandmothers.

3. Transkei represented a historic turning point in South Africa's policy of apartheid and "separate development." It was the first of four territories (referred to as Bantustans) to be declared independent of South Africa. In creating bantustans or homelands, the vast majority of Black people were forced out of urban South African cities thus entrenching the segregation of Whites from Blacks. Although intended as a self-governing area, the homelands were unable to support themselves as the agricultural land of those areas were dry and inhospitable. "As a result, millions of Blacks had to leave the Bantustans daily and work in the mines, for White farmers and other industries in the cities. The homelands served as labor reservoirs, housing the unemployed and releasing them when their labor was needed in White South Africa" http://www.sahistory.org.za/article/homelands. The homelands were incorporated into the new nine provinces in 1994 when apartheid ended in democratic South Africa.

4. In Community and Conscience (The Jews in Apartheid South Africa), Gideon Shimoni provides a detailed account of the emigration of Jews to South Africa.

5. Nelson Mandela, *Long Walk to Freedom* (Boston: Little, Brown and Company, 1994, 62).

6. Bruce Murray, Mandela and Wits University. *Journal of African History* 7, Issue 2 (Cambridge, July 2016), 271–292.

7. Franklin Adler, South African Jews and Apartheid. *Macalaster International* 9, Article 12 (2000), 185–197, http://digitalcommons.macalester.edu/macintl/vol9/iss1/12.

8. In both Zulu and Xhosa (two African languages spoken in South Africa), Umkhonto we Sizwe means "Spear of the Nation."

9. Accessed May 28, 2020, at https://www.hollywoodreporter.com/news/bob-dylans-spirituality-explored-new-biography-1011277.

10. "Without music, would we even be Jewish?" by Norman Lebrecht in The Guardian, March 1, 2014.

11. Information accessed May 29, 2020, at https://www.cinchreview.com/leonard-cohen-on-being-jewish/13585/.

12. Bonisile John Kani is a Tony Award-winning South African actor, playwright, director and activist. He was born in 1943 in the Eastern Cape in South Africa. Kani joined the Serpent Players (a group of actors whose first performance was in the former snake pit of the zoo) in Port Elizabeth in 1965 and helped to create many plays that were performed and very well received. His most famous work is Sizwe Banzi is Dead and the Island, cowritten with Athol Fugard and Winston Ntshona, in the early 1970s.

13. The Progressive Party, established in 1959, was a liberal party in South Africa that opposed the ruling National Party's policies of apartheid. Its only member of parliament for thirteen years was Helen Suzman. In 1975, it was renamed the Progressive Reform Party; in 1977 it was called the Progressive Federal Party; today the Democratic Alliance names the party as its earliest predecessor.

14. An Afrikaans-speaking person of European descent, especially Dutch.

15. Punk rock music is defined as "rock music marked by extreme and often deliberately offensive expressions of alienation and social discontent." Accessed May 16, 2018, at http://www.merriamwebster.com/dictionary/punk%20rock.

16. Accessed March 18, 2016, at http://janiallan.com/2016/03/18/afrikaner-pride-passion-mixed-fun-laughter-new-era-boere-punks/.

17. "The NGK until 1986 supported the government's policy of apartheid (separate development for the races) and had commissioned several studies to develop theological justification for it. Their findings were rejected by Reformed churches in Europe and the United States and the NGK was excluded from membership in the World Alliance of Reformed Churches (WARC) at Ottawa in August 1982. [. . .] In 1986, however, the Dutch Reformed Church denounced its own former attempts at the biblical justification of apartheid, and in 1989 it condemned apartheid as a sin." Accessed August 16, 2017, at https://www.britannica.com/topic/Dutch-Reformed-Church.

18. Volk is an Afrikaans word meaning "people."

19. Accessed May 20, 2018, at http://www.sahistory.org.za/article/township-uprising-1984–1985.

20. The Casspir referred to an armored vehicle deployed in South Africa during the apartheid era. The name is coined from an anagram of Council for Scientific and Industrial Research (CSIR) and South African Police (SAP). Accessed May 23, 2018, at https://www.collinsdictionary.com/dictionary/english/casspir.

21. The Bantustans or homelands were areas designated by the apartheid government where the majority of the Black population was relocated to prevent them from living in the urban areas of South Africa. It was a mechanism of the apartheid system aimed at the removal of Blacks from the South African political system.

22. "Andries Treurnicht (born February 19, 1921, Piketberg, (South Africa)—died April 22, 1993, Cape Town), SouthAfrican politician. A preacher in the Dutch Reformed Church (1946–1960), he later achieved high office in the National Party as a strong supporter of apartheid. In 1976 his insistence that Black children be taught Afrikaans led to the Soweto uprising. In 1982 he left the National Party to form the Conservative Party, which opposed F.W. de Klerk's decision to end apartheid. He came to support the idea of a separate White homeland within South Africa." Accessed May 23, 2018, at https://www.britannica.com/biography/Andries-Treurnicht.

23. Essentialism is "the view that categories of people, such as women and men, or heterosexuals and homosexuals, or members of ethnic groups, have intrinsically different and characteristic natures or dispositions." Accessed June 3, 2018, at https://en.oxforddictionaries.com/definition/essentialism.

24. Woza Friday was Juluka's first release. It was rejected by SABC's Zulu radio station because the combination of English with Zulu was considered "an 'insult to the Zulu people'; a form of cultural censorship by language purists" (Baines 2008:107).

25. "The school of thought that race is not biologically identifiable." (Accessed June 3, 2018, at https://sociologydictionary.org/social-construction-of-race/.

26. Accessed May 24, 2018, at https://www.britannica.com/biography/Johnny-Clegg.

27. Accessed August 22, 2017, https://bobdylan.com/songs/times-they-are-changin/.

28. Accessed October 30, 2016, at http://www.pophistorydig.com/topics/tag/crosby-stills-nash-ohio/.

29. Accessed October 30, 2016, at http://ultimateclassicrock.com/csny-ohio/.

30. Accessed September 2, 2016, at http://overcomingapartheid.msu.edu/sidebar.php?id=65-258-3.

31. Accessed September 2, 2016, https://genius.com/Peter-gabriel-biko-lyrics.

32. "A person is a person through other persons, or——I am because we are. In his explanation, Mandela touches upon the multifaceted nature of Ubuntu, as well as the way one feels Ubuntu as an innate duty to support one's fellow man" (C. E. Oppenheim, 2012, 369).

33. Accessed September 7, 2016, http://www.allmusic.com/song/bring-him-back-home-nelson-mandela-mt0030437954).

34. Accessed January 30, 2018, http://www.rollingstone.com/music/news/read-joan-baezs-moving-rock-hall-of-fame-speech-w475770.

35. Accessed January 30, 2018, http://www.rollingstone.com/music/news/read-joan-baezs-moving-rock-hall-of-fame-speech-w475770.

36. Accessed January 30, 2018, http://www.rollingstone.com/music/features/joan-baez-the-life-and-times-of-a-secret-badass-w474962.

37. Accessed March 26, 2017, at http://jonimitchell.com/music/song.cfm?id=75.

38. Accessed July 9, 2015, at http://downloads.bbc.co.uk/rmhttp/radio4/transcripts/20060428_reith.pdf.

Chapter 3

Glimpses of Musical Activism on a Transcontinental Journey

The time is right today. Let's get together South Africa (America)
The world is changing, and the time is right
To walk together into the light
It's time for changing and rearranging
We've got to sing together black and white
The time is right today. Let's get together South Africa (America)

—*The Time is Right Today* by Sharon
Katz (1993/Adapted 2016)

EXPLORING ACTIVISM

When I first contemplated documenting the musical activism of Sharon Katz & The Peace Train, my focus was the Peace Train Tour of 1993. I planned to go from the United States to South Africa and interview the participants of that 1993 tour. Besides, I also wanted to meet with Mama Mary Lwate of the Good Shepherd Organization in Mabopane, an hour's drive from Johannesburg, South Africa. I believed that a visit would provide a more detailed understanding of the relationship between Mama Mary Lwate and the nonprofit organization Friends of The Peace Train, founded by Katz in the United States. My research evolved into a multi-case study as knowledge of significant cases emerged.

At the beginning of my investigation, I did not know that Katz had been trying to complete the documentary, *When Voices Meet*, which premiered in July 2015. The American Peace Train Tour of July 2016 was created only after my interviews with participants of the first Peace Train Tour of 1993 and the documentary's screenings in July 2015. This study became a dynamic process. I realized that the documentary and the tour of 2016 were too substantive to omit from my analysis. As it relates to Katz's life, the background material provides the backdrop against which I outline three of my five cases in this chapter, which constitute a part of my research's multiple case study. Stake (2006) clearly outlines the rationale for a multiple case study:

> A multi-case study starts with recognizing what concept or idea binds the cases together. Sometimes this concept needs to be targeted [. . .] the cases to be studied may each have a different relationship with the quintain.[1] Some may be model cases, and others may have only an incidental relationship. If other considerations are satisfied, cases will be selected because they represent the program or phenomenon [. . .] when cases are selected carefully, the design of a study can incorporate a diversity of contexts. (p. 23)

There are pros and cons to using this type of research design. While evidence from this type of study is considered robust and reliable, it can also be extremely time-consuming and expensive. These are challenges that I have worked hard to overcome. The parameters of my research extend to the end of The American Peace Train Tour of 2016. However, Sharon Katz & The Peace Train have continued with their goal of transcending barriers. They are traveling, collaborating, and performing in Mexico, Cuba, and other parts of the United States, celebrating diversity and promoting unity (Katz, personal communication, February 18, 2020).

Three Case Studies of Musical Activism:
Music Therapy: "From Gang Members to Band Members"
Performances: The South African Peace Train Initiative beginning in 1993
Humanitarian work: Friends of The Peace Train

Case Study One: Music Therapy "From Gang Members to Band Members"

Katz studied English, African Government, and Law in South Africa and then Music Therapy at Temple University, Philadelphia, in the United States in 1981. Katz has practiced as a music therapist, educator, social activist, performer, and conflict resolution consultant since 1983. She has worked in prisons, schools, universities, mental health facilities, drug and alcohol rehabilitation centers, youth empowerment projects, HIV/AIDS orphanages, and community development programs. Katz's use of music therapy techniques to heal individuals and communities has earned her a reputation for converting "gang members into band members."

As part of her music therapy studies at Temple University, Katz served an internship, working with prisoners in Pennsylvania. The residency was at a mental health wing of a detention center housing prisoners who were at risk among the general prison population for various reasons (suicidal, at risk of being attacked because of the nature of their crimes, and so on). According to Katz, this was a unique program undertaken by the Hahnemann University Hospital in Philadelphia, affiliated with Drexel University College of Medicine. It was an opportunity for Katz to work with prisoners using group music therapy.

The detention center's music studio had drums, keyboards, guitars, xylophones, and other percussion instruments. Katz used songs with which they were familiar as a point of entry to building trust within the group. This experience eventually led to songwriting and improvisation. Katz recalls that the prisoners with whom she worked were mostly men, many of whom had been convicted of heinous crimes from rape to murder. Katz reflected that it was challenging for her as a woman to deal with this group of individuals. She also realized that many of the prisoners had been victims of abuse themselves. It was rewarding when they reached places in themselves through this group music therapy that may not otherwise have occurred. A similar experience is documented by Mikail Elsila (1998) at Ryan Prison in Detroit, Michigan, whose conclusions speak to aspects of social change and healing described by Katz:

> Maybe the best the songwriting class can do is allow me to learn more about prison, allow people in prison to gain personal power, and allow all of us to critique and analyze the nature of crime and punishment. This jibes with imagining social change as a combination of people with privilege learning how to share power and people who have been denied privilege learning how to demand power, while all parties learn compassion and how to analyze larger systems of oppression. Before power can be demanded, however, one must feel good about oneself and feel as if one deserves power. Music in prison has this potential to forge feelings of personal power. (p. 8)

During Katz's internship, the prison assigned a deaf woman prisoner— removed from the general prison population—to Katz for music therapy. The woman's infanticide crime (drowning her children during an attempted suicide) made her a target of violence among the women prisoners. According to Katz, she was a mentally ill woman who reached a significant breakthrough in music therapy. Katz recalled the woman rolling up the rug in the room to feel the music's vibrations through her bare feet. This case was incredibly compelling among Katz's many music therapy experiences (Katz, personal communication, October 15, 2016).

During these years of practicing as a therapist, Katz also worked with middle-school boys at a Reform School in Philadelphia. Every class of approximately twelve students worked with Katz to create bands, one for each unit. These were groups of heterogeneous students from the streets of New York to the inner cities of Philadelphia. They were Black, White, and Hispanic young boys with musical preferences that ranged from country to rap to pop. Katz describes these groups of students as initially insulting each other and fighting with one another. She taught them to listen to each other's music. Katz reminded them that they were not forced to like the music, but they did not have to attack each other. Using what Katz describes as the "Group Therapy Music Model" she had developed, it was the beginning of converting these gang members into band members playing keyboards, guitars, drums, among other instruments. Without realizing that her return to South Africa would take place in the early 1990s—it was not preplanned—Katz continued her work in music therapy settings, gaining extensive experience over ten years in the United States. Katz describes this experience as her preparation for her next endeavors in South Africa, as it served her well in the years that followed.

In the years leading up to Katz's return from the United States to South Africa, Katz was actively immersed in training and working as a music therapist. Her work with prisoners and disturbed youth in small group settings, using music as the vehicle for healing and rehabilitation in the United States, provided the foundation for the large-scale musical endeavors she developed in South Africa.

In an article written for *Voices: A World Forum for Music Therapy*, Katz (2011) articulated her understanding of the connection between music therapy and music performance in creating her "Peace Train" model. Since this is a model that draws heavily on group participation and community engagement, it is worth noting that Katz's initiatives may be seen as Community Music Therapy where the larger cultural, institutional, and social context is taken into consideration. Ruud (2004) describes this practice as "music therapists crossing the boundaries between therapy and community music-making" (p. 12). Herein lies Katz's strength. She is both a trained music therapist and an accomplished musician.

This marriage of music therapy and community music is not new. For instance, in indigenous cultures, the entire community may participate in rituals that include music (See Stige 2003, Gouk 2000). Ansdell (2014) distinguishes music therapy and community music, describing each as its own practice and discipline that "has developed further along its own path, with forms of compelling alignment and collaboration." The role of Community Music Therapy as it applies to the work of Sharon Katz & The Peace Train is best encapsulated in the following description:

[as] systemic interventions, how music can build networks, provide symbolic means for underprivileged individuals or use music to empower subordinated groups. Music has again become a social resource, a way to heal and strengthen communities as well as individuals. [. . .] Musicking thus will be seen as a kind of "immunogen behavior," that is, a health performing practice, in the same spirit as Pythagoras when he practiced his music at the root in our [Western] culture. (Ruud 2004, p. 13)

Sharon Katz embarked on her unforgettable return to South Africa in the spirit of healing and strengthening communities.

Case Study Two: The South African Peace Train Initiative

Prelude to the South African Tour

Nelson Mandela (1994) describes the opening speech of F.W. de Klerk before the South African Parliament on February 2, 1990, as a "breath-taking moment" (1994, 485) as the head of state "truly began to dismantle the apartheid system and lay the groundwork for a democratic South Africa" (ibid.). Mr. Mandela was released from prison on Robben Island after 27 years on February 11, 1990. This momentous event energized South Africans eager for change. It prompted a global response with Mr. Mandela receiving "telegrams from all around the world, from presidents and prime ministers . . . so many journalists, from so many different countries (1994, 494–495).

After an extensive African tour following his release, Mr. Mandela flew to London in April 1990 to attend a concert held in his honor at Wembley Stadium in London. Mandela (1994) describes the experience as follows:

> Many international artists, most of whom I never knew, were performing, and the event was to be televised worldwide. I took advantage of this to thank the world's anti-apartheid forces for the tremendous work they had done in pressing for sanctions, for the release of myself and fellow political prisoners, and for the genuine support and solidarity, they had shown the oppressed people of my country. (1994, 500)

In Philadelphia, the release of Nelson Mandela and the enthusiasm of musicians and activists created a sense of urgency in the heart and mind of Sharon Katz. She was determined to return to South Africa to do whatever she could to support this tide of change. Katz knew that democratic elections would soon occur, even though negotiations were ongoing (Katz, personal communication, October 15, 2016). In 1992 Katz, accompanied by her

American-born partner, Marilyn Cohen, returned to South Africa without any
financial support. Katz (2016) describes this period:

> I had my guitar, and I just went around trying to find work. One of the places I
> went to was the Playhouse (Theatre) in Durban. It was called NAPAC.[2] There
> was an opportunity [. . .] they hired me for a couple of workshops because they
> could see my experience with children, with youth. There was a spot open for a
> multicultural production. I took that opportunity and ran with it. We had to do
> something huge. Let's bring 500 children together [. . .] to make it into a 500-voice
> choir. They had never had anything like that before. In fact,—I knew they didn't.

Figures 3.1 and 3.2 (a salvaged poster and a ticket for the 500-voice concert)
represent the realization of Katz's vision for an integrated choir. Choral
competitions for each of the four racially segregated education departments (Black, White, Colored, and Indian) were common in the 1990s. The
Education Director of NAPAC recommended the best choirs in Kwa-Zulu
Natal to Katz based on her knowledge of these competitions. Armed with a

**Figure 3.1   The Upper and Lower Portions of a Salvaged Poster Advertised the 500-
Voice Concerts at the Durban City Hall.** Courtesy of Sharon Katz. Used with permission.

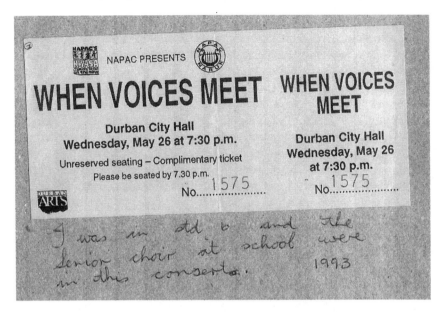

Figure 3.2 An Entrance Ticket to May 26, 1993, 500-Voice Choir Concert at the Durban City Hall. Courtesy of Sharon Katz. Used with permission.

list of winning choral groups, Katz began meeting with the music superintendents from each separate education department to get their project's approval. Her experiences at the Indian, Colored, and Black schools were very positive, where music teachers were willing to performing in this production. Katz (2016) recalls that "the [administrations of] White schools were harder. They were much more stand-offish about the whole thing because they were nervous. The music teachers, however, were open."

Without a doubt, Katz readily acknowledges that recruiting singers was expedited because she had this knowledge of the very best choirs. Katz refers to the words of one of her "graduates" of The Peace Train, Priya Shukla (a young woman I interviewed in Durban). She also appears in the documentary *When Voices Meet* (2015). Shukla states that "the tide was turning" in South Africa, making people more receptive to any effort to bridge the racial divide among South Africans.

Interviews with Participants on the South African Peace Train

During my visit to Durban, South Africa, in July 2015, I conducted interviews with nine individuals who had been participants in the South African Peace Train Tour of 1993. Unfortunately, two individuals with whom I had intended to meet, a medical doctor (a child during the tour of 1993) and a school administrator (a teacher, parent, and chaperone during the tour of 1993), had urgent professional matters to attend to during our scheduled times. Although I tried to reschedule our interviews, the potential interviewees were unavailable. All nine interviewees appear in the documentary, *When Voices Meet*, and the two individuals I did not meet. Nine of the eleven individuals articulate some of their experiences in the documentary. I attended the screening of the film in July 2015, after the completion of my interviews.

The purpose of the interviews with the South African Peace Train participants was to obtain multiple Peace Train experience perspectives. As the primary technique for data collection for this case study, I contacted potential interviewees or critical informants who had different backgrounds based primarily on race. Since the apartheid policies had separated South Africans based on race, it was essential to listen to people's insights from different backgrounds, using a sampling strategy. This method facilitated an understanding of the phenomenon under investigation. "Such persons not only provide insights into a matter but also can suggest sources of corroboratory or contrary evidence" (Yin 1994, 90).

Since the qualitative approach of thematic analysis is appropriate for interviews, this analysis method was selected. According to Braun and Clarke (2006), thematic analysis is a method used for "identifying, analyzing, and reporting patterns within the data" (p. 79). The "rigorous thematic approach can [also] produce an insightful analysis that answers particular research questions" (ibid., 97).

The data collected through interviews with South African Peace Train participants underwent a three-stage process. First, the data was prepared through transcriptions of all nine interviews. Second, the interviews were analyzed using NVivo software. This process was efficient, both in terms of time and the analysis of words and texts. The third and most challenging phase of the study was the development of themes. As Ishak and Bakar (2012) assert:

> NVivo is just another set of tools that will assist a researcher in undertaking an analysis of qualitative data. However, regardless of the type of software being used, the researcher has to dutifully make sense of all the data himself or herself, without damaging the context of the phenomenon being studied. Inevitably, the software cannot replace the wisdom that the researcher brings into the research because at the back of every researcher's mind lies his or her life history that will influence the way he or she sees and interpret the world. (p. 102)

Although all nine interviewees indicated in their informed consent letters that the condition of anonymity might be removed, each participant received a pseudonym with attention to both gender and race. The initial insights explored using the NVivo software revealed clusters of interviewees based on the similarity of words used during the interviews. A graphic depiction of these clusters may be found in Appendix 2, Figure 7.1.

At the most fundamental level of inquiry, it is worth noting that the word similarities of the first cluster of three interviewees includes Linda, Ethel, and Mary. They are three women who are teachers by profession. All three women have contributed their teaching and performance skills to advancing the South African Peace Train.

Teachers Share their Experiences

Ethel is a retired colored teacher. She served as a vocal coach and a chaperone on the South African Peace Train Tours of 1993 and 1995. In speaking of the 1993 tour through South Africa by train, Ethel describes the intense excitement of interacting with Ladysmith Black Mambazo, a singing group. She had only seen them on television previously. There she was, traveling on the same train with them. The excitement she reveals extended to her students as well:

> *My children were very excited. Think of it this way, some of these kids came from homes where they weren't even taken out on an outing to the beach, and the beach is right here [near Wentworth in KwaZulu-Natal]. They have never gone there. So, for them to be going out of Durban into entire South Africa was really something awesome. [. . .] I wasn't a seasoned traveler at the time, but I had studied in Cape Town. [. . .] So for me, it was also a first experience going through all these cities [in South Africa].*

Linda is a Black teacher who works on both songs and dance choreography with children for Katz's ongoing South African performances. Since joining the Peace Train as a high school student for the South African Peace Train Tour to the United States in 1995 and several performances throughout South Africa, she is in a unique position. I had the privilege of watching her perform with her students alongside Sharon Katz and the band at the Elizabeth Sneddon Theatre in Durban on July 24, 2015 (see Chapter 4). Her memories of the tours are vivid:

> *So many to remember. But the biggest was Grahamstown [. . .] just before performing in Cape Town. There is always a show during the June-July school holidays. They always have festivals there, so we'd just go there and perform. And it was such a great experience because the first point is that we were touring, which my mother could not afford. Because my father was the one who passed away earlier, so my mother was the one who brought us up. So, she couldn't afford it. Going to Grahamstown was such an opportunity and meeting*

different people to stay in boarding schools. And then we'd eat in restaurants.
[. . .] My mother couldn't afford it; she could only afford to feed us at home. But
Sharon with the Peace Train. [. . .] Sharon and Marilyn told us you could order
whatever you like. Sometimes you don't know what this is but you just want to
try it out. It was quite an experience, a memorable experience for me.

Among the South African Peace Train teachers was Nonhlanhla Wanda (her
real name used with her permission). As a Black music teacher, she brought
a unique set of skills to the Peace Train. Not only did she assist Katz with
reaching out to the Black community, but she assisted in teaching the songs
and dance routines to her students and working with other students in the
group. Wanda declares that meeting Katz and being part of the Peace Train
was a "miracle" for her school because this was an experience that her students and her school community have never forgotten. Being a part of the
500-voice choir was the first time that her students visited the City of Durban
(only half an hour away), and it was the first time that her students had the
opportunity to engage with children from different races. Wanda states:

The greatest moments for learners from rural areas was when we toured the
whole of South Africa by train with megastars Ladysmith Black Mambazo and
performing in the New Orleans Jazz Festival . . . also touring the USA, which
made a great impact on their lives. It was something that they cherished in their
lives. They learned more about other races and cultures. Today those children
are professionals, business people, etc., which is an amazing thing we have
accomplished.

Wanda also describes the strides that she has made at her school. She is
running after-school programs with learners from her community. She has
also formed an NPO (parents, educators, and street community committee).
They have secured funding from "Suncoast," a hospitality and entertainment
group, to build an Amphitheatre and Support Centre for students with learning disabilities. Three more classrooms have been created to accommodate
the yearly increase in enrolments. Wanda believes that the school still lacks
adequate facilities to cater to many learners' needs and pay extra teachers.
She says, "The work hasn't been finished yet."

Wanda has continued to tour the United States and Canada with the Peace
Train. In an interview with her, she indicated that Friends of The Peace Train
often donate her flights from South Africa to overseas destinations using air
miles. Some Friends of The Peace Train members provide aid to her school
with donations such as windows, recorders (Barbara Novick from the United
States), and snacks for learners' after-school programs. During my fieldwork
in 2015, it was my privilege to bring the recorders from the United States to

South Africa. Wanda expresses sincere gratitude to all who have assisted her school. She describes her goal as being able to give back to South Africa's economy so that the country could give back to others.

South African Children on Tour in 1993 and 1995

The second cluster of the remaining six interviewees—Madeline, Robert, Natalie, Shandhini, Candice, and Tanuja (all pseudonyms)—were relatively young adults between thirty and thirty-eight during the interviews of July 2015. They were all children when they participated in the South African Peace Train. The subcluster represented by Candice and Tanuja is also striking as Candice, aged nine during The Peace Train tour in 1993, was one of the youngest participants while Tanuja, aged fifteen in 1993, was among the oldest of the children on tour. Although they describe their experiences from different perspectives, in terms of race, age, and performance backgrounds, their memories of The South African Peace Train are similar. Derived themes and subthemes emerged from extensive word and text queries using NVivo (see Appendix 2, Table 7.1) and detailed readings and analyses of the nine transcripts.

The highest number of words refer to emotional aspects of the Peace Train experience represented by "feelings excitement wonder" and the "impact of the experience." A reflection on "personal growth," "memories," and "peace and unity" has the second-highest number of references. Strikingly, "performances and auditions" and "cultural and racial differences" were mentioned but did not dominate the interviews. Figure 7.2 in Appendix 2 provides a detailed list of se

Central Themes of the Peace Train Experience

Reflections of young adults (in their own words) interviewed in 2015 were children participants on the Peace Train tours of 1993 in South Africa and 1995 in the United States. A close reading of the transcripts with attention to the frequency of words in context revealed the following central themes:

Feelings of Wonder and Excitement

When Voices Meet was quite fantastic. It was overwhelming in a lot of ways because of the sheer volume of people [who were there], and it was live and with a band and a lot of rehearsal, but it was an awesome experience. (Tanuja)

There was this excitement. It's like almost under the surface excitement because this was something so different for us. [. . .] I was only in grade seven, and it was just so surreal. At first, you are in awe and a little bit nervous but also excited. You don't know why you are excited until you get on the stage, and you start

*singing [. . .] we all realize that we are there to sing because we love singing.
[. . .] It's so far removed from what everybody else is doing that nobody could
quite understand the excitement.* (Shandhini)

*I first heard about Sharon Katz in 1992, and I was quite young. I think I was 16,
if not 15. I was doing standard nine at a high school in Umlazi, and everyone
was excited. We had a White lady coming to teach us how to sing, and it was
an exciting time for us. When she came to our school, and I was already in a
choir. We were told that we were going to join other schools, they're going to
combine all the choirs and form one big choir made up of about 500 kids from
South Africa around the country.* (Robert)

*Goodness. Our American tour. Leading up to it was exciting. Rehearsal times,
just the different songs [. . .] the energy and the whole vibe leading up to it. [. . .]
It was tiring, it was grueling, but it was so exciting at the same time because I
mean this was an experience for all of us that we went through, this huge group
of us that was going out there to perform, going to sing South African songs to
people in America.* (Natalie)

*I remember having the concert [the 500-voice concert in Durban]. I think that
I've said this before; for me, it's about how I feel. The experience for me is far
more important than the details of the event. I know that it sounds random, but
I remember feeling excited, and it's something new and interesting and vibrant,
taking [you] out of your norm. [. . .] Anyway, so we went on the Peace Train,
and we were with Ladysmith Black Mambazo, the most amazing experience
[. . .] the Peace Train was amazing.* (Madeline)

Impact of the Peace Train Experience

*1990 for me was a critical year because I entered high school; I joined the
choir; Nelson Mandela was released and that year. I discovered who Nelson
Mandela was. I discovered what he'd done, and I discovered the state of the
country on a larger scale. It was like an awakening for me, and then I was
exposed to the Peace Train, exposed to these different communities, so it's
almost as if my awakening was also supported by this interaction. I was given
these opportunities that other kids weren't given. I was given a different glimpse
into a life that most of the country wasn't given, and I'm extremely grateful for
that.* (Shandhini)

*Where I came from and the school that I was attached to didn't give the chil-
dren much opportunity, especially in this kind of thing, even though I was at the
forefront of the music, and the dancing and the acting. I even went into Spanish*

dancing. But we would have never gotten funding for that kind of thing. And what changed, for me, was that Sharon could have come in and offered these children such an opportunity. I mean, nobody else was going to do it for them and me. It made me realize that out there in the world; there are these opportunities. They are the possibilities for our children to go beyond their circumstances and even for me. (Ethel)

When you go on a train which is an enclosed space, and you don't have anywhere to go [. . .] and then a bus later on, so you tend to pick up a lot of things about people's culture, about the different ways people think and how they react to the different lives they've led compared to yours. It takes you out of that comfort zone where everybody you know went to a certain type of school and did a special type of thing. Then you realize that, no, not everybody had what you had, and yes, some people did have more than you and some people—a lot of people have less than you. It really opens your eyes to that sort of thing. The South African condition that we just don't see what people have—the more is not as important as seeing, the less, I think. (Tanuja)

We had mentors, people who told us anything is possible. Forget the color; forget where you come from. We grew up in and out of the township; back then, things were difficult. There is something that [. . .] God created [. . .] when you're in a difficult position or situation; you don't really realize at the time. That you are in a very, very awkward or difficult position, only when you passed that, then you look back and say, you know what, things were tough. [. . .] At a time, by the time, when we were doing it, we didn't really understand the impact and effort of what we were doing and what it was going to do for the country. (Robert)

It's not about her; it's about what she can do for other people, and if nothing else, I think that's what she's instilled and ingrained in all the kids that have ever had the fortune of meeting, of being part of the group. It's not about just you; it's about what you can do for other people. What can you do to be a part of, to assist other people and she's just been phenomenal in—I mean, all of us I think have turned out successful human beings, strong human beings, human beings with a work ethic [. . .] we're not afraid to work hard, we're not afraid to put in those hours and not to take things for granted. Just to be so appreciative of things that you do have because we got to see people that had less, people that had more. We got to see all that and just to be so thankful for everything that we do have. (Natalie)

Personal Growth

I mean, I would have never thought—I grew up as a child who was practically thrown away. And for me to have been accepted to and given the responsibility

*to be part of an endeavor like this, that for me was awesome. Awesome. Just
to know that there are people out there who really see your worth, as well, see
the worth in other people. Because I mean, those children that I was teaching,
some of the parents didn't want them. They just didn't care about them.* (Ethel)

*I feel that I am the strong independent person that I am today because of all
that I learned back then. We were 9 or 10 years old and traveling, and we had
to learn to be independent. It was not where mummy was doing this at home or
mummy is busy hanging up clothes, or mummy is folding up things putting them
away. You had to do it. We had our set times. "Okay, it was practice, it was your
lunch, your breakfast, back to your rooms." There was order. We had to learn
time management back then as well, but this was instilled in me back then, and
it's things that are being carried out today.* (Candice)

*I finished [with the Peace Train] when I was 17, so five years of my life. It
definitely affected the way I responded and associated and the level of comfort I
felt with other kids and other race groups. It was a fantastic foundation, a starting point for me for my life basically because it prepared me for where I am
now with the kind of work that I do, the associations I have, the temperament I
maintain with work and clients, and colleagues and friends. It was the perfect,
perfect foundation for me. I could see that.* (Shandhini)

*The kids had to vote for a person to lead the group. Even when we went on the
Peace Train—Black, White, Indian—for some reason, all of them, [. . .] wanted
me to be the president of the group. [. . .] It was a huge surprise for me, and
when we went on stage, whenever someone was supposed to talk on behalf of
the group, as a president, I had to do that. Remember, I grew up in Umlazi. The
only English that I knew was during that 45-minute English class that I had.
We never spoke in English. It was really difficult. But for some reason, it didn't
worry me because when I engaged Sharon, she seemed to understand what I
was saying, and everybody else understood what I was saying. That built my
confidence, and even going forward, that's when I started being who I am. [. . .]
You can't be the same person after going through such an experience.* (Robert)

*We just shared. We danced and rehearsed and sang with what we had. That was
lovely because I think that—now, when I reflect, I think that had such a huge
impact on molding the type of person that I've become. I think you don't judge
somebody; you are also very sympathetic towards people's situations and way
what if you have, yes, it's lovely to have, but if you're not able to share it with
somebody else who's less fortunate, then what's the point of having. How does
it make you happy? Sharon was instrumental in that, in encouraging what's
mine is yours, what's yours is mine. The sharing and caring policy, that's just*

how it was. That, for me, I think, has been such a crucial thing that has been ingrained, that has been instilled in me. Just not judging, having this openness, seeing people for who they are, and accepting people for who they are. (Natalie)

Performance Preparation

What happened was while we were at school, Sharon sent some music, but I suppose she just sent out the music. Some of it we were [inaudible] with the names of the songs and the type of music that was going to be done. I do play a little piano, so I just got onto the piano, and I got the tunes into my head, and while I was doing that, the children also got into it, and they started singing. So, when Sharon came in, she said, "Right. I'm going to teach you this song today. Did your teacher tell you about it?" and they smiled, and they said, "Yes." And she wouldn't understand why they were smiling. And then when she started playing the guitar, the children started singing. And she said, "Wow! Gosh, you people have been working." So, in that way, I think she could see herself through how excited these kids were about being part of the project. And that's how we did it. On the tours, I did voice training with the children. [. . .] It was an audition, and those children, who passed the audition, were the ones who went on the tour. [. . .] We had a Black choreographer with us, and he was a vibrant guy. And the children just took to him because he didn't tell them what to do. He showed them how to do it, so for them, that was it. (Ethel)

There were many rehearsals during school time, and sometimes we had to leave school early to rehearse before we went and stuff like that. (Tanuja)

My goodness. The rehearsals were Saturday morning. I think we started at 8:00 every morning. Every Saturday morning from 8:00 until I think it was 3:00 or 4:00. It was a full day. There were other times I remember that it went on until 6:00, if not a little later, that's when we were getting ready for a show, we needed extra rehearsals with something else. It would go on as long as that, but it was every Saturday. (Natalie)

Organization and Structure

Closely associated with rehearsals' rigor is the theme of organization and structure provided by Katz, Cohen, and the chaperones. The following excerpts attest to this:

We had a very, very good organizer. We had Marilyn Cohen. She is the most well-organized person I know. To conduct and plan such an operation is something that is very, very difficult. [. . .] They planned and organized everything quite well. We never got to think about what is going to happen; instructions were quite clear. Now, it's time to eat, take a bath, change into this; we had different uniforms, even during the performances. We had to change into this, change into that, everything was well-organized, and we were programmed. You think about it now; you realize that it wasn't that easy, but when you were doing it, it just becomes natural. Every performance, you got better and better, and probably things got easier and easier for Marilyn as well. She never never relaxed; she wanted to make sure that everything was perfect. (Robert)

We performed at Disney World. And I mean organizing all that, getting all these kids into Disney World. When you think of the managing side, I don't know how Marilyn pulled all these strings. [. . .] Five weeks. Five weeks. But do you know, it was so structured. Like I'm saying, I don't know how Marilyn did all that. We never went to bed unless we had had a meeting and reflected on the day's activities. What went wrong? What can be fixed? What can we improve upon? And really, the kids used to fall up to sleep. My son used to fall off to sleep all the time. But it was so important for her because she said, "We cannot take today's mistakes with us tomorrow." And for me, that was awesome. It was a learning curve for me. (Ethel)

It was very structured. Amazingly, I don't know how they did it, and I think we still have these conversations now, Sharon, Marilyn, and I about things that they did and how they did it. (Shandhini)

Racial and Cultural Differences

Oh, the children were absolutely fantastic. We had a few glitches here and there, and cultural glitches, but the good thing was that they interacted, and they learned that their culture—we were all different cultures, which we had to respect. So, I think that's what the kids learned, that even though we're in the same country, we have different cultures. We have to respect each other. And for me, that was one of the learning curves that the children learned on the Peace Train. (Ethel)

Ethel explained further:

The school that I came from was predominantly Colored. So, the children who came from my choir were Colored kids. Then we had predominantly White schools. So, the White children came from there, and then we have predominantly Black schools. So, it was a good mix because the children who were chosen from the different schools blended. And so here, we have a rainbow nation traveling on the Peace Train. They worked well together, or they learned to work well together. I was very appreciative of that, especially exposing my children from, I mean, my area to that type of cultural diversity. (Ethel)

Once you realize that you are not so different because you share the same passions, you realize you are not so different in other aspects of your life. You treasure your family. You care about what your parents think of you. You want to grow up to be somebody. You want to lead a good life. You want to make something of yourself. That's what we all wanted. We weren't that different. (Shandhini)

When you met all sorts of people from different cultures, backgrounds, ethnicities, it was really amazing because there was really no racial tension. I don't think I felt that at all. I think it was just some people you liked and some people you didn't, and in a group of 500 people, that's always going to happen. It's not something that you can ever predict, and it's got absolutely nothing to do with apartheid, race, or anything. We were kids. We were there. We were having fun, and when the rehearsals got stressed out, people got stressed out, crabby, and miserable, which would happen with any group of kids. But apart from that, I didn't feel the race thing. I never noticed it. Never. It wasn't—I know it was for the greater audience. It was something that was wow, but I think from the inside, I don't really feel like I felt it. (Tanuja)

It was actually such a natural thing. I went from Metropolis [another production Katz directed] to the Peace Train, and yes, there was this huge number of kids—I'd say 50. Maybe more than 50, but yes, they were White, Black, Indian Colored, just a whole real rainbow nation of kids. Sharon and Marilyn [. . .], everybody was just another person from the time we got in there. It wasn't a White person or an Indian person or a Colored person or an African person. We were all just children that were there; we were coming to sing together; we were coming to sing about our country to sing about each other's cultures. Really, it was easy and comfortable and natural. (Natalie)

Natalie provided greater detail and clarification:

When you go on the Peace Train [. . .], you were exposed to other cultures, other languages. It just made you appreciate so much more who we actually were, but who we thought we were because there was even more out there. This is what we thought we were. No, there's actually more to us than what we know. Learning from each other, learning the different cultures from each other, learning religion, and different religions. Even that, that was never an issue with us. Sharon and Marilyn always said—we are all just one. We are all just one family. Don't judge somebody on their religion, on their culture. Rather than learn about somebody's religion, learn about somebody's culture. Embrace it. (Natalie)

Family and Community Support

I remember having a meeting at my school one evening with parents from the choir or whatever else. Apparently, there was a heated debate. I mean, I just wanted to go. My mom stood up and said, "You know what, why not? My child's going." What if there's danger? I didn't know there was danger. [. . .] The support of my mom as well, because she didn't stop me. I think that was the best thing ever. She's always been supportive in saying, "You know what, [Madeline], just go for it." Going for it has made huge changes. It influenced her, as well. (Madeline)

My father's been very supportive. My father and mother, in fact, have been very supportive of my dancing, my singing. With having two other siblings, my parents had to split themselves. My mom would be busy taking my brother to cricket or karate and taking my sister elsewhere. My dad would have to drop me because it was early on a Saturday morning as well. He would have to drop me often. He wouldn't just drop me over and drive off. He would drop me off and sit and watch. (Natalie)

The parents, relatives, neighbors, and everyone wanted to see Black and White, Indian, Colored performing on one stage. This is something that was never heard of. It's just the first in the country, and the numbers, of course, made it unique. Everyone wanted to see what was happening. My parents were also skeptical, but they were so impressed when they came to see what was happening. My parents never missed any of my performances, especially in Durban. The response was just unbelievable. (Robert)

I come from a very conservative family, a very traditional Indian family, and for them to put that much trust in me and then also in Sharon and Marilyn, they barely knew them. They'd meet with our parents and our teachers and stuff, but obviously, my parents understood that this was something huge, and even though it was possibly beyond their realm of understanding, they put a lot of faith in us. (Shandhini)

The South African Peace Train was created in 1993 after the success of the concert production *When Voices Meet,* which showcased a 500-voice multiracial choir. Subsequently, the children of the South African Peace Train choir (almost all of whom had been a part of *When Voices Meet*) ranging in age from nine to seventeen were selected through an audition process to travel and perform in a train tour through South Africa. This selection of students speaks to the fact that Katz believed not only in bringing a message of racial harmony and hope to communities in South Africa but she also displays a commitment to excellence in performance. The interviewees corroborated Katz's musical requirements with references to the rigor of their rehearsals. The impact of the first Peace Train Tour of 1993 with Ladysmith Black Mambazo with subsequent performances at several festivals as well as an extensive visit to the United States shaped, to some extent, the personal growth of each of the interviewed participants.

The most intense recollections of my childhood and growing up as a young adult of color came flooding back when I interviewed the adults who had been children on the South African Peace Train. Although I was a student and then a young adult teaching in a segregated school with Black and Indian students, the 1980s and 1990s were a time of intense protest. As a university student, I remembered the instances of being tear-gassed in the university cafeteria. I recall the panic of running away from police officers' rubber bullets as they charged through our campus. There was also the sense of unity and camaraderie I felt with other students, playing my guitar as we sang "We Shall Overcome" and other songs of protest. One of the verses that still elicits an emotional reaction in me was from the song, *Dona,* a version I had heard by Joan Baez. The most poignant lines for me were "Calves are easily bound and slaughtered, never knowing the reason why. But whoever treasures freedom, like the swallow, must learn to fly." My connection to these words was relevant in many ways.

It was gut-wrenching to lose my Honors Degree supervisor from the University of Natal. He was killed in Zululand—an area that was the Inkatha Freedom Party's stronghold—for being a supporter of the opposing African National Congress. Members of my family and friends suffered imprisonment for anti-apartheid nonviolent actions. These were times of great personal and societal angst. In the years leading up to Nelson Mandela's release, my students, my fellow teachers, and I were engaged in several marches, boycotts, and protests, all of which were peaceful. As passive protestors, we were the "calves" of the struggle.

The children who went on the Peace Train to bring this message of hope, peace, and unity among children from different racial groups shared uplifting, compelling testimony that both contrasted and resonated with my own experiences. The remarkable realization for me was that race was not my focus in listening to my respondents. I tried to interview at least one Indian, White, Black, and Colored participant to have a balanced range of responses. I listened to their narratives, their experiences, and their attitudes while feeling that I could relate to each respondent in similar or different ways. The children on the Peace Train tours were caught up in the social, political, and performance aspects of their experiences. They were blissfully unaware that their interactions and growth were being carefully nurtured by a professional in her field, the musical activist and music therapist, Sharon Katz.

The Healing Power of Music

As a music therapist, Katz describes The Peace Train project in her article entitled "The Peace Train" (2011, para. 14) as follows:

> I conceived of a project which would use the therapeutic power of music to bring together youth of the previously separated races and cultural groups in South Africa in a shared experience and a shared experience that dealt with the potential for a more normalized future in the country. [. . .] In February 1993, after three months of negotiation with the nine communities, approval was received to begin a weekly music therapy process with youth from all the diverse groups within the Kwa-Zulu Natal region. I composed songs for the youth to sing, which focused on issues of trust, understanding, peace, and unity for the future.

In her doctoral thesis, Wooten (2015) examines the effects of this form of music therapy on participants' lives in the Peace Train experience of 1993. Wooten introduces her discussion by comparing the work of pioneering music therapists such as Edith Boxill. The latter advocated for using music therapy to promote peace with the efforts of Sharon Katz. She asserts that "Sharon Katz utilized this concept to advance her music therapy model to bring peace and harmony to the people of South Africa." Besides, Wooten contends that Katz was "determined to bridge the cultural gap that was created by the apartheid regime from 1948–1994, [focusing] particularly on the children because they represented the first generation that would benefit from a South Africa without the constraints of apartheid" (ibid., p. 1).

An article entitled "Music Therapy, War Trauma, and Peace: A Singaporean Perspective" by Wang Feng Ng (2005, para. 9–10) refers to Katz's work. Ng describes the role of music therapists in postwar societies where healing and rebuilding are paramount. Ng asserts that several programs, not specifically related to music therapy, developed in postwar contexts that used musical and other creative artistic experiences to rehabilitate trauma survivors and promote peace, healing, and reconstruction (Barenboim 2004; Gould 2000; Zelizer 2003). Specific to peace activism, Ng also highlights the music therapist's work, Edith Hillman Boxill, the founder-director of Music Therapists for Peace, Inc. (MTP), an international movement. Their mission is to "have music therapists maintain a conscious awareness of contributing to the healing of our wounded planet" (Boxill 1997, p. 158).

Ng (2005, para.16) describes Katz as a "South African music therapist and 'multi-talented peace emissary'" (Weinstein-Moser 2003, 9). Besides, Katz initiated the Peace Train project in 1992, in KwaZulu-Natal, known for the civil strife between two political parties, namely, the Inkatha Freedom Party and African National Congress. Ng describes Katz's 500-voice choir as a "community music therapy project . . . [of children and youth from] previously separated races and cultural groups in South Africa in a shared experience" (Katz & Cohen, n.d., 3). The event is described as "a tradition-defying multiracial and multilingual choir to perform at the culminating event, *When Voices Meet*." Ng confirms that following this concert, Katz led a subset of the original group on a nationwide and international tour to spread the message of democracy and peace to educators, community leaders, and youth (Katz & Cohen, n.d.). Ng provides a detailed description of the Peace Train children's social circumstances gleaned from personal communication with Katz in 2004. According to Ng's (2005) commentary:

> These youths were from impoverished, violent, and oppressed communities. In their attempts to achieve status and a sense of belonging in their communities, many were gang members [. . .]. Fundamental to Sharon's work is the use of music performance as the transformational tool to break down barriers, and to facilitate dialogue and resolve conflicts peacefully. [. . .] Outcomes of the project were extremely positive: "marginal students began earning top rankings; introverted individuals became much more communicative; gang membership disintegrated, and initiative and creativity blossomed." [. . .] Presently, all members were gainfully employed, and many had success stories to share.

In July 2015, I had the opportunity to meet young men and women who had been participants in the South African Peace Train project of 1993. While my conversations with them revealed that they had all grown up in an abnormal society—as did I—where an apartheid government segregated people based on race, I disagree with Ng's generalization that all the participants came from violent and disadvantaged communities. My interviews with some participants revealed much better stability and support in their home environments than Ng suggests. My interviews in 2015 contradict Ng's claim. Besides my interviews, immediate family members' excitement is palpable in actual footage of the documentary *When Voices Meet*, discussed in Chapter 4. While Katz's work in the United States was with individuals who had been gang members, Ng's characterization of "many members" of the Peace Train as gang members is inherently flawed. There is no substantiation of this claim.

Sharon Katz, as an academic, has authored articles that explain the nature of her activism. In a section entitled M*usic Therapy for Children and*

Families with Mass Trauma Exposure (Katz in Stewart 2010), Katz presents a compelling narrative of the Peace Train from its beginnings in the early 1990s and the transformative role the experiences have played in the lives of its participants. Katz (2011) delves into the part played by the Peace Train with a detailed narrative of the role of music in fostering peace and harmony in a country torn apart by decades of discriminatory practices.

Sociological Implications

Beyond the role of musical activism, Gay Seidman (1999) provides commentary on what she sees as South Africa's importance in social science studies. With the end of legal apartheid, Seidman sees South Africa as being "poised to move into a new position in the annals of social science. From being an outlier, South Africa will be used increasingly as an exemplar in discussions of democratic transitions, development strategies and globalization, and post-colonial transformations" (p. 419).

Seidman hoped that future comparative studies would draw on insights from other parts of the world to reexamine aspects of South African society left relatively unexplored. Ironically, these include issues around racial identity and changing patterns of race relations as South Africa continues with its efforts to construct a nonracial democracy. This noble ideal of a nonracial democracy espoused by Mr. Mandela has been thwarted in no small part by a post-apartheid government that has failed to honor its promises to its citizens more than twenty years later. However, the country's constitution is a guiding light for South Africans who hold the optimistic view that this is a country with a long road to travel before it is whole again. This optimism is reflected in the words of a young Black entrepreneur who traveled as a high school student with Sharon Katz & The Peace Train through South Africa, the United States, and Ghana:

> My wife says I am a dreamer. Things that people usually think are impossible, we've done them. Working with Sharon and the Peace Train [. . .] if you can take the train for a couple of weeks [on a performance tour through South Africa], take kids overseas [on an extended performance tour of the United States], what's stopping us from building empires or anything else that we want to do (Robert, personal communication, July 23, 2015).

Case Study Three: Humanitarian Efforts—
Friends of The Peace Train

The little we have, we share
That's the way it must be

In the world everywhere
I carry you, you carry me
—(Chorus from *The Little We Have We Share* by Sharon Katz)

The Influence of Rathebe

In 1998, with very few prospects in South Africa due to a lack of funding, Katz went to Ghana to perform at a music festival with the Symphony Orchestra. Katz met Professor Nketia[3] at this performance. He invited her to a music therapy conference and subsequently asked her to teach music therapy at the University of Ghana. She remained in Ghana for two years. Katz describes the events that followed as a fortunate series of circumstances that motivated her to establish her humanitarian efforts. While she was in Ghana, Professor Nketia invited her to present a paper on The Peace Train at a Bloomington, Indiana Ethnomusicology Conference. It was there that she met Dolly Rathebe.[4] Dolly was touring with Peter Davis. Katz describes their meeting as an "instant falling in love—you know as musicians do—as people do." Davis filmed this fateful first meeting. Katz and Rathebe became friends very quickly and jammed together that night after Katz's presentation. The next night they performed together at the conference (S. Katz, personal communication, October 15, 2016).

Despite Katz's efforts to create performance opportunities for Rathebe in Ghana, Katz admits that she "could not pull it off." Upon Katz's return to the United States in 2001, Rathebe invited Katz to visit her in South Africa. This open-ended invitation was life-altering for Katz. During the six weeks Katz stayed with her, they recorded together, and Katz simply shadowed Rathebe. She was in awe of the work Rathebe was doing:

> She was building. That's where I got the idea to build. She was giving back to her community like you wouldn't believe. She created this fantastic place for the pensioners and tried to create a development in a poverty-stricken area. And she was always going around and buying cement and bricks, and I just loved her. (ibid.)

Once a sought-after actress and singer, achieving success in South Africa and the United Kingdom, Rathebe occupied herself in her later years with community work and development. Motivated by the need to give a helping hand to the poor and the underprivileged, she was instrumental in building a community hall in Mabopane. She also funded the construction of a center called Meriting kwaDolly ("Dolly's Retreat") at Sofasonke village near Klipgat, north of Pretoria. Rathebe was also a member of the executive committee of the Ikageng Women's League.[5]

The Good Hope Community Organization (2001–Present)

During her first stay with Rathebe, Katz met Mama Mary Lwate (pictured in Figure 3.3), the founder of the Good Hope Community Organization. Rathebe was helping the children's group by bringing them uniforms for their dance performance. This meeting established a relationship between Katz and Mama Mary that continues today. Katz describes her relationship with Mama Mary as being "close" since 2001, when she also began working with the children from the orphanage (Katz, personal communication, October 15, 2016).

Inspired by Rathebe's community work and her meeting with Mama Mary and the orphanage children, Katz decided that she would find a way to provide meaningful assistance to the Good Hope Community Organization. These early efforts led to the formation of the nonprofit organization, Friends of The Peace Train, in the United States a few years later. Katz explained the nature of her humanitarian efforts:

> I brought tourists (from America) there every single year. I used to stay with them. We started raising money (in America) to put down the floors in one of the buildings. And then I got the tourists that come with me every year to contribute money and help buy school uniforms, get driver's licenses, computers—at one time, I helped four to six kids into the university. But only two of them graduated, and I realized tertiary education would not work very well. We got them into other situations such as computers and helping them reach their drivers' licenses—skills rather than the university, which is not easy. But one of them

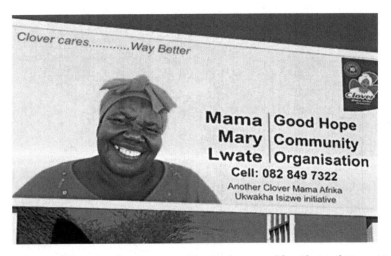

Figure 3.3   A Billboard at the Entrance of the Orphanage with a Photo of Mama Mary. Photo by the author.

graduated in hospitality as a chef. We have one young woman right now that we're financing now to be a social worker—so it's a long relationship. (ibid.)

The young woman studying to be a social worker named Angela, who grew up in the orphanage, met me on July 12, 2015, at a central location to bring me to the orphanage and Mama Mary's home. She was a vibrant and very personable young student in her early twenties. Angela was very excited to share with me that she was driving a car donated to her. Within a half-hour of meeting her, Angela communicated with me the dire circumstances of her life. These struggles included many years of abuse before coming to live at the orphanage. She had been less than ten years old at that time. When Angela and several other young people had aged out of the orphanage, they had nowhere to go. Mama Mary took them into her own home.

Serendipitous Research

The unstructured interviews with the young adults at Mama Mary's house was not a predetermined plan. When Angela met me on July 12, 2015, at a location close to Mama Mary's family, the purpose of her meeting with me was to take me to meet with Mama Mary and see the orphanage as I did not know my way around the area. On my arrival at Mama Mary's home, I was greeted by the young adults and Mama Mary, all of whom I had the privilege of conversing with after visiting the orphanage. Fortunately, I had copies of my "Informed Consent" document that they were all willing to sign before speaking with me about their experiences with Sharon Katz. All participants indicated that they did not object to having their names used for my research. Every young adult participant has both an African and an English name. I observed that they often reverted to the use of their African names when speaking among themselves. All participants, including Mama Mary, agreed to my audio-taping our conversations, with the option to review my transcripts.

As I set up my digital recorder, I could see that the young adults were somewhat shy to speak, as being recorded was somehow intimidating. After this observation, I spontaneously asked them if they wanted to sing "Amazing Grace" with me as I sensed that that would be a song they would know. I began singing the melody, and what ensued was a beautifully harmonized spontaneous rendition of the song with everyone joining in. This impromptu singing was an "icebreaker" that resulted in easy conversations with the three young adults and Mama Mary at her home. It was more than I hoped for, as they explained how they were each preparing to become independent and gainfully employed by pursuing their interests and acquiring skills supported by Mama Mary. They also expressed deep gratitude to Katz and the Friends of The Peace Train from America, who have made an enormous difference in their lives through their financial contributions.

Conversations at the Home of Mama Mary

Angela, a young woman, aged twenty-three, studying Social Work (with financial assistance from Sharon Katz, Marilyn Cohen, and Friends of The Peace Train), began her recollections thus:

> I remember Sharon with her music and many people visiting us [. . .] with guitars, music stuff like drums . . . from America. They will start with music, performing for us. They were singing (Angela starts singing) "Sanalwami ne bongo . . ." Because it is a South African song, how can you not sing that. Of course, you will be able to get it and sing. The atmosphere was amazing. The kids here (in the orphanage)—we love drama. We love singing, acting, dancing. And after we were done dancing, we would start building a relationship with the people. I would spot who I wanted to sit with—Sharon, Nonhlanhla—and they would talk about me. They did not make me feel like I'm in an orphanage. They wanted to hear about my dreams.

Angela also recalled how a question from one of the tourists about her interest in studying drama inspired her to get Mama Mary's blessing to attend an after-school program at the Pretoria State Theatre for four years. She also shared many memories of Katz, inviting her to perform with the children and how impressed Katz was with their local production of the musical, *Sarafina*,[6] performed by children from the orphanage. Katz began bringing them instruments (guitars and keyboards). Angela refers to Sharon "as part of the family." When asked if there was anything she wanted to add, Angela stated very poignantly, "I was once an orphan, and now I can do something for other children and make a difference in the community." She added, "Sharon is a wonderful child to Mama with her respect and loyalty to this family. The Peace Train and Good Hope Community is a family" (Angela, personal communication, July 12, 2015).

Margaret, a young woman in her early thirties, stated that she was one of the first children to be raised by Mama Mary. She did not have a personal relationship with Katz:

> I don't know much. [. . .] I used to come for the weekend and go back to work at the Correctional Facility, where I stayed nights [. . .], but I know that Sharon is a daughter to Mama. I know that she sponsored children for school [. . .] we used to see many people on buses with instruments . . . she's a singer . . . she's a daughter . . . she's one of our own (Margaret, personal communication, July 12, 2015).

Daniel, a shy young man, aged nineteen, was completing high school in 2015. After a little coaxing from Angela, he shared that he was interested in music and that he had a three-man, a cappella group with one of the boys from the orphanage and another from the community. Daniel sang one of his original songs. It was a melancholy song in English entitled, "I was thinking of you," accompanied by his beatboxing. Although he was very passionate about music, having taught himself to play the keyboard, he wanted to study Agriculture to assist Mama Mary with her community projects. He recalled that Katz had come to the orphanage with Cohen. "The thing that I like about her is that she sings songs from Africa" (Daniel, personal communication, July 12, 2015).

My recorded conversation with Mama Mary provided more profound insights into her relationship with Sharon Katz. She recalled meeting Katz through Dolly Rathebe when the children from the orphanage performed for one of Rathebe's events for the elderly. Katz showed a keen interest in the children. She purchased dance costumes for all the children because she was very impressed with their artistry, and she knew that they were children from an orphanage. Mama Mary states that Katz has developed a very close relationship with her "as a daughter." Katz has visited Mama Mary and the orphanage children "too many times to count over the years" (ibid.).

Mama Mary expressed her gratitude to Katz and confirmed that Katz always financially assists the young men and women as they complete their schooling. They provide computers, help get their driver's licenses, bring instruments, and secure sponsorships from Friends of The Peace Train for higher learning. Katz's visits, sometimes with tourists, are always accompanied by music-making. Katz creates this music with the children and the tourists. Angela laughingly sums up the conversation for Mama Mary when she says, "There are some very White people singing in Zulu . . . we love Sharon" (Mama Mary Lwate and Angela, July 12, 2015). Angela was very expressive in animatedly describing many experiences, always tinged with a sense of humor. de Caro (2012) makes an astute observation when he states:

> Far from being distractions or amusing asides, the "little" stories embedded in a formal interview can be looked at to provide insights we might not otherwise have and to supplement other forms of discourse about the past and the construction of the past and its society or about the mentalité of those who inform us about it and these stories should, of course, be viewed as a valuable resource. (275–276)

Themes and Subthemes

In working with the audio-recordings and transcriptions of my unstructured interviews, I reflect on the experiences of Seidman (2006), who states:

When working with excerpts from interview material, I find myself selecting passages that connect to other passages in the file. In a way, quantity starts to interact with quality. The repetition of an aspect of experience that was already mentioned in other passages takes on weight and calls attention to itself. (p. 127)

In comparing the texts derived from my audio-taped conversations with the three young adults and Mama Mary, the goal was to analyze how the texts were similar or different from each other to extrapolate common themes. Glaser and Strauss (1967, 101–116) provide descriptions of this technique, which utilizes a method of constant comparison. When scrutinizing each line of the text, the focus remains on the data rather than preconceived notions or assumptions.

Five common themes and related subthemes were extrapolated from these unstructured interviews with the three young adults who were all raised in the orphanage (several years apart), as well as my interview with Mama Mary. *Musical performance* was a striking theme. Music was described as a joyful experience that facilitated forging connections with tourists and displayed artistic skills. *Gratitude or thankfulness* was also crucial to the interviewees. They expressed gratitude for the monetary support from Katz and Friends of The Peace Train, for having each other as "family," and for the visits of tourists who engaged with the children from the orphanage. They voiced thankfulness for every person and organization assisting with their daily needs. The theme of *familial love* was significant among the interviewees, where the orphanage (The Good Hope Community) provides the space for "family" bonding. Sharon Katz & The Peace Train were described as part of their extended family, with Katz described as a "daughter" by Angela and Margaret (two of the young adults) and Mama Mary.

The interviewees were candid in describing the *racial and socioeconomic impact* of engaging with White tourists who are Friends of The Peace Train. They were acutely aware that the racial contrast is stark when White people visit a Black community in South Africa.

From their perspective, the instruments the children received and the monetary assistance provided over time represent the wealth of the White benefactors. Finally, one of the central themes was that of *professional aspirations and loyalty*. The young adults interviewed all aspire to jobs that would benefit the community, reflecting a deep respect for Mama Mary as the family's matriarch. Katz was also viewed as loyal and respectful.

My interviews in Mabopane, at the home of Mama Mary, sparked mixed feelings—compassion for the children and the young people; a kindred spirit with the young men and women who had been raised by Mama Mary when they spoke of the visits of Katz and the Friends of The Peace Train. I also remembered White friends of my father who visited us at my home in a segregated "Indian" suburb. I could identify with how it was so unusual to see them there. I also felt an intense sense of injustice for myself as a child and for the children in the orphanage in Mabopane today who continue to be victims of circumstances. Understanding the humanitarian work of activists like Sharon Katz offers hope for the children and young people in these communities. In my interview with Katz, she explained the formation of the Friends of The Peace Train:

It's a non-profit that I formed in 2004 because I found myself back in the United States. I felt as if I'm here physically, but I'm still emotionally in South Africa. So, in 2004 we founded a non-profit called Friends of The Peace Train. We raise money for projects in South Africa. The exception was when we decided to raise funds for the documentary—we did that with Friends of The Peace Train. They are individuals who have helped us because they believe in the project.

Katz goes on to describe their engagement with the nonprofit organization:

Some have been on tours with us in South Africa; many of them have come to concerts, and many of them have come on this 2016 (American) Peace Train Tour. Some went on the first tour in 2003—Emma was 5 when she arrived—it's been a part of their soundtrack or something [. . .] some people call it the soundtrack of their life. The Peace Train has been in their lives for a long time. As a part of that, I've been helping Mama Mary, and that was the one thing I'm continuing to do my best [. . .] trying to help her. (Katz, personal communication, October 15, 2016)

Sharon Katz has been working as a humanitarian and a musician to raise awareness and funds for children who have lost their parents because of HIV/AIDS or other circumstances. One of the primary goals is to help young adults become self-sufficient. Funding from Friends of The Peace Train provides meals for the hungry, homes for the homeless, training and jobs for the unemployed, and music therapy to give hope and aid in the healing process. Besides their ongoing support to Mama Mary's Children's Home, Katz is determined to support the entrepreneurial businesses of Mama Mary. A small truck is currently needed to transport supplies and finished products from their bakery, farm, and recycled jewelry businesses to stay self-sufficient. The need for funding at Mama Mary's is ongoing as she prepares young people to take over all future endeavors.

On March 3, 2017, Mama Mary was acknowledged in an article entitled, "Mama Mary Lwate recognized vastly!" by Seiso Modisenyane in the *Winterveld News*. The writer documents the work of Mama Mary as follows:

WINTERVELDT-Clover Mama Afrika, Clover's CSI project, has announced Mama
Mary Lwate as Performer Extraordinaire at an award ceremony. . . . Mama Mary
Lwate from Winterveldt, started the Good Hope Community Organization in 1997
to care for abandoned and abused children. Her extended family has grown from 18
girls to over 150 children from new-born to 20 years of age. The crèche alone has 44
children who are cared for on a full-time basis. (Modisenyane, March 2017)

Modisenyane describes Mama Mary's role in the children's lives, from ensur-
ing that they attend school regularly to teach them skills such as baking, dress-
making, and knitting. Professor Elain Vlok, Founder of Clover Mama Afrika,
explained that Mama Mary was awarded "Performer Extraordinaire" for her
strength in continuously empowering members to manage self-help projects.
Besides, Mama Mary has the creative ability, finding success with her projects
such as her jams and medicine supplies. Her center's design is commendable
as it ensures a clean and healthy environment for all her members (ibid.).

This article speaks to the enormous respect that Mama Mary Lwate has
garnered in South Africa through her leadership and humanitarian work.
During my visit to her home and the orphanage in 2015, Mama Mary's efforts
were apparent. Besides an inspirational mural (see Figure 3.4), the bedrooms
and the kitchen at the orphanage were clean and organized meticulously. The
caregivers were gracious (pictured with the author and children in Figure
3.6), even though they shared with me that they had not received salaries
owing to a bureaucratic glitch. The respectful demeanor and work ethic of the
young adults at Mama Mary's house also reflected her influence.

Figure 3.4   An Inspirational Mural Inside the Orphanage. Photo by the author.

Sharon Katz's efforts through the Friends of The Peace Train in America and other such humanitarian efforts are vital for the Good Hope Community Organization's sustenance in South Africa. Mama Mary Lwate, in her own words, states: "We want to help the world to see South Africa like it used to be, and this can be done by the help of others" (Lwate in Modisenyane, 2017).

Figure 3.5 articulates one of the principal philosophies of the Good Hope Community Organization. This motto states, "The little we have we share." It has inspired a popular song with the same title written by Sharon Katz. The lyrics of this song deliver a powerful and universal message that resonated with the children and adults at the orphanage and the participants of the American Peace Train Tour of 2016 (see Chapter 5).

Katz embarked on yet another humanitarian project in 2008. This initiative came to fruition because of the enthusiasm of a young man named Malcolm Nhleko, who was a

"graduate" of the Peace Train. Katz describes him as "an amazing success story of the Peace Train." He and another member of the Peace Train had traveled to Ghana in 1998 with Katz and her partner, Marilyn Cohen. Katz felt that the experience in another country would be a positive one for both young people. Nhleko became very successful in subsequent endeavors, and he is currently the sound engineer for Ladysmith Black Mambazo. This position is a notable accomplishment for a young man living at St. Philomena's Children's Home in Durban when Katz first met him. He auditioned to be in the 500-voice choir of 1993, and according to Katz, Nhleko credits the Peace Train for "turning his life around" (Katz, personal communication, October 15, 2016).

Katz's engagement with a new and ambitious humanitarian effort in KwaNgcolosi followed an unexpected set of circumstances. Although Katz traveled between South Africa and the United States following her stint in

Figure 3.5 Large Posters on the Interior Walls of the Orphanage. Photo by the author.

Figure 3.6 The Author Getting to Know the Caregivers and the Children at the Orphanage. Photo by the author.

Ghana, Katz and Cohen maintained a very close relationship with Nhleko, having taken on a parental role in his life.

Kayamandi Township Music Project (2006–2016)

When financial constraints almost prevented Katz from returning to South Africa regularly, Distell, the wine distribution company from Cape Town, invited Katz in 2006 to work in Kayamandi township, developing youth empowerment using music therapy with young adults. A short article, under the banner of "Rural Project Partners" listed under "Community Engagement" on the University of Stellenbosch website reads:

Vlottenburg Music Project
  Sharon Katz, Director of the Peace Train, works with Distell Foundation to implement music therapy projects on farms in the Western Cape and Kayamandi township, South Africa.[7]

Katz also auditioned and trained unemployed young women in Kayamandi township. By 2008 she had formed a group called *Masande* that performed together very successfully for several years.[8] According to Katz, all the group members, Thandeka Ndwalaza, Nolubabalo, and Andiswa (surnames not known), Zandile Batweni, Thobela Maliwa, and Busi Maki, gained much self-esteem from their performances and participation in The Peace Train/Distell Foundation project. Besides, they all joined the workforce and received promotions in their positions. Katz asserts that this music project allowed her to provide a service to the people of Kayamandi township and allowed her to return to South Africa from the United States every year.

KwaNgcolosi School Project

On one of those trips back to South Africa, Nhleko expressed excitement about what he saw as a beautiful area outside Durban that needed development. When Katz saw the location close to the *Valley of a Thousand Hills* in Kwa-Zulu Natal, she describes it as "love at first sight." She decided that she would work with the community of KwaNgcolosi. Katz met with the Chief and the councilor from the district. The selection of a plot of land followed. It was considered perfect for the building of a school. Katz explained that she had seen a school had burned down by ANC/Inkatha violence and that children were walking many miles to attend another school. Katz (2011) describes this initiative in detail:

> Children were walking 3 hours a day to the closest school. Most had lost their parents to the HIV/AIDS crisis and were living in child-headed households, hungry most of the time. Just at a time when equal opportunities were becoming available for all South Africans, the oldest child in each of these households had to stay home from school to care for the youngest ones or try to find food for the next day. He (Nhleko) asked Friends of The Peace Train to help him build a school for the community, and we immediately began staging concerts and presentations to raise the money needed to build the school.[9]

In the summer of 2008, Katz went to the area for two months with three volunteers and began the building process. Katz describes the activities of the days that ensued—in her words, "ordering and delivering cement and stone, and supervising the leveling of the land, digging of foundations and building of the walls" (ibid.). She ran music therapy, recreation, and arts programs for a core group of about fifty at-risk children. At the end of the summer, with the community hall and school building walls already built up, Katz had a ribbon-cutting ceremony attended by the Chief of the area to officially hand over the school to the community. By the following summer, Katz had found a partner on the ground in the Rotary Club of the neighboring very affluent area called Hillcrest. Then, in August 2010, Katz brought a group of twenty-five American tourists to visit KwaNgcolosi (see Figure 3.7). They enjoyed a concert and minifestival inside the new school walls. This close-up view of the humanitarian work in progress with American tourism's support is vital to the survival of Friends of The Peace Train (ibid.).

In an interview in 2016, Katz explained the traumatic events that led up to the handing over of the school:

> Before we could put the roof on, we were attacked. I was held up at gunpoint and robbed. Absolutely everything was taken in the area, right on the way to a *Valley of a Thousand Hills*. It was November 1, 2009, and everything, even my glasses. [. . .] I was coming from a gig, so I was wearing my contacts, but the car, everything was in it. My amp, my guitars, my computer, everything that you need that you take for granted. I was left on the side of the road. And I couldn't stay because I didn't have anything. So, I came back to the States. And it happened to be right about the time the economy crashed and the contract I had here in Philadelphia had also ended. We had to withdraw somewhat from the project, but I continued fundraising. I was traumatized by the hijacking because I could have lost my life. They were pointing guns at me. (Katz, personal communication, October 15, 2016)

Despite this experience, Katz continued fundraising in the United States to complete the construction of the school. Katz realized that she could not live

Figure 3.7   Sharon Katz Is Pictured with American Tourists (*Friends of The Peace Train*) at the KwaNgcolosi School with Adults and Children from the Community. Courtesy of Sharon Katz. Used with permission.

in KwaNgcolosi, as was her original plan. She realized that this area was dangerous. Upon returning to South Africa, Katz ensured the completion of the construction of the school (see Figure 3.8). An official ceremony followed to hand over the school to the community. However, every attempt to use the building for the benefit of the community failed. The Rotary Club from Hillcrest tried to establish a sewing project, but they were not successful.

The Pietermaritzburg Department of Education said the children do not walk far enough. They could not give the school a number to get the school up and running as a school and allocate teachers. "Time after time of going to meet with them and sending higher up people and talking to the mayor and the deputy mayor [. . .] no-one could get things up and running in KwaNgcolosi. Teachers training [. . .] we had carpentry—everything would just last for a while and just not continue, and so the school is not functioning as I want it to operate now" (ibid.). Katz reflects that this is a project that did not work out how she envisioned.

> It's just one of those stories of a development project [. . .] you know it's there; it has plumbing because we got that done; it has someone who looks after it to make sure it's not ransacked; and every time I go to South Africa, I try to do something more, to see if something can ever happen there. Malcolm [Nhleko] also built in the area. He built rondavels, and he was also robbed. Mbongeni Ngema[10] has bought the property from Malcolm. The house we bought to live in was always supposed to go to a teacher that would be teaching at the school, and now a friend of Nonhlanhla[11] is living in the house. She is a teacher, but not in the area. And you know the story continues. [. . .] I plan to go back to Durban. (ibid.)

Katz's experience of crime within the volatile and often dangerous circumstances of living and working in South Africa has not deterred her resolve "to go back." These incidents are also not isolated or unique. Crime statistics in South Africa have, sadly, trended upward since the 1990s. Louw (1997) discusses the contradiction between the achievement of democracy in 1994 and the complex reality of the high crime rate in South African society. The most significant feature of South Africa's transition from a racially divided apartheid government to democracy has been the peaceful nature of the transformation through negotiation instead of revolution. But for many South Africans, one of the dominant features of the transformation process over the past two decades has been and continues to be crime and violence. The social and psychological effects of violence on a large portion of the population and sections of the security forces are significant. These effects will continue to have implications for the quality of life of South Africans well into the future. In terms of the country's general stability, burgeoning crime rates cause feelings of insecurity and undermine popular confidence in the democratization process (137–138).

This article highlights the widespread nature of crime in various parts of South Africa that continues today. This scourge of the criminal element in society may stymy the progress of humanitarian work in areas that most need assistance. Still, individuals' resilience and strength, such as Katz and communities, such as KwaNgcolosi, cannot be underestimated. Katz may be an "edge walker"[12] whose cross-cultural experiences allow her to overcome many challenges in different situations. In a published article on The Peace Train in *Voices, A World Forum for Music Therapy*, Katz (2011) was optimistic regarding the school's future in KwaNgcolosi. She concluded by stating:

> In just two years, the community hall and school have been completed, and the first two classes will attend school beginning in January 2011. In addition, a pre-school or crèche will also begin in January 2011. Young children will no longer have to walk three hours a day to get an education; a breakfast program for at-risk and vulnerable children has been implemented; a training program has started for local women who will work in the food and recreation program, and a Music Therapy program will begin shortly.[13]

During my interview with Katz in 2016, she expressed deep disappointment that the property could not acquire its status as a school. Katz remains connected with the community of KwaNgcolosi by putting on musical events whenever she visits. As she says, "I get emails and Facebook messages from kids I met there in 2008. They were little kids in that area then, but they still idolize me because we built that school. I am tearfully talking about it. It's

Figure 3.8   An Acknowledgment of the Building of the Hall and School at KwaNgcolosi.
Courtesy of Sharon Katz. Used with permission.

testimony to the power of hope" (Katz, personal communication, October 15, 2016). Katz believes that despite the transitional use of the facility, it symbolizes positive development in the community of KwaNgcolosi.

Sharon Katz credits Dolly Rathebe for inspiring her humanitarian efforts in South Africa. Through the creation of the nonprofit organization, Friends of The Peace Train, Katz provides financial support and resources, whenever possible, toward the upliftment of communities in South Africa. Katz is significantly invested in The Good Shepherd Community Organization in Mabopane, with Mama Mary Lwate at its helm. It comprises an orphanage and home industries such as bread-making, growing crops, and sewing, among other endeavors, to empower this rural community with job-creation, self-sufficiency, and small business entrepreneurship. Primarily through workshops and performances in the United States, Katz keeps the message of hope and upliftment alive to raise awareness of the ongoing needs of children and young people in South Africa. Although Katz's earlier humanitarian initiative of building a school in KwaNgolosi in KwaZulu-Natal did not pan out as she originally intended, the community has a well-built physical space for other projects.

Since 2004, Katz's performances for international audiences have addressed the need for financial support through her nonprofit organization, Friends of The Peace Train, that benefits South Africa's underprivileged children. Ingrid Monson (2007), an ethnomusicologist, describes the role of musicians as significant catalysts in social and political landscapes as follows:

> During the 1960s, the civil rights and Black Power movements were so strong that they demanded that musicians and entertainers take a stand. [. . .] On September 17, 2005, I watched the television broadcast of Marsalis's Higher Ground live benefit concert and was filled with emotion as the sounds of the New Orleans style were drastically re-contextualized and infused with new relevance and poignancy by the tragic breaking of the levees and the destruction of the neighborhoods that birthed jazz. (p. 320)

Monson argues that despite the efforts of musicians from many different genres of music who have held benefit concerts, raising funds, and establishing networks "for aiding New Orleans musicians and other hurricane survivors, [. . .] this nascent movement has not captured the attention of the national media" (ibid.). Her concerns speak to the uphill climb faced by many musician activists, like Sharon Katz, whose reach through the media may be even more limited than musicians whose output may have a more commercial appeal. However, Monson's research on jazz through the changing political, social, and musical landscape of the civil rights era provides insights into the impact of performers in recurring situations that demand engagement, both musically and politically. In performing as agents of change, musicians are essential to shaping public discourse and creating an environment that promotes activism.

NOTES

1. "A quintain (pronounced kwin'ton) is an object or phenomenon or condition to be studied— a target" (Stake 2006, p. 6).

2. NAPAC refers to the Natal Performing Arts Council which was founded in 1963. NAPAC took up residence at the Playhouse Theatre Complex in 1986. All the art departments including the Natal Philharmonic Orchestra, the NAPAC Dance Company, the Loft Company and the Musicals Department operated from this venue.

3. Joseph Hanson Kwabena Nketia (born June 22, 1921) is a Ghanaian ethnomusicologist and composer. He is one of the most celebrated, published, and best-known authorities on African music. *The Music of Africa*, W. W. Norton. ISBN 0-393-02177-7. ISBN 978-0-393-02177-6 is one of his best-known books.

4. Dolly Rathebe was born in Randfontein, west of Johannesburg in 1928, but grew up within the unique cultural and political milieu of Sophiatown in the 1930s and 1940s. Rathebe is best known as an actress and singer in South Africa and abroad.

5. Information accessed November 9, 2016, http://www.sahistory.org.za/people/dolly-rathebe.

6. See endnote 10.

7. Information accessed November 10, 2016, http://www0.sun.ac.za/music/rural-project-partners/. Included with this information is a video that demonstrates Katz's work on some of the farms in 2012.

8. The YouTube video features *Masande* performing the song, *Serantabole*, (Umbrella Song) with Sharon Katz on guitar, and Schalk Joubert and his band (Accessed November 10, 2016, https://www.youtube.com/watch?v=3fBIWOBJ1Ug).

9. Accessed November 10, 2016, https://voices.no/index.php/voices/article/viewArticle/284/439.

10. Mbongeni Ngema (born in 1956 in Verulam, Kwa-Zulu Natal) is a South African composer, lyricist, director, and theater producer who won international acclaim for his musical, *Sarafina,* among others. Notably, in 2001 during the African Renaissance festival, his name was engraved on the entrance of the City Hall in Durban, Kwa-Zulu Natal, alongside those of Nelson Mandela, Oliver Tambo, Miriam Makeba, and other heroes of the liberation struggle.

11. Nonhlanhla Wanda is a singer, dancer, and teacher in Kwa-Zulu Natal who played a pivotal role during the formation of the 500-voice choir in 1992. She remains an integral member of the Peace Train.

12. Chang, H. (2015) describes the identity of an "edgewalker" as follows: "By having lived in different cultural communities, edgewalkers develop cross-cultural competence that helps them to become comfortable and functional that helps them to become comfortable and functional in multiple cultural settings" (Accessed June

6, 2018, https://www.researchgate.net/profile/Heewon_Chang/publication/23808636
1_Self-Narratives_for_Christian_Multicultural_Educators_A_Pathway_to_Unders
tanding_Self_and_Others/links/55b9183e08aed621de086175.pdf).

13. Accessed February 7, 2015, https://voices.no/index.php/voices/article/viewArt
icle/284/439.

Chapter 4

Tracking and Triangulation through Film

We've been hoping for change and at last we can see
Without color blinding our vision of peace
We won't miss a beat
When Voices Meet

—*We are the Children of South*
Africa by Sharon Katz

SOUTH AFRICA IN FOCUS

Case Study Four: The Documentary Film "When Voices Meet"

It was the optimism of Sharon Katz that struck me most powerfully during a chance encounter in 2013 at one of her intimate performances at Caffè Lena in Saratoga Springs, New York. I knew that musical activism would be at the heart of my research, but I was not prepared for the wealth of information that I discovered along the way. During my fieldwork in South Africa, I attended the eighty-six-minute documentary film, *When Voices Meet*, on July 24, 2015, at the Elizabeth Sneddon Theatre in Durban. This screening was a part of the Durban Film Festival. The premiere of this documentary directed by Nancy Sutton Smith of the United States had taken place two days earlier at *Suncoast*, an extravagant entertainment facility in Durban, South Africa.

This documentary's release was most fortunate for me, especially since I had no prior knowledge of this film's development when I began my research. The film served as a central document in understanding The Peace Train Project (a term that the founder, Sharon Katz, uses). It also served as an invaluable tool to improve this qualitative research's validity and reliability since one of the critical components of my research process was triangulation. Merriam (1995) draws from the experience and writings of Guba and Lincoln (1981), Merriam (1985), and Patton (1991), which speak to strategies such as "triangulation" that may be employed to strengthen the internal validity of a qualitative study (p. 54). The process of triangulation comprises the following:

> The use of multiple investigators, multiple sources of data or multiple methods to confirm the emerging findings (Denzin 1970; Mathison 1988). For example, if the researcher hears about the phenomenon in interviews, sees it taking place in observations, and reads about it in pertinent documents, he or she can be confident of the "reality" of the situation, as perceived by those in it, is being conveyed as "truthfully" as possible (ibid.).

The Peace Train experience is validated in several ways. There are detailed transcripts of my interviews with the 1993 South African Peace Train Tour participants. Katz and the interviewees shared photos and artifacts with me. Further, it was possible to triangulate the interviewees' narratives with a critical document, *When Voices Meet* (the documentary released in 2015), that contained video footage of the South African Tour.

The informational piece advertising the films at the festival had already created excitement and joyful anticipation among attendees. Evidence of this enthusiasm was reflected by a sizable crowd at the Elizabeth Sneddon Theater at the University of Natal in Durban, with its capacity of four hundred people. A description of the documentary stated:

> Music therapist Sharon Katz joined with singer and educator Nonhlanhla Wanda to form a 500-voice multiracial choir that would break through apartheid's barriers. Threatened with bombs and thwarted at every turn, they prevailed and railroaded across the country aboard the Peace Train. They performed together for seven years, never lost touch with one another; and then reunited 20 years later to tell their stories and reflect upon the Peace Train's impact on their views of the country today.

The director bio read as follows:

> Nancy Sutton Smith has a Master's in education and teaches digital cinema, video editing, graphics, journalism and mass media at Northeast Community College in Norfolk, Nebraska. Prior to teaching, she spent 30 years as a television news broadcaster, producer, and video editor. Nancy collected six regional Emmys during her career.[1]

Understanding the Documentary

Any critique of this documentary necessitates an understanding of the documentary film. John Grierson coined the term in the 1920s to refer to a genre that he saw as a "creative treatment of reality" (Hartwig 2001, para. 2). In *Representing Reality,* Bill Nichols (1991) speaks of the expectation that documentaries' sounds and images would bear an indexical relation to the historical world. He posits that viewers expect little or no modification of the material that has been recorded on film (p. 27). Hartwig (2001) presents the argument that in the postmodern age—even before the widespread use of digital tools—there has been the ability to manipulate and alter images. While recognizing the documentary's social importance and a champion of the genre, Nichols (1991) acknowledges that objective representation can sometimes be problematic. Gunthar Hartwig (2001, para. 5) offers the following insights:

> The representation of the thing can never be the thing—it always passes through both a technical filter (the camera and display devices) and a psychological or social filter (the filmmaker). Postmodern theory often argues that reality itself is a social construction. The practices and activities that we undertake create our world. Documentary can be seen as being a part of this constructive process, in the same company as such discourses as law, education, economics and politics.

Most significantly, Asch, Marshall, and Spier (1973) see the value of a camera as its ability to do and record what the human eye cannot. The writers discuss the difficulty of recording an event and the handling of the film after shooting. They describe the camera as having a "position in both time and space," which imposes a particular perspective on any action. By turning the camera on and off, one automatically structures events as determined by the camera operator. When editing the film, it goes through another layer of structuring. This editing can lead the viewer to "almost any desired conclusion." Finally, the third layer of restructuring occurs since every viewer is impacted differently by any film segment depending on their individual backgrounds (ibid., 179–180). These many perspectives inform and create a greater awareness among viewers, which ultimately impacts one's response to a film.

Besides the interpretative considerations that come with making every documentary, Katz's physical challenges in trying to piece together this film seemed insurmountable. According to Katz, the quality of some of the footage was so poor, and the projected cost with a potential director was more than she could afford to pay. Finally, in 2010, Nancy Sutton Smith, who had worked for the television station, CBS in the United States, agreed to take on the task of trying to piece together the journey that Sharon Katz had undertaken. Her purpose was to spread a message of peace through music during the political transition in South Africa. Through her musical activism, Katz wanted to bridge the racial divide perpetrated by the apartheid government and the Group Areas Act that created separate residential areas for people from the four South African classifications of race (White, Black, Colored, and Indian).

Williams (1993), in her article, *Mirrors without Memories: Truth, History and the New Documentary,* argues that there are rich contradictions inherent in documentaries. In analyzing several documentaries, she points to the fact that "the postmodern deluge of images seems to suggest that there can be no a priori truth of the referent to which the image refers." However, "in this same deluge, it is still the moving image that has the power to move audiences to a new appreciation of previously unknown truth" (p. 10). For audiences in South Africa, the revelation of the "unknown truths" was for young people who had grown up in a post-apartheid South African society. For audiences at the many film festivals abroad, this documentary created a renewed curiosity in the political transition of South Africa from a country segregated through apartheid to a "rainbow nation" intended to represent all its people.

The ideas of peace and healing expounded by President Mandela were carried forward in many ways: The Truth and Reconciliation Commission[2] created in 1994 after the democratically elected government came into power played a significant role, hosting the Africa Cup of Nations[3] in South Africa was a source of national pride, and then there was an explosion of international musical greats (Michael Jackson, Whitney Houston, Luciano Pavarotti, among others) who graced the concert arenas throughout the country. Through it all, musical activists like Sharon Katz were engaged at the grassroots level. They were reaching out to the most important commodity of any nation and harnessing the power of children and youth irrespective of race—singing and dancing together to promote harmony and peace even before Nelson Mandela was elected president.

Comparing Musical Collaborations

Sharon Katz is the central figure in the 2015 documentary, *When Voices Meet,* directed by Sutton Smith. In 2012, the documentary *Under African Skies* featured the American musician Paul Simon as the essential character. Both documentaries deal with musical collaborations and political ramifications for the artists during the apartheid era. Although the documentary, *When Voices Meet* stands in stark contrast to *Under African Skies,* directed by filmmaker Joe Berlinger, there are exciting intersection points among these documentaries' main role-players. Berlinger enjoyed successes previously with *Brother's Keeper* (1992), *Metallica: Some Kind of Monster* (2004), and the *Paradise Lost Trilogy* (1996, 2001, 2012).

In *Under African Skies,* he explores the history, the controversies, and the impact of Paul Simon's *Graceland* album recorded in 1986 with the South

African all-male *a capella* choral group, Ladysmith Black Mambazo. This collaboration with South African artists defied the United Nations-sanctioned cultural boycott, intended to pressure the apartheid government to end racial segregation policies. At the time, Paul Simon appeared to be tone-deaf to his actions' political and social ramifications. Harry Belafonte had advised him[4] to consult with both the ANC[5] and Artists Against Apartheid (founded in 1983 by Dali Tambo[6] with musician Jerry Dammers). One of their initiatives was to encourage international artists to respect the cultural boycott of South Africa. The boycott meant that artists should not perform or sell their music in South Africa. Paul Simon went ahead with his recordings, the album sold worldwide, but anti-apartheid protests followed at his concerts with outrage expressed in the media. The documentary reveals that on July 1, 2012, Simon still found himself explaining his rationale in a conversation with Dali Tambo more than two decades later.[7]

Paul Simon and Ladysmith Black Mambazo's artistic connection is unmistakable from the documentary's clips and indeed in the *Graceland* album itself. Berlinger cleverly weaves his narrative with archival footage and clips of Paul Simon's return to South Africa in 2011. He includes interviews with political figures, musicians, and celebrities to present many differing viewpoints. The essential points gleaned from the debate of the documentary are through the comments of Simon and Tambo. Simon poses the question early in the film when he asks, "When the artist gets into some sort of disagreement with politics, why are the politicians designated to be the ones to tell us, the artists, what to do?" In contrast, Tambo, who was very troubled by Simon's actions, articulates very clearly that "This situation was not about Paul Simon, it was about the liberation of the people of South Africa."

The fame of Ladysmith Black Mambazo did not diminish through their collaboration with Paul Simon. If anything, their fame increased, and they drew crowds wherever they performed (both in South Africa and abroad), due in no small part to their exceptional choreography and rich choral harmonies. They describe their partnership with Paul Simon as follows:

In the mid-1980s, Paul Simon visited South Africa and incorporated the group's rich tenor/alto/bass harmonies into his famous "Graceland" album—a landmark recording that was considered seminal in introducing world music to mainstream audiences. A year later, Paul Simon produced Ladysmith Black Mambazo's first worldwide release, "Shaka Zulu," which won a Grammy Award in 1988 for Best Folk Recording. Since then, the group has been awarded two more Grammy Awards ("Raise Your Spirit Higher" (2004) and "Ilembe (2009)") and has been nominated a total of fifteen times.[8]

Storhoff (2015) describes the effect of Paul Simon's impact in working with Ladysmith Black Mambazo at a pivotal stage of South African history very succinctly:

> The story of Paul Simon's *Graceland* has been told on film before, but *Under African Skies* brings important nuance to the narrative and demonstrates how artists claiming purely musical objectives can become embroiled in political situations that raise complicated ethical and artistic questions. While Simon argues that his good intentions brought awareness to South African music, the film shows that he still does not fully understand why his actions were problematic. *Under African Skies,* [. . .] entertains viewers but also provoke them to consider issues that continue to impact international cultural exchanges and the advancement of human rights. (p. 172)

Another critical perspective is that of Joseph Shabalala, the founder of Ladysmith Black Mambazo, who described Paul Simon in favorable terms in 2011 footage in the documentary, as someone who "has a special magic." Figure 4.1 captures the close relationship between Simon and Shabalala. Muller explores the opposing dimensions of Paul Simon's collaboration with South African musicians in the mid-1980s. On the one hand, she speaks of *Graceland* as being created at a time "when political oppression of Black South Africans by the apartheid government was at its peak, and resistance (both internally and internationally) to apartheid was mounting" (2008, 68). On the other hand, Muller also sees *Graceland* as a project that demonstrated that musicians could bridge the racial divide and work successfully together. This collaboration speaks to the "process in the creation of 'world music' . . . a highly successful story about the capacity of very different musical practices to find a way to blend, harmonize, to become palatable to a wide range of tastes both in South Africa and the world at large" (ibid.). Muller's analysis may apply to the very different context of Sharon Katz & The Peace Train—another project that demonstrates the power of collaboration through singing, *When Voices Meet.*

The music of Ladysmith Black Mambazo is featured in the documentary *When Voices Meet.* In 1993, when Sharon Katz decided to create The Peace Train, her prominent musical ally on that journey was Ladysmith Black Mambazo, who traveled on the train with Katz's 120-voice choir accompanied by ten band members. They were not only a musical drawcard for audiences at every performance along the way, but they have also always championed the activism of Katz.

Through a series of fortunate circumstances, the young man, Malcolm Nhleko, realized a dream. He sang with Katz in the 500-voice choir as a teenager, traveled with the Peace Train through South Africa, and the 1995 tour to the United States. He inspired Katz to build the school in KwaNgcolosi, and

Figure 4.1 Joseph Shabalala and Paul Simon Perform at the Library of Congress Awards Ceremony in 2007 When Paul Simon Received the First Gershwin Prize for Popular Song. Photo courtesy of Scott Suchman (photographer).

he is currently the sound engineer for Ladysmith Black Mambazo on their national and international travels. I had an opportunity to meet with Nhleko in February 2016 when Ladysmith Black Mambazo performed at Troy Music Hall in New York. He described his experience with the group as having "come full circle" (M. Nhleko, personal communication, February 10, 2016). I had first met Nhleko briefly at the Durban Film Festival at a screening of the documentary *When Voices Meet* in July 2015.

While Paul Simon, a White American artist of international fame, created controversy through his music-making with Black musicians during a politically tumultuous time in South Africa, Katz was embraced by many as an unofficial "goodwill ambassador" in the early 1990s. She was a South African with a very different purpose. Katz worked through music at the grassroots level with children and young adults from many different racial and socioeconomic communities. She was trying desperately to help foster understanding, harmony, and healing among people who had all (White, Black, Indian, and colored) been subject to the effects of apartheid.

Both Berlinger (*Under African Skies*) and Sutton Smith (*When Voices Meet*) create compelling narratives authenticated by actual footage. Their many interviews include credible voices of people whose memories create a living document of a time when artists navigated the difficult roadblocks of apartheid South Africa while trying to preserve their integrity as performers. There is a significant difference, however, between the interviewees in both documentaries. *Under African Skies* features many well-known artists and celebrities, from Ray Phiri to Oprah. *When Voices Meet* relies predominantly on parents, chaperones, young adults (who were children on the South African Peace Train), and a few well-known artists like John Kani and Abigail Kubeka to provide the viewer with a window into this experience of musical activism.

When Voices Meet lacks the professional videography apparent in the film *Under African Skies*. The footage of Katz in rural areas of South Africa shows her working with underprivileged children in schools with broken windows and scant furniture. These clips do not have the sound quality or picture quality expected in twenty-first-century technology. Rather than detract from the documentary's substance, the absence of professional videography adds poignancy to the moment. It reminds the viewer of the challenging circumstances under which children were living and learning. It also reveals the courage of one White woman who challenged the status quo, who often went into segregated areas, where she was a stranger representing the unknown. Katz pressed forward with her goal of bringing the joy and healing power of music to children from diverse socioeconomic and racial backgrounds to showcase a 500-voice choir at the Durban City Hall.

This artistic and organizational feat that overcame the bureaucratic red tape of a segregated society would lead to the formation of The Peace Train in 1993. As the documentary progresses, the quality of the images and the sound improves (due in no small part to having a five-member television crew in tow). A historic, racially integrated journey on a train with 120 children, fifteen teachers and chaperones, ten band members, and the renowned choral group, Ladysmith Black Mambazo, is revealed. Katz provided the statistics of this tour in an email communication dated July 7, 2017. This journey through South Africa, followed by a tour in the United States and other performances, reflect a microcosm of the optimism that many South Africans shared for a country that would eventually free itself from the stranglehold of an apartheid government.

Activism through Another Lens

When Voices Meet documents a journey that was twenty years in the making. The video footage, clips, and powerful still images are informative, compelling, entertaining, and sometimes amusing. Still, it is the narration (by Sharon Katz) and the memories of the interviewees—by famous South African personalities such as John Kani and Abigail Kubeka alongside teachers, parents, and children [now adults] of the Peace Train experience—that provide the context and a deeper level of understanding.

The documentary spans several years, beginning in August 1992. Katz goes to schools in the areas segregated into four separate education departments of KwaZulu-Natal and works on music with teachers and students in preparation for the 500-voice choir that would perform together for the first time at the Durban City Hall in May 1993. Katz's first visit on film is at the Abambo Primary School, where Nonhlanhla Wanda is a young, energetic teacher. In this scene, the viewer is drawn immediately into Katz's world of music. The words of the song, "When Voices Meet," is written on the chalkboard. The African children are singing joyfully. Wanda is encouraging the children by singing English words very clearly with them. Cohen (Katz's partner) moves in time to the music while engaging the children, and Katz is playing the guitar and singing. As explained fully in Chapter 6, Wanda's role as a "culture-broker" for Katz and Cohen, mediating access to African children in a segregated Black township, cannot be overstated. These were children whose first language was Zulu. Despite the broken windowpanes and the overcrowded room—with little evidence of furniture or learning materials—the children's focused singing accompanied by guitar engages the viewer.

The stark contrast among each school's facilities as Katz rehearses from one racial group to the next is a reminder of the iniquities of the apartheid system. The 500-voice choir's performance on-screen showcases the attention to detail in Katz's conception of this event. She achieves this through subtle gestures: the inclusion of the tablas (Indian drums); an eclectic mix of dance styles from Zulu dancing to Indian folk dance; the singing of songs in several languages from Zulu to English; and her not-so-subtle message of unity and peace with a multiracial choir. Her nod to the Indian community of KwaZulu-Natal does not go unnoticed as the largest community of Indians outside India lives in Durban, South Africa.

This event sets the stage for the South African Peace Train Tour. We are transported to 1993 as the train leaves Durban Station with its very excited passengers on board. We catch glimpses of a train journey and performances throughout South Africa with 120 voices and ten band members as well as Ladysmith Black Mambazo on this historic tour. Words alone cannot adequately describe the children and adults' energy and vitality depicted in this documentary.

One of the South African Peace Train's powerful performances with footage of the choir singing to choreographed movements and a clip of Katz dancing with Joseph Shabalala, the leader of Ladysmith Black Mambazo, is that of the Cape Town Jazz Festival of December 1993. The Peace Train performing alongside Ladysmith Black Mambazo draws the attention of crowds of onlookers at the festival, many of whom are dancing in time to the music. The Peace Train's enthusiastic reception at the Cape Town Jazz Festival inspired thoughts of a tour to the United States.

In the documentary, Malcolm Nhleko (Sound Engineer for Ladysmith Black Mambazo), a teenager with the Peace Train in the 1990s, recalls the excitement of just thinking about the possibility of a trip with the Peace Train to the United States after one of their many performances. Then, in a letter dated October 13, 1994, from the Consul General of the United States, shared in the documentary film, the realization of Katz's developing vision to bring The Peace Train message to an international audience is confirmed. This letter recognizes significant aspects of The Peace Train message. It states (in part):

I am very pleased to endorse the upcoming visit to the United States of the KwaZulu-Natal based "Peace Train" singers and musicians as ambassadors of goodwill and peaceful conflict resolution. Their efforts to deflect negative responses for positive ones have been highly recognized and commended in this province and throughout South Africa. The group is representative of the myriad of races and cultures which make up the rich cultural heritage of KwaZulu-Natal.

The letter goes on:

It is an honor for me to inform you that they have been invited to the United States as well as to Israel to spread their music and methodology for peaceful co-existence. The people of this region and throughout South Africa are pulling together to assist in financing this visit. Their music, methodology, and message have much to contribute to easing tensions in the troubled cities and in the United States, where gang rivalries have proven disruptive.

I bring the visit of the Peace Train to your attention in the hope that you may know of organizations, individual(s) or entities which might be able to assist South African sponsors and organizers in financing and supporting their travel to key cities in the U.S. while the group is performing at the New Orleans Jazz Festival in May.

The letter is signed by Pamela E. Bridgewater, The Consul General of the United States of America.

The tour of 1995 with the South African Peace Train Tour to the United States with twenty-nine singers, chaperones, and a full band (keyboards, drums, bass guitarist, a horn section including a trombone, trumpet, and saxophone with Katz on lead and rhythm guitar) took these young performers on a five-week, eight-city tour of the United States performing at venues such as Disney World's International Festival to the New Orleans Jazz Festival, from Harlem to Hampton, to Memphis and Cincinnati, and from Philadelphia's Penn's Landing to Washington, DC's Duke Ellington School of Performing Arts. This unlikely journey of Sharon Katz & The Peace Train was made possible through sponsorships from the government and the private sectors in both South Africa and America. Speaking on camera, a music critic, Don Albert, at the New Orleans Jazz Festival praised the performances of Sharon Katz & The Peace Train. He exclaims enthusiastically, "To see the South African group [. . .] with music spread over forty acres [. . .] to see the crowd that gathered just to watch the Peace Train was incredible to see."

This documentary also reveals footage of what Katz describes as a most fortuitous meeting with her "childhood idol," Joni Mitchell, at Maximo's Restaurant in New Orleans, referenced in Chapter 2. In footage featuring Mitchell at the restaurant where the choir spontaneously bursts into song, Mitchell smiles and says, "We've just been graced with this heavenly choir. The whole restaurant is kind of stunned [. . .] it's beautiful [. . .] they are just great ambassadors for Africa."

This film serves as an essential research document that provides a chronology of some of the highlights of Katz's work through actual video footage and interviews with individuals, some of whom have a keen understanding of the South African political landscape dating back to the apartheid era. In contrast, others have been an integral part of the South African Peace Train experience. This documentary also corroborates information gathered through interviews with the Peace Train participants described and analyzed in Chapter 3.

Screenings and Awards of the Documentary, When Voices Meet

The following table provides an outline of the screenings of the documentary, *When Voices Meet*, at film festivals in South Africa, the United States of America, and Canada. The documentary has also earned awards at several festivals. Table 4.1 depicts the screenings and awards received.

The release of the film, *When Voices Meet,* in 2015, created renewed interest in the grassroots efforts of Sharon Katz & The Peace Train. Participants of the original tour of 1993, and other members, such as Lenore Goss Matjie, who joined the group in 1995, found themselves in the spotlight. Besides their documentary interviews, they received media attention answering questions from television hosts at the film's premiere. At subsequent screenings of the film at the Durban Film Festival, Katz acknowledged all participants in the audience. In lieu of a "Question and Answer" session that typically follows such screenings, Sharon Katz entertained Durban's audience with a miniconcert performance. Informants, whom I had interviewed a few days before the screening, were invited to join the performers on stage. They had first performed with Katz in the first *When Voices Meet* concert in 1992 when they were children, young teachers, or chaperones. This concert of 1992 inspired the formation of The Peace Train and the many shows and tours

Table 4.1   Details of the Screenings of the Documentary and Awards Received. *Details provided by Marilyn Cohen.*

Date	City	State and Country	Festival/Event	Award
7/22/15	Durban	South Africa	Durban International Film Festival	World Premiere
8/21/15	Washington	DC, USA	World Music & International Film Festival	Best Documentary, Best Director, Best Original Soundtrack, Humanitarian Award
9/19/15	Chicago	IL, USA	Chicago International Social Change Film Festival	
9/26/15	Toronto	Canada	Community Global Film Festival	Best Documentary
9/30/15	Wilmington	DE, USA	Depth of Field Film Festival	
10/16/15	Jersey City	NJ, USA	Jersey City International TV & Film Festival	Best Documentary
10/24/15	Antigonish	Canada	Antigonish Film Festival	
10/25/15	Philadelphia	PA, USA	Philadelphia Film Festival	Audience Award
10/25/15	Yonkers	NY, USA	YoFi Fest	
11/7/15	Springfield	IL, USA	Route 66 Film Festival	Notable Documentary
11/7/15	St. Louis	MI, USA	St. Louis International Film Festival	
11/8/15	Teaneck	NJ, USA	Teaneck Film Festival	
11/21/15	Ft. Lauderdale	FL, USA	Ft. Lauderdale International Film Festival	President's Award
12/9/15	Nassau	Bahamas	Bahamas International Film Festival	
12/26/15	49 Countries	Africa	AfriDocs	
1/2/16	Big Island	HI, USA	Waimea Ocean Film Festival	Best Inspirational Film
1/12/16	Oahu	HI, USA	University of Hawaii	

Date	City	State and Country	Festival/Event	Award
1/31/16	St. Augustine	FL, USA	St. Augustine Film Festival	
2/17/16	Chestnut Hill	PA, USA	Chestnut Hill College	
3/11/16	Dover	DE, USA	Schwartz Centre for the Performing Arts	
3/13/16	Omaha	NE, USA	Omaha Film Festival	
3/18/16	Harrisburg	PA, USA	National Music Therapy Association Conference	
4/24/16	Beacon	NY, USA	Towne Crier	
4/27/16	Palm Springs	CA, USA	Palm Springs Women in Film & TV	
4/29/16	Fresno	CA, USA	CineCulture	
5/1/16	Santa Cruz	CA, USA	Reel Work Film Festival	
5/3/16	Berkeley	CA, USA	Berkeley Film Foundation	
5/6/16	New York City	NY, USA	New York University	
5/21/16	Whallonsburg	NY, USA	The Grange	
5/22/16	Brooklyn	NY, USA	Ethical Culture Society of Brooklyn	
6/25/16	Woodstock	NY, USA	Upstate Theatre	
7/2/16	Madison	WI, USA	National Women's Music & Film Festival	Kristin Lems Social Change Through Music Award
10/5/16	San Francisco	CA, USA	California Institute of Integral Studies	
10/25/16	Philadelphia	PA, USA	Temple University	
11/19/16	Toronto	Canada	Toronto South Africa Film Festival	

that followed. Nonhlanhla Wanda (see Figure 4.2), the African music teacher from South Africa and cofounder of The Peace Train, attended many of the screenings of the documentary with Sharon Katz, Marilyn Cohen, and Wendy Quick throughout the United States and Canada.

Creating a 500-voice multilingual and multiracial choir with its first performance in 1992 is highlighted in the documentary *When Voices Meet*. The

Figure 4.2   (From Left to Right) Nonhlanhla Wanda, Sharon Katz, and Wendy Quick at the Screening of *When Voices Meet* on September 26, 2015, at the Community Global Film Festival in Toronto, Canada, Where the Film Received the "Best Documentary" Award. Photo courtesy of Marilyn Cohen (photographer).

founding of the South African Peace Train emerged out of this endeavor. This initiative occurred at a time when South Africa had apartheid entrenched in its constitution. In taking 120 children between nine and seventeen years from different racial and socioeconomic backgrounds on a ten-day concert tour traveling together on a passenger train, Katz challenged the political and social status quo. She created a racially integrated experience for children who had grown up isolated from one another through the government's policy of separate development.

The formation of what became known as "The Peace Train" interrupted the political order of apartheid. It broke down social barriers among children and adults through integration, from sharing sleeping cars to eating meals together to engaging in recreational activities such as card-playing and chess, to performances of music, song, and dance. From a therapeutic perspective, creating an atmosphere of unity through music among South Africans from different backgrounds was Katz's primary focus. Her broader goal was to promote a peaceful transition to democracy. Within a global context, musicians are increasingly prepared to harness the power of music, creating musical experiences that are inclusive, both culturally and geographically, to tap into a universal language that speaks to our shared humanity.

This shared humanity is also evident in the documentary film, *The Music of Strangers: Yo-Yo Ma and the Silk Road Ensemble,* released in June 2016. It unveils a sixteen-year collaboration of exceptional musicians. They came together from different cultural backgrounds to celebrate the universal power of music. This collaboration was the brainchild of the acclaimed cellist Yo-Yo Ma who recruited musicians from the ancient trade route linking Asia, Africa, and Europe. The *Silk Road Ensemble* is an international collective that further demonstrates music's ability to transcend geographical boundaries, blend disparate cultures, and inspire hope for artists and audiences. This documentary introduces the viewer to a varied range of performers, including instrumentalists, vocalists, composers, arrangers, visual artists, and storytellers, as they gather in locations across the world, exploring the ways art can both preserve traditions and shape cultural evolution.

The documentary films discussed, such as *When Voices Meet, Under African Skies*, or *The Music of Strangers: Yo-Yo Ma and the Silk Road Ensemble*, are essential documents to understand the context of this research. All these documentaries showcase the power of collaboration and a celebration of music, and they all represent sustained effort to realize their ultimate goals. As Mandela famously declared, "It always seems impossible until it's done."

NOTES

1. Accessed August 22, 2015, http://www.durbanfilmfest.co.za/index.php/film/item/599-when-voices-meet.

2. The TRC was set up in terms of the Promotion of National Unity and Reconciliation Act, No. 34 of 1995, and was based in Cape Town. The hearings started in 1996. The mandate of the commission was to bear witness to, record, and in some cases, grant amnesty to the perpetrators of crimes relating to human rights violations, as well as reparation and rehabilitation. Bishop Desmond Tutu chaired this Commission.

3. South Africa hosted the 20th ACN competition in 1996, marking their first ever appearance after a decades long ban was lifted with the end of apartheid in the country and a failed attempt to qualify in 1994. Bafana Bafana, the South African soccer team won their first title on home soil, defeating Tunisia in the final.

4. Harry Belafonte (born in 1927) is a multitalented African American performer also known for his social and political activism. His early song successes include "The Banana Boat Song" (Day-O) and "Jamaica Farewell." https://www.biography.com/people/harry-belafonte-12103211.

5. African National Congress.

6. Dali Tambo is the son of the late ANC president, Oliver Tambo. He and his family lived in exile for thirty years in England. http://www.sahistory.org.za/people/dali-tambo.

7. Accessed August 30, 2015, at https://www.bbc.co.uk/programmes/p00vl8rm.

8. Accessed June 29, 2017, at http://mambazo.com/our_story/.

Chapter 5

Replicating the Peace Train Model in the United States

Listen everybody, can you feel the beat
We can be united, just stand up on your feet
Take a look around you; the world's a mess right now
So brothers and sisters, we can play our part somehow

—*We Can Be The Change, We Can Be*
The Change We Want by Sharon Katz
with Zulu lyrics by Nonhlanhla Wanda

WIDENING THE APERTURE

Case Study Five: The American Peace Train Tour 2016

When Sharon Katz left South Africa as a young woman in 1981 to study music therapy at Temple University in Philadelphia, Pennsylvania, she could not have foreseen the impact that she would have more than thirty years later back in the United States. Katz was encouraged by potential sponsors and well-wishers to create a Peace Train tour after the successful release and the screenings of the documentary, *When Voices Meet*, at several film festivals in South Africa and abroad. The aim was to promote peace and harmony among young people in America, where racial and socioeconomic inequalities fuel unrest in communities.

The Global North to South Shift

Katz's experience speaks to the South to North global shift. A model for racial integration and a message of peace and hope implemented successfully in the South is applied to situations that beg for healing, peace, and hope in the North. A South African introducing a model of integration in the United States goes against the grain of thinking that emerged in the 1980s with the Brandt line,[1] which suggests that more economically and politically significant "first-world" countries of the Northern hemisphere, such as the United States, are leaders of research and innovation. The circumstances leading up to Katz's return to the United States also highlight the country's dark underbelly. A North-South divide exists within its borders, manifesting itself through acts of racism and the growing disparity between the rich and the poor.

The United States in Crisis

The shooting deaths of young unarmed African American youth and men in various parts of the country have exacerbated this divide. On April 27, 2015, Rachel Maddow, the host of a television program that expounds news stories and opinions, *The Rachael Maddow Show*, on MSNBC in the United States, provided an informative timeline of instances of police violence against minorities in 2015 alone. The case of Michael Brown of Ferguson, Missouri, who was shot and killed by a police officer, received widespread media coverage in the United States and elicited outrage from communities across the country. Other examples in 2015 of police brutality against unarmed minorities included Eric Garner of Staten Island, who was choked to death in a headlock by police officers for selling loose cigarettes. Tamir Rice, a child of twelve, was shot in a park by Cleveland police for waving a toy handgun. Sarreshbay Patel, of Alabama, was slammed to the ground by police officers so hard he was paralyzed. Antonio Zambrano-Montez was shot seventeen times in the back for throwing rocks. Floyd Dent of Michigan was beaten so severely during a traffic stop that he suffered a cracked eye socket and broken ribs. Eric Harris of Tulsa, Missouri, was shot by a "reserve deputy" with no police training, and Walter Scott was killed during a traffic stop by a South Carolina policeman.[2] In many of these American states, days and weeks of protest ensued to effect change, demand accountability, and highlight the plight of minorities within the country.

In the light of these and ongoing atrocities, Katz's goal in 2016, as it had been in South Africa, was to bring young people out of a sense of despair and provide an atmosphere of unity and healing. Through social and musical interactions of young people from different racial and socioeconomic backgrounds, Katz worked toward realizing this objective through The Peace Train Tour of 2016. However, the work of grassroots is never done.

In 2020, amid a global pandemic, the United States found itself in a very similar situation once again with the murder of a forty-six-year-old Black man, George Floyd, by a White police officer. On May 25, 2020, Floyd was killed in Minneapolis, Minnesota, during an arrest for allegedly using a counterfeit bill. This incident sparked the resurgence of the *Black Lives Matter* movement. Sandra Susan Smith (2020), a sociology professor at the University of California-Berkeley, points out that the protests surrounding George Floyd's murder are unlike past protests against police brutality and racism—the racial and class composition of protesters alone makes this moment different. Smith asserts that more people who have felt alienated now "feel seen and heard, and this has bred a sense of optimism." However, she states that history preaches caution. Smith affirms that despite some apparent differences, this outrage has occurred many times before. She adds that "with the certainty that the sun will rise, we will probably be here again in the not-too-distant future."[3] This observation also speaks to the ebb and flow of social, political, and musical activism as societies respond to the issues at hand.

The Belafonte Connection

Harry Belafonte (referenced in Chapter 4), an American musician and activist, has always been an outspoken critic of political and social policies, especially those of the United States that disenfranchise poor and underprivileged communities. Coincidentally, I met Harry Belafonte and his daughter Shari Belafonte at two separate events in the United States. During the apartheid era, Harry Belafonte advised Paul Simon against collaboration with South African musicians during a United Nations-sanctioned cultural boycott. Paul Simon disagreed and bore the brunt of the ensuing controversy (discussed in Chapter 4).

On November 11, 2017, it was an honor to attend "An Evening with Harry Belafonte," a sit-down conversation between WAMC/Northeast (New York) Public Radio's Alan Chartock and the Grammy, Tony, and Emmy Award-winning performer, Harry Belafonte. The program, which is part of the New York Living Legacy Series, also marked Belafonte's ninetieth birthday. On this night, Belafonte reiterated his commitment to humanitarian efforts in the United States and other parts of the world, including Africa. Harry Belafonte has inculcated this spirit of activism in his children, one of whom is Shari Belafonte. I had the privilege of sharing a table with her and other nominated actors at the World Music and International Film Festival in Washington, D.C., on August 21, 2015. At this festival, *When Voices Meet* received many accolades, including awards for "Best Documentary," "Best Director," "Best Original Soundtrack," as well a "Humanitarian Award" for Sharon Katz.

Shari Belafonte (the daughter of Harry Belafonte), an actress and activist who also met Katz at the film festival for the first time, was impressed with her humanitarian work and music. In an article dated September 11, 2016, that appeared in *Trend Privé Magazine* in the United States, Shari Belafonte describes her father as an activist first. She notes that his artistic output is secondary to his activism, describing his advocacy for Civil Rights, Native Americans, Incarcerated Youth, African Relief, and the end of apartheid. Shari Belafonte expresses her joy at meeting both Sharon Katz and Marilyn Cohen at the screening of the documentary *When Voices Meet* at the International Film Festival in August 2015. This interest in Katz & The Peace Train resulted in her promoting and screening the film in Palm Springs, California, in April 2016. Then, Katz declared that she was planning another Peace Train tour with American children from around the country to spread a message of peace. Shari Belafonte, pictured with members of The Peace Train in Figure 5.1, describes the excitement that followed:

> Sharon told me, "We're starting in N.Y. and going down to D.C. with stops along the way." Less than three months to prep and plan, and raise the capital to fund this event? I thought, "Ok, here we go again, I am in." [. . .] with six (6) stops along the way to spread the word of PEACE and UNITY, through wonderful music and dance [. . .], there's still a youthful underground root system that cannot be killed which is seeking PEACE. Kids of all races, sizes, and shapes gathered in a small amount of time to learn the songs and dances and spread the word of PEACE. Grassroots. It's where it always starts.[4]

Putting the "United" Back into the USA

The Itinerary

The original itinerary for the tour across America with a 100-voice choir included the following concerts from July 4 to July 18, 2016, including the cities of St. Louis, Chicago, Albany, New York City, Jersey City, Trenton, Philadelphia, Baltimore, and Washington D.C. However, streamlined plans for this tour were necessary because of financial constraints. The American Peace Train Tour of July 2016 became a five-concert tour which started on Saturday, July 9, 2016, according to the following schedule and details:

New York City: Saturday, July 9, 2016 at 8:00 PM
New York Society for Ethical Culture
West 64th St. at Central Park West, New York, NY
Special Offer: Advance Tickets only $15
Jersey City: Sunday, July 10, 2016 at 5:00 PM
Summerfest at Liberty State Park, Jersey City, NJ.
Bring a blanket or chair. Free
Trenton: Tuesday, July 12, 2016 at 12:30 PM
On the lawn at Covenant Presbyterian Church
471 Parkway Avenue, Trenton, NJ. Free
Philadelphia: Wednesday, July 13, 2016 at 7:30 PM
World Cafe Live, Downstairs
3025 Walnut St., Philadelphia, PA

Figure 5.1   Shari Belafonte (Second from Right), Pictured with Sharon Katz, Wendy Quick, Nonhlanhla Wanda, and Marilyn Cohen, Receives an Award on July 9, 2016, on Behalf of Her Family for Being "Champions of Social Justice & The Arts, Worldwide" at the First Concert of the American Peace Train Tour in New York. Courtesy of Sharon Katz. Used with permission.

Tickets for World café—Save $5 with Advance Purchase Here
Washington, DC: Sunday, July 17, 2016 at 12:00 Noon
Nelson Mandela Day Celebration with UNESCO Center for Peace
Washington Monument's Sylvan Theater
Bring a blanket or chair. Free

The Performers

Listed in the table below are the demographic details of gender, race, and age of the eighty-six (*N* = 86) participants in the American Peace Train Tour of 2016.[5] Table 5.1 summarizes the composition of the participants on tour by gender, age, and race. Excluded from the data are participants who performed for only one event.

It is striking that the female to male ratio of participants on this tour was almost four to one. Against the backdrop of police violence against Black youth, the angst, the outrage, the sadness, and the hope for peace were the call to musical activism for young people in the fifteen to twenty-four age categories. My informal conversations with this group of young people and

Table 5.1   Demographic Data of the American Peace Train Tour of July 2016.

Participants on Tour (N=86)	Female	Male	Percentage Rate
Gender	69	17	100%
Age			
Under 15	14	2	18.6%
15–24	23	10	38.4%
25–44	8	0	9.3%
45–64	20	3	26.7%
65+	4	2	7.0%
Race			
White	29	9	44.1%
Black	20	7	31.4%
Hispanic	7	1	9.3%
Asian	1	0	1.2%
Hawaiian	4	0	4.7%
Mixed	8	0	9.3%

listening to their creative output on this tour allowed me to gain insights into their commitment to creating an atmosphere of trust and harmony through their music and performances. I also learned of the feelings of uncertainty of young African American males. They feared that they could suffer a similar fate to victims of police brutality in the United States.

The racial mix of participants on the American Peace Train Tour is reflective of a complex confluence of factors. According to the U.S. Census Bureau, the racial make-up of the American population across the United States in 2015 indicated that the White population was in the majority with 77.1 percent while Blacks made up 13.3 percent, Asians 5.6 percent, Hispanic 17.6 percent, Hawaiian 0.2 percent, and people of mixed-race 2.6 percent.[6] A comparison of the statistics reveals a higher level of participation among Black and Hawaiian performers. This engagement by people of color may have been triggered by the social issues that precipitated this tour in the first place. The police's increased brutality against young Black men in America with its ensuing unrest in several cities was a primary cause for alarm and a call for peace and harmony. A secondary issue raised during the tour was the state-supported proposal for a massive Thirty Meter Telescope (TMT) proposed for a designated conservation district (sacred grounds of Native Americans) near the summit of Mauna Kea, a mountain in Hawaii.

The Show

Sharon Katz provided teachers and adult participants with a detailed outline of the concerts on this tour. This precise information offers insights into Katz's creative process and the structure and sequence that she provides

PEACE TRAIN TOUR PROGRAM JULY 2016

1. *SHOSHOLOZA*   C   with Gumboot & Stepping at end
Hawaiian conch & Zulu vuvuzela and blessings in Hawaiian & isiZulu

2. *WE ARE THE CHILDREN OF AMERICA* w brass section G mod to A /
Break dancing to 2nd verse to end

3. *SALA NGOANA*   A   intro by Barbara Novick on flute   AFTER APPLAUSE GO RIGHT INTO

4. JAM IN C   Salsa dancing

STOP! By Mohana & Jamey

5. *THE TIME IS RIGHT TODAY*   B with Zulu dance at the end

6. Choir sits down for *TOGETHER WE RISE*   C (Hawane Rios on Ukelele & voice)

7. Choir stands up for *SANALWAMI* in D with brass section All do movements

8. *GO WELL MANDELA* in G with middle section in D listen for Sharon's guitar figure to switch back to
slow A section

9. *THE LITTLE WE HAVE WE SHARE* in Am

10. *WE CAN BE THE CHANGE* in Gm mod to Am

After second rap modulation to Am / We Can Be the Change etc.
plus, Get up onto that train 2 X, Get up onto that Peace Train 2 X / band jams while some of the choir go
into the audience

After they come back to the stage, we start the song from the top 14 bars
"Be the Change We Want"

PEACE TRAIN FINALE

ENCORE ELAMANQAMU in E for Philadelphia and D.C.

Figure 5.2   Second Draft of the American Peace Train Concert of July 2016. Courtesy of Sharon Katz. Used with permission.

for performers. The first concert outline was emailed to teachers and adult participants in June 2016. Katz's second draft of the concert (see Figure 5.2) resembles the performances very closely as follows:

Inclusiveness as the Key to Unity in Harmony

The outline of "The Show" reveals a multilayered strategy employed by Katz to create a concert performance that unequivocally appeals to as many members of an audience as possible. Figure 5.3 captures the unity Katz hopes to inspire. While her narrative draws on her experience of growing up and living in apartheid South Africa and Nelson Mandela's teachings, Katz demonstrates a keen understanding of music's nuances necessary to engage her audiences. The gumboot dancing[7] (also described in Chapter 1) and stepping[8] to *Shosholoza* is a dynamic introduction to the show that draws in the audience.

Immediately following the singing and dancing, Katz invites Nonhlanhla Wanda from South Africa to blow the vuvuzela while Hāwane Rios from Hawaii blows the conch. This act is a spiritual ritual to send out good vibrations into the universe, with two women from different continents leading the way. This cultural mingling of the show is evident in the songs. Several languages prevail, from Zulu to Ndebele to English and Polynesian. Various dance styles are included, such as breakdancing, salsa, stepping, ballet, and gumboot dancing. The instruments range from the flute to electric guitars to djembe to the ukulele. Always, the singers represent a cultural mosaic from different backgrounds.

Hāwane Rios, an activist from Hawaii, performed on the American Peace Train Tour. Katz included Rios based on a relationship that Katz describes as having developed "organically" with Rios and her family as they protested the use of a Hawaiian mountain (Mauna a Wākea) (considered sacred by the indigenous people), for the installation of a thirty-meter telescope. On October 6, 2016, Hāwane Rios provided written testimony explaining the reasons for her protest:

> My advocacy work for the Protect Mauna Kea Movement and my life work as a musician has taken me to the far reaches of the world to stand in solidarity with many movements rising to protect the rights of the earth. [. . .] The constant questioning and belittling of my spiritual connection to Mauna a Wākea, my beliefs, traditions, and cultural practices in the court system, the Astronomy community, and the University community has been wearing on my emotional, physical, and spiritual wellbeing. The pain in me recognizes the pain in my own people and the people from around the world that are dedicating and risking their lives to protect what is left of the clean air, land, ocean, and water.[9]

Katz expressed her admiration for Rios during her October 15, 2016, interview at her home in Philadelphia. Informal conversations with a few band members and the adult performers shared Katz's genuine appreciation for Rios and her music.

The Songs

For many years, the music of Sharon Katz has been described by the media in several ways. Katz encapsulates her varied musical styles in a June 17, 2011, interview:

> The audience can expect to be transported to South Africa—without needing a passport—and start singing and dancing with us from the first song, "the Grammy-nominated Katz promises." "We blend traditional South African musical styles like Maskanda, Mbaqanga, and Township Jive with Afro-Jazz

Figure 5.3 Sharon Katz (Pictured with a Guitar in the Center of the Photo) and the Participants of the American Peace Train Tour 2016 Perform at the New York Society for Ethical Culture Centre in Manhattan, New York, the United States on July 9, 2016. Photo Courtesy of Brian Klasewitz (photographer).

and a little rock to round out the fusion" (Tad Hendrickson for *The Star-Ledger*, 2011).

In one article, the writer describes Katz's music as follows:

Her music reflects a hodgepodge of influences—high-life Afropop, R&B funk, folk, and jazz. But its distinctive African rhythms and message-driven lyrics have their roots in Katz's own sensibilities. (Annette John-Hall in Philly.com, posted August 22, 2002)

The concerts of the American Peace Train Tour begin with the singing of *Shosholoza*. This choice of song is wholly appropriate as it ties in with the contemporary meaning of this song. It reflects solidarity with the struggle for racial and economic equality in the United States. As singers move onto the stage, the choreography also suggests the movement of the Peace Train as it arrives at yet another concert venue with its message of hope, peace, and unity. The positive significance of the train in this context of Sharon Katz's activism contrasts with the train's original symbolism during the days of oppression and apartheid, described by Hugh Masekela (2003) in *Amandla! A Revolution in Four-Part Harmony*:

> When all our land was taken, and we had to go to the urban areas to look for work, the train is what we had to get on. The train has always been a symbol of something that took away your mother or your father or your parents or your loved one [. . .] because the train was really South Africa's first tragedy.

Shosholoza is a traditional Ndebele folk song that was initially sung by groups of men from the Ndebele ethnic group who traveled by steam train from their homes in Zimbabwe to work in South Africa's diamond and gold mines. The song expressed the angst and hardship of working in the mines. The lyrics mix Ndebele and Zulu words, although it originated in Zimbabwe. Katz's positive message of the song is more in keeping with that of researchers Booth and Nauright (2003, 1). They explain that the melody's repetitive rhythms helped Zulu mine workers alleviate the stress and monotony of their jobs. The miners sang in time with the rhythm of their axes' swinging with one man singing a solo line and the rest of the group responding by repeating the line after the soloist, usually referred to as "call and response." The song, *Shosholoza,* was also sung by prisoners in call and response style where the call was sung by one row of prisoners with the response was sung by the second row of prisoners. This form of music was described by the former South African President Nelson Mandela when he wrote of his imprisonment on Robben Island. He described *Shosholoza* as "a song that compares the apartheid struggle to the motion of an oncoming train" and went on to explain that "the singing made the work lighter" (1994, 394). In contemporary times, this song shows support for any struggle. The lyrics of the song vary, as do the transcriptions. Sharon Katz & The Peace Train use the following transcription:

Shosholoza
Kulezo ntaba
Stimela siphume South Africa
Kulezo ntaba
Stimela siphume South Africa
Wen' uyabaleka
Kulezo ntaba
A loose translation of the song is:
Go forward
Go forward
from those mountains

on this train from South Africa
Go forward
Go forward
You are running away
You are running away
from those mountains
on this train from South Africa

The word *Shosholoza* or "chocholoza!" means *go forward* or *make way for the next man*, in Ndebele. It is a term of encouragement and hope for the workers as a sign of solidarity. The sound "sho" uses onomatopoeia, which is reminiscent of the steam train's sound (*stimela*). Stimela is the Zulu word for a steam train. "Kulezo ntaba!" means (At those far away mountains), "Stimela Siphume South Africa" (the train comes from South Africa), "Wen' uya baleka" (Because you're running away/hurrying). In South Africa, *Shosholoza* enjoys immense popularity, such that it is known as South Africa's second national anthem. Katz's arrangements of this song (see Figure 7.3) and other songs discussed in this section are available in Appendix 3.

We are the Children of South Africa (America) was originally written by Sharon Katz for the South African Peace Train Tour of 1993. In 2016, the song was adapted by Katz for the American Peace Train Tour. The Spanish words "Somos los hijos de America," meaning "We are the children of America," are appropriate for an American audience since Spanish is spoken widely across the United States, especially among immigrant populations. Spanish is also a foreign language elective at many schools across the country. Although this is one sentence in a song (see Figure 7.4), it is an example of Katz's sensitivity to the audience to which she brings her message. This single sentence allows the performers and the audience to engage with the idea of belonging to a country and national identity. My observation of audiences from New York to Washington D.C. in 2016 demonstrated the power of this single sentiment where people were clapping, dancing, and singing along with the choir, "We Are the Children of America." This idea of inclusiveness and unity in harmony permeates Katz's repertoire.

Sharon Katz originally composed *The Time Is Right today* in 1993 for the South African Peace Train. In 2016, the message remained the same, with an adaptation for the American Peace Train. As an up-tempo song, it has an energetic rhythm with instrumental interludes and accompaniments, including a brass section, electric keyboards, and guitars with the driving rhythms of the drums. The singers' choreographed dance routines convey the text's meaning, like the dance routines of *maskandi* songs in South Africa. In a recording of the original song on the compact-disc, *Crystal Journey* with South African singers, Katz begins the song with flute (with jazz improvisation) and table,[10] reflecting her collaboration with Indian musicians in South Africa. This eclectic mix of instruments and musical styles creates a hybrid form that attracts diverse audiences.

The following lines of the song are noteworthy. In the first line: "The time is right today, let's get together America," Katz immediately summons all people in America to come together in unity and harmony. This line has a strong and powerful message in the South African version, which states, "The time has come today, Mayibuye iAfrica." Mayibuye iAfrica are Zulu words that refer to the "return of Africa," or "bring back Africa," a slogan from the liberation struggle calling for justice and the rights of the people to self-determination. In many ways, the South African version suggests a strong call to action, while the American version suggests a reconciliation. The punctuated *staccato* delivery of the notes on "Black and White" in measure 16 (see Appendix 3, Figure 7.5) draws attention to issues of racial prejudice and the need to join forces for a more effective outcome. The lines, "We do not work for nothing brothers, now it's time to right those wrongs; We do not work for nothing sisters, we have been waiting too long!" are equally effective in both South Africa and the United States. Workers' rights—usually protected by unions—have been decimated by the wealthy upper class and the government. The bright and energetic introduction for horns in the song, *The Time is Right Today*, is repeated during the song (see Figure 5.4). The ascension of the melodic line landing on the top D flat in the tenor saxophone reverberates toward a climax with determination, mimicking the song's message. This motif is reminiscent of a military bugle call, assertive in its resonance.

The song *Sanalwami* is a traditional Xhosa song arranged by Sharon Katz for voices and contemporary instruments (electric guitars, electric keyboard, and drums). Katz also includes a horn section with trumpets and saxophones (see Figure 5.5). The musical form follows the traditional call and response (see Glossary) pattern used widely among traditional African songs. In contrast, the instrumentation and the fast tempo are reminiscent of High Life Afro-Pop's musical style with its jazzy horn section. The dance-like quality lends itself to energetic choreography, as displayed by participants in both the South African and American Peace Train Tours. This choreography highlights the idea of embodied rhythm, as the participants' movements reveal the song's meaning. Each performer interlocks their hands as if cradling and rocking a baby. This movement synchronizes with the exciting rhythm and pace of the music in fast 4/4 time. When a song is in a language other than English, enhancing the understanding of a song through movement is vital to Katz's appeal. She draws in audiences who may not speak or understand African languages in both South Africa and abroad.

The inclusion of songs in commonly spoken South African languages (Zulu, Xhosa, and English) speaks to Katz's desire to create an atmosphere of inclusivity in the Peace Train performances. The singing of songs in African

Figure 5.4   Score for Horns for the Song, *The Time Is Right Today,* **by Sharon Katz.** Courtesy of Sharon Katz. Used with permission.

languages on the American Peace Train Tour established its founder's identity. It also plays well with American audiences who sympathize with the South African fight for freedom from oppression and recognize the challenges of the present-day American society, where issues of race and prejudice served as a springboard for this tour of musical activism.

The high energy of this song contrasts with its English meaning. However, the joyful spirit embodied in the rocking of a baby is unmistakable. The lyrics of *SANALWAMI* (My Baby), a Xhosa traditional song arranged by Sharon Katz (see Appendix 3, Figure 7.6 for the vocal score), are as follows:

Call: NDI NO SANALWAM
Response: SANALWAM NDI NE BONGO (2X)
Call: NDIZALU BELEKA
Response: SANALWAM NDI NE BONGO (2X)
Together: NO MA NDILE (3)

HORNS   **SANALWAMI**

SHARON KATZ

Figure 5.5 Score for Horns for the Song, *Sanalwami*, by Sharon Katz. Courtesy of Sharon Katz. Used with permission.

Call: NDIZALUBELEKA
Response: SANALWAM NDI NE BONGO (2X)

A loose translation of the song as provided by Katz is: "My baby, I am proud of you, and I will carry you on my back while you are asleep." The horn section, which features saxophone, trumpet, and trombone—bolsters this up-tempo song's dynamic quality. As indicated previously, the horn section is reminiscent of the sound of Highlife Afro-Pop music.

The tension between music that is high in energy with driving rhythms and strenuous choreography contrasts with some of Katz's more poignant and contemplative songs. This contrast provides the audience with an opportunity to be more reflective. It allows the performers to regroup, physically speaking, before returning to spirited choreography and singing that usually follows slow songs at the concerts. An example of a slow-paced, intense, and thoughtful song is *Sala Ngoana* in Sotho, composed by Katz. The song repeats a memorable line, *Sala Ngoana Sala,* which means "Be at Peace My Child" or "Prayer for the Children" (see Appendix 3, Figure 7.7).

The song that takes me back to the orphanage in Mabopane, South Africa, and the children's sweet faces there is "The Little We Have, We Share," based on their inspirational wall hanging. Although Katz sings the verses, the chorus with its simple choreography entices audiences to sing and imitate the hand gestures. The song's only Zulu language words are "Kancane Sizofika," which means "Slowly, it will come." These are the lyrics:

The Little We Have We Share by Sharon Katz
Chorus:
The little we have we share
That's the way it must be
In the world everywhere
I carry you, you carry me
Verse:
And what of those who have fallen down
How can they get up again?
Hearing their cries, don't say goodbye
Don't you know you can be a friend?
Verse:
And how can I know I'll see you around
While this War is gaining ground
Don't hesitate; it might be too late
Don't you know that it's more than just fate?
Chorus
Kancane Sizofika
Slowly but surely, we must reach for the sky
Let's give it away; let's give it a try
Don't say goodbye
Don't say goodbye
Chorus

Katz has performed this song using a variety of musical styles. The instrumentation for this song varies depending on the availability of musicians. The opening chorus embraces a harmonic choral style with only keyboard accompaniment on the American Peace Train Tour. The chorus repeats with the hand gestures added this time. The entire ensemble moves in time to the music. This movement leads to a jazz-style singing of individual syllables, "parap," by the whole choir as the drummer set a fast-paced beat with all other instruments, including Katz, on electric guitar joining in. The chorus's voices came in after Katz sang the verses with a flute counterpoint playing a similar jazz melody vocalized at the beginning of the song.

Another example of different styles' blending was when Katz played a lead guitar interlude, reminiscent of a rock performance, which showcases her musical talent. At the same time, individual children came to the front of the group to perform dance solos. These ranged from a ballet twirl to break-dancing, hip-hop, and salsa. This eclectic mix of cultures reflected through the dance solos enhanced the song's lyrics with its underlying message of "sharing." The horn section for this song provides a rich counterpoint played by the jazz saxophone and trumpet on her CD *Double Take*.

The lyrics of this song are not only a call to humanity to share and lend a helping hand but also a need for reciprocity in the world with the words, "I carry you; you carry me" (see Figure 7.8). There is also the message of not giving up and always having hope. In the line, "Don't say goodbye," there is the need for ongoing engagement. This idea is not unlike the message of Yo-Yo Ma, the famed cellist who says in the documentary *Music of Strangers*, "If you don't have hope, you're in trouble." The spirited performance articulated these messages of "sharing" and "hope" in a manner that was both joyful and heartfelt.

Both Nonhlanhla Wanda and Wendy Quick played an essential role in keeping the young participants on track with movements and clapping in time during the song. The students' actions reflected the preparation level for this performance, with everyone singing their harmonies with accurate entries. The expressive choreography and singing demonstrated a commendable level of comfort with both the music and movement. Since Katz had ensured that all participants had received their scores by sending them to all adults who were assisting with students' rehearsals beforehand, her later practices with groups in different areas were very successful before the concerts in America. The essential roles of Nonhlanhla Wanda and Wendy Quick within the Peace Train are detailed in Chapter 6.

Impact of the American Peace Train *Tour on Participants*

On July 16, 2016, a dark and gloomy day in Washington D.C., I arrived by taxi, drenched from the pouring rain at Catholic University, where the Peace Train tour participants stayed. This gathering was the night before the final Mandela Concert scheduled for July 17, 2016, at the Sylvan Theatre (open-air) at the Washington Monument. Many participants had been writing and composing their music during the tour when they were not performing or rehearsing. Katz decided to allow all participants to share their creative work with the group in what she called a "Talent Showcase."

The presentations, hosted by a well-spoken and confident young African American teenager, included dance, instrument-playing, singing, and prose/poetry recitations. Most songs and writings were original compositions by the participants themselves, created on tour. One particularly strikingly poignant original poem, entitled "When Will It All Change" (transcribed from a video recording by the author), was shared with the group of Peace Train participants by a young nineteen-year-old African American student named Ziare Bellamy. An excerpt of his writing follows:

When Will It All Change
By Ziare Bellamy

I used to think that life was fair
Yet everything you do never really matters
I used to think that the brilliant ideas of a person
Were more than just a gateway to making money
I used to think that mothers and fathers would die
Before their sons and daughters
I used to know that life that grows
Enhances the mind as they start to mature
I used to think it was all simple-
Simply because all I ever saw in my mind was a lie
I used to run around the city asking people for nickels and dimes
As I greet them on the street
Because they drove nice cars and had nice things
Not knowing that it was all a part of a system [. . .]

Printed with the permission of Ziare Bellamy

These are creative thoughts from the mind of a young African American man in America, at a time when police brutality toward African American people is continuously highlighted through the media. It shines a light on the personal struggles created by social injustices. Bellamy's decision to join the Peace Train grew out of these feelings of angst and hoped that he could, in some way, contribute toward peace and healing. *To Kill A Mocking Bird* by Harper Lee (1960) is as relevant today as decades ago. The words of the character Atticus Finch states, "You never really understand a person until you consider things from his point of view . . . until you climb into his skin and walk around in it" (p. 30). Katz & The Peace Train demonstrate this sense of compassion with its goal of creating understanding and peace.

Katz reaches out to people using an eclectic mix of musical genres that appeal to audiences across several generations throughout her performances.

The following rap written and shared with me by a forty-nine-year-old White woman of the American Peace Train Tour (when she returned her responses to my questionnaire) is entitled "Baggage." It speaks to the influence of youthful energy with rap music and an attitude of kindness and concern, revealed through the texts, instilled among members of the Peace Train. I have included the complete rap to demonstrate the arc of this composition. The playful quality of the opening lines builds as the narrative progresses until the reader (listener) hears the apprehension and compassion that culminates with a sense of relief at the end.

Baggage
By Linda Pollack-Johnson (Written September 23, 2016)

I've got this fat backpack. I know! I don't travel light
I don't need most of this stuff, but you never know when you might!
I've got cough drops and tea bags, a good book, and some hard candy
It may be extra baggage, but one time it came in handy.
I had traveled with my choir down to Washington D.C.
To the Institute of Peace, to learn about our democracy.
We talked about peacebuilding as if it were a recipe
With ingredients like listening, creativity, and empathy.
Inspired but hungry, we moved on to tour the town
Have a picnic, maybe ice cream, take in the sights and sounds.
In smaller groups, we wandered, and with monuments behind
We posed for lots of selfies, then trudged back to the Red Line
The Metro was our ticket home; young and old all knew
To head back to the dorms and to bed by our curfew.
While in the moving metro car, I chatted with my friends
Of all that we had done and seen, and of how the day might end.
Suddenly I heard a shout, a domestic spat perhaps
But worse, an intense wrestling match with her struggling in his lap
So many questions came to mind, was it really a fight I was seeing?
If it was, were we in danger? Should I run or intervene?
And if I do step in at all, what should I do or say?
What were those peaceful lessons we had learned earlier that day?
Quick be creative! Find just the right vibe!
Even though they're going to see me as not one of their tribe.
I should offer something helpful as a way to defuse
The tension in the Metro. But what could I possibly use?
I pulled something from my backpack and meekly extended my hand,
Speaking in a timid voice, I was trying to understand.
"Do you need this little band-aid? I saw blood on your shin.

Maybe it will help you mind less the pain you must be in."
It was more than just a bandage to help heal the skin
It was an act of kindness to reach the heart within.
I could see from both their eyes that their hands would do no harm
And as we all left the station, they walked together arm in arm.

Printed with the permission of Linda Pollack-Johnson.

Furman (2007) explores existential principles through autoethnographic poetry and narrative reflections. In his discussion, he demonstrates that poetry and narratives are valuable tools for presenting people's lived experiences. Furman asserts that "Poetry may be thought of as the emotional microchip, in that it may serve as a compact repository for emotionally charged experiences" (ibid., p.1). The subjective experience of an individual is honored and presented in a manner that is "metaphorically generalizable" (Stein in Furman 2007, 1).

The talent showcase provided participants with an outlet for their creativity and a safe space for feelings of angst and joy to be expressed. Members of this tour demonstrated a remarkable comfort level with each other as they laughed or cried during their presentations. The presentations elicited responses of chuckles and applause or empathy and kindness from the group, as appropriate. After one particularly anguished revelation, Katz and Cohen called for a break to ease the room's pain-filled tension. This response was a clear demonstration of Katz's work as a therapist. There was no judgment, no analysis, and no advice. Everyone simply listened, and through this respect, validated every presentation. After drinks of water and snacks and a short period of conversation, the showcase resumed. There were also humorous little songs and dance routines (from salsa to breakdancing), creating a mosaic of cultures that represented the make-up of this diverse group called the American Peace Train.

Demographic Survey of Adult Chaperones: Respondents to a Questionnaire

Unlike the interviews I had scheduled with Peace Train participants of the 1990s in South Africa a year earlier, I had limited opportunity to interact with the adults from the American Peace Train Tour of 2016. Since they had a busy travel and performance schedule, the participants did not have time for individual interviews on tour. I did have informal conversations with a few adults. The night before their final performance in Washington D.C., I received Katz's permission to ask the adults who wished to answer a short questionnaire on their experience voluntarily and read and sign the "informed consent" letters. I subsequently sent out short demographic surveys together with the questionnaires via email for their responses. Although I did not receive all questionnaires sent out to the participating adults, the responses I did receive were informative and revealing, with a few respondents choosing to remain anonymous. Pseudonyms were used for all respondents in this section of analysis to preserve a few respondents' confidentialities.

All adult chaperones on the American Peace Train Tour, many of whom also performed with the group, were over forty-five years old. As already established in this chapter, from the overall statistics recorded, there were twenty women and three men in the forty-five to sixty-four age category, four women, and two men in the 65+ category (see Appendix 4, Table 7.2) for details of the survey). The results of this survey highlight an aspect of activism that is worth noting. The concept of biographical availability notes that some members of a society will be more likely to engage in activism activities than others (McAdam 1986). Although people within a society may have different reasons for joining a group, they often weigh the potential costs and risks of participation. As Waren argues:

> Young people who often have the least investment in the status quo and thus the least to lose, take the lead in many social movements. Biographical availability argues that it is easier for a young person to take on the costs and risks of activism than a middle-aged person with a spouse, children, and a steady job. The most common characteristics associated with biographical availability are age, marital status, family status, and occupational status. Alternatively, the idea of intergenerational activism hypothesizes that older activists have an important role to play by bringing their experience to bear on new political opportunities. (p. 441)

Johnston and Aarelaid-Tart (2000) emphasize the role of generations or cohorts as distinct, identifiable social units. Zeitlin (1970) observes that as each cohort passes through the formative ages of eighteen to twenty-five, significant historical events shape their political views. When political opportunities arise and social movements begin, cohorts will respond differently based on their historical perspective. Importantly, older cohorts may become more influential in framing political speech and social action than more recent cohorts (Waren, 2012).

The adults who responded to my questionnaires represent one-third of the total number of adults who served as chaperones. The demographic survey of these adult chaperones revealed that they were majority women; majority White; between fifty and seventy years old; tertiary-educated professionals; almost all performers; almost evenly split between single and married individuals—all engaged with a younger cohort in promoting the message of peace, harmony, hope, fairness, and equity espoused by Sharon Katz & The Peace Train. The individual responses to the specific questions on my questionnaire provided more significant insights into their backgrounds and the impetus for their involvement with the American Peace Train Tour.

Responses to the Questionnaire

Written responses were elicited through a questionnaire with six questions to understand the adult participants' lived experience in the American Peace Train of July 2016. Pseudonyms were created for all respondents to the questionnaire to respect their anonymity. The first question targeted their initial involvement with the Peace Train: *How were you selected or invited to participate in the Peace Train Tour of July 2016?* The responses revealed varied points of entry to the Peace Train experience, as reflected in the following:

It was serendipity. I contacted Sharon and Marilyn to inquire about screening their film at the Trenton Film Festival [in Pennsylvania, United States]. I hoped that the Trenton Children's Chorus could perform at the screening. During that initial phone conversation, we were invited to participate. (Leanne)

Because I was involved with getting the film off the ground, I was involved with the tour from the very beginning in helping to organize it once Sharon and Marilyn made the decision to do it this summer. (Beatrice)

I was introduced to Sharon and Marilyn by my friend, a music teacher at PS11, and when I asked about joining the tour, I was told they had more than enough applicants—but that I could fill out a form anyway—so I did—see attached. You would have to ask Sharon and Marilyn how I got selected!! (Brianna)

I was asked by Sharon Katz to chaperone and help with coordinating some of the tour activities. (Jasmine)

I saw an email/flyer about an information session near our home. I thought our son might be interested in it. He started somewhat skeptical, but once Sharon started auditioning the young folks, he was motivated. I was interested in being a chaperone if it would not negatively impact our son's experience to have his parents along. Since he was okay with that, I then felt strongly about wanting to be on stage as well as a chaperone. (Jennifer)

As a producer of *When Voices Meet* [the documentary], I was aware of the requests for a US Peace Train Tour that arose from our festival appearances and was involved in the planning of this project from the beginning. (Frank)

In trying to ascertain the participants' mindsets in supporting the Peace Train, I posed the question: *What was your understanding of the tour's purpose?*

My understanding of the tour was to impart the same vision in the U.S. that took place during the original South African Peace Train Tour, one of bringing peace and reconciliation into communities through the healing powers of music, song, and dance. The tour was to bring together a choir of youth and adults to sing empowering songs of peace and to embody those same principles toward one another. (Jasmine)

To promote the unity of kids and adults working and singing together to show unity and diversity. (Joelene)

To raise awareness about peace, equality, and social justice. (Leanne)

Initially, I figured we would be a healing presence in communities that had been traumatized by the racially divisive violence of the previous year. My personal goal for the trip was to do something as an antidote to all the negativity I heard during the presidential campaign. I am not really into politics that much but wanted to be part of the solution to reduce the racial tension that was building in the country. (Jennifer)

To create a demonstration of interracial harmony in music and in living together to inspire positive action in the U.S. (Frank)

To offer a voice for positive and peaceful change; to cut through the prevailing and abundant e negative discourses by affecting this change through music, dance, and voices raised as one. To try to put the "united" back in the USA. (Brianna)

The following two inquiries provided further insights into American respondents' demographic:

Did you know about South Africa's history and apartheid policies before the tour? And *Did you see any similarities between South Africa and America?*

While all respondents indicated that they had some knowledge of the apartheid policies of South Africa, some were aware of not having an in-depth level of understanding. In the words of Brianna who asserts that she "knew many things, but it was not until I saw *When Voices Meet* [the documentary film] that I realized how little I knew. I had no understanding of the depth and breadth of apartheid." Identifying similarities between apartheid South Africa and America in 2016 is encapsulated in the following responses where

Beatrice speaks of the "divisive rhetoric [and] the ongoing police brutality towards Blacks" while Jennifer states that there is "the lack of trust between different communities." Brianna argues that "America appears to be getting closer and closer to its form of apartheid, and despite all the progress made, there is an underbelly in the United States that is very powerful and destructive." Jasmine expands on this sentiment when she declares that "there are similar issues in America regarding our political system and all the social injustices we still experience regarding race, gender, class, religion, and disparities when it comes to our health and educational systems, housing, and fair wages."

One of the research questions delved into aspects of personal transformation: *In what ways did this experience affect your: attitude toward others, your personal views, your political views, your everyday life, your confidence and your self-esteem?* These are a few responses:

It helped me empathize. It helped me think of myself as an activist. It strengthened my resolve to work to create change. It made me more reflective. (Leanne)

It reinforced my intention not to judge any of my fellow human beings but to embrace each of them, to be open to all, even to those I may not be immediately drawn to. It made me think more about my White privilege—which, until now, I have not thought much about in-depth. It confirmed the need to stay involved in the fight against all discrimination and actively speak out against it and, when possible, to act—not just voice my opinions, to effect change. It made me determined to be available to any of the young people on tour—as a life resource, support system, or even financially if they are in need. One young man has already reached out, and he knows that he can call me at any time. It drew me out of my usual initial shyness when around a large group of mostly strangers. Marilyn and Sharon are very skilled in helping people "break the ice"—to the point that in the space of two weeks, we really were a "family." (Brianna)

As a young person, I had a lot of diversity among my friends. I attended comfortably integrated schools and had very progressive parents. As an adult, that diversity had begun to wane. The Peace Train gave me a whole new crowd of friends of diverse backgrounds. I feel that we are an extended family. I hope to stay in touch with these people forever. I have begun to think a lot about leadership skills. Some can lead overtly, by being charismatic and organized, while others lead more by example, from the sidelines. I am still sorting out where I fall on that continuum. I started a leftie and am still a leftie. Maybe I am a more convinced leftie now. I monitor social media more to keep in touch with the Peace Train crowd. I am eager to hear of any follow-up concerts, events, etc. We have reached out to one young singer and have done a lot of outings with that person. I lost some self-esteem in realizing that I do not have the organi-zational skills (visionary, planning, proactive problem-solving skills) that I saw displayed in Marilyn Cohen and Sharon Katz. I admire them for these strengths. On the "up" side, the two of them and others in the group seem to value me for the skills I do bring to the Peace Train community (listening, one-on-one atten-tion, behind the scenes problem solving, reliability, honesty, low maintenance ego, willingness to do grunt work) so that gave me confidence. (Jennifer)

The questionnaire's final question was open-ended to encourage more flexibil-ity and range in terms of the participants' responses to the Peace Train experi-ence. Respondents were encouraged to *"Please share any aspect of the tour that impacted you or others on tour in some way."* One respondent asserted:

I saw my students blossom and grow and watched many of the kids come out of their shells and really find themselves. My most cherished memory is of one of the girls who was sixteen. In the beginning, I could barely hear her when she spoke to me. She was a big girl, very overweight, and she and I had a long talk one day about the difficulties she had growing up and how she was teased and made fun of. She seemed to shrink inside of herself, as though if she kept very quiet, maybe no one would notice her. On the last evening of the tour [. . .], she got up in front of the whole group and spoke forcefully and with joy. What a pleasure to see that! Many kids seem to grow in their self-esteem and willing-ness to move outside of their comfort zones. It was beautiful to watch. (Beatrice)

Moments that stand out for one adult is explained as follows:

Shadrack was the first teen to reach out to me, helping me to learn a dance rou-tine (I have never really danced since I was a child.) Mary—one of Shadrack's classmates—when we were in Washington at the end of a 100+ degree day, fix-ing my disheveled hair so gently, ending with "You are so beautiful"—totally unexpected interaction and deeply affecting. The care and effort that was put into planning the surprise birthday party for the 16-year-old twins [by Sharon and Marilyn] when we were in Baltimore. Baltimore train station, where we all came together around Jeremiah's pain to lift him and comfort him in our circle of song and caring—led by Hāwane and Malia. The wonderful and often unspo-ken deep connections made with different people—you included! (Brianna)

I enjoyed going to the rehearsals and watching the performances come together. It was a great experience to see the youth interact with each other, take care of each other, observe how well they got along, and how well they were able to articulate on several occasions what they learned from the tour. Although I didn't sing in the choir, I never got tired of hearing the songs. I danced and had a good time interacting with the audience. It was overwhelming to see how the spirit of the songs/music moved people each time. (Tania)

The questionnaires and follow-up conversations with Beatrice and Brianna in August 2016 provided two different perspectives regarding Rios's inclusion into the American Peace Train Tour. On the one hand, Brianna saw Rios as a caring individual who was a strong advocate for her cause. Beatrice admired Rios' musical talent but felt that the addition of a lengthy musical rendition to explicate a separate issue into the Peace Train concert detracted from Sharon Katz's message and the Peace Train.

During my interview with Katz on October 15, 2016, I addressed Rios's inclusion into the Peace Train concert since opposing views were expressed. This clarification was essential to understand the process behind Katz's creative choices. Katz was gracious in her response. She was clear that she wanted "indigenous representation of the Hawaiian people" in an American tour. The indigenous people's struggles to preserve their sacred lands resonated with her when she thought about most people's struggles during the apartheid era in South Africa. Katz describes herself as being "intuitive as far as music and collaborations go." As the artistic director, Katz addressed the length of Rios' narrative and song with grace, merely shortening Rios' presentation in future concerts. Katz sees that as a function of fine-tuning a production since there was no dress rehearsal before the opening concert in New York (Katz, personal communication, October 15, 2016).

Reflections of Children on the American Peace Train Tour of 2016

The young people recruited for the American Peace Train Tour went through the audition process. All students from the Trenton Children's Chorus in New Jersey were included through their school chorus affiliation. The choir's Executive-Director had already attracted the attention of Katz. Eleven members of the Trenton Children's Chorus, many of whom I had spoken with during informal conversations while they were on tour, were among the diverse 100-voice youth choir and band that traveled and performed from New York to Washington D.C. from July 9 to July 17, 2016. Their understanding was that their mission was to inculcate ideas of peace, respect, and mutual understanding through music. These are the student's reflections created for the Trenton Chorus website.[11]

My experience with the Peace Train can only be described as extraordinary. The bonds I made will be a part of my life forever. To be honest, my favorite performance we did was in Jersey City, NJ. The scenery was beautiful, and the performance was outside. If I had to sum up my experience in one word, it would be amazing! [Tabia]

When I first heard that I was going to be on the Peace Train, I didn't know how much sweat would go into preparing for it. After a month of practicing with ten other Trenton Children's Chorus members, we met the other 89 Peace Train performers from all over the country in New York City. Our first full rehearsal was powerful because all 100 voices met in the songs that we had been practicing. While on stage at the Centre for Ethical Culture, I grew excited as I heard all the voices bouncing around the room—different but the same.

Later in the trip, we visited the Peace Institute in Washington, D.C. There we discussed how to resolve conflicts with small and large issues with people, groups, or even countries. [To] resolve a problem, it is important not only to talk but also to listen to what the other needs. I realized that to avoid conflict with my brother, I must listen to what he needs. So maybe peace starts at home and can move through the community from there. The songs that we sang spread a message of peace and may also spread hope to those people who are in need.

My favorite performance was in Jersey City because of the spectacular view behind us as we were performing. At that moment, I realized that even though I'm tall for my age, I am so small as far as what happens in the world. But when I joined my one voice with the 100-voice choir, our songs were heard by what felt like all of New York and part of New Jersey. So maybe our songs of peace can influence the world. [. . .]

Overall, the Peace Train trip was an awesome experience. Over ten days, I met new friends from all over the country. I met with my Congresswoman, Bonnie Watson Coleman, Visited the Liberty Bell, Statue of Liberty, Capitol Building, many museums, and discussed how to resolve conflict at the Peace Institute. As part of the Peace Train Project, I sang and danced on stages in New York, Jersey City, Trenton, Philadelphia, Baltimore, and Washington, D.C. If the Peace Train comes back to the station, I want to be the first in line.
[Jeremy]

I have never really traveled with a group around my age before, so being on the Peace Train tour with other choirs and other kids/teens has been great! We sang at different places in New York, Jersey City, Trenton, Philly, Baltimore, and Washington, D.C. We also went sightseeing. My favorite place was New York because there were many beautiful attractions, such as the Statue of Liberty. As a member of the Peace Train, we sang nonviolence songs and made Responsible Action Plans to stop hate in the world. We don't need violence and conflict; we just need love and support. That's what the Peace Train is all about; spreading the word to make a change we want for the better.

Overall, my experience with the Peace Train has been amazing. Throughout the whole trip, Sharon has inspired me to have a voice and share my personal opinions. With this, I finally understood why Sharon went to these different places where we performed (and in South Africa where she started it all)—it was to stop violence and spread the love. So, will you join us in bringing the "United" back to the USA? [Paola]

When I was first introduced to Sharon Katz, I had no idea about who she was and why she was standing in front of my choir, teaching us songs in other languages about peace. I instantly took a liking to who she was and what she stands for, and when I learned about the huge opportunity of joining the Peace Train Choir, I knew I just HAD to do it. I was confident in myself and nailed the auditions. The Peace Train Tour 2016 was a great experience for me. I [could] meet people I never thought I would have the opportunity to meet.I made friends with people from all over the country, Hawaii, Kansas, and California, as well as people that I never knew lived by me! Performing with Sharon has given me confidence in my performance skills and has shown me a whole different experience of expressing myself on stage.

One of my favorite events from this experience was the talent show we had at the Washington DC dorms. I got to see what other talents my friends have. I was really surprised by the results, which ranged from beautiful original songs, spoken word poetry, and dance to comedic improv.We also went to many interesting workshops that were informative and fun; yes, the juggling workshop was AWESOME. The last day reminded me of senior speeches before the last performance of a musical at my school. Not a single dry eye in the room, and not a single person uncomforted; all the new friends were hugging each other, promising to text and call once we were all back home. I believe that the Peace Train experience will help me find better opportunities because I know it has brought out a new confidence in me. I am very thankful for this experience! [Payton]

[Tobias shared his reflection through a poem]

I've been on the Peace Train
To help the light shine again.
They put more peace inside our lives
For each of our sons, daughters, husbands, and wives.
I came to the program without any hassle,
Thinking of new friends and places to travel.
My experience was always extremely fun
And like most people, I'm sad that it's done.
Many friends and moments that I will now keep,
And the sound of "Shosholoza" playing while I sleep.

I found it fun to be traveling around to different states, singing and dancing at nice venues. On the Peace Train Tour Across America 2016, I met new friends, took lots of pictures, learned new songs and dance moves, learned things about people that I never knew before, and learned lots of lessons about being a musician. It was a lot of work, but it paid off in the end. Each performance was better than the last, which made our hard work worth it. [. . .] Also, Nonhlanhla Wanda, from South Africa, gave my grandmother the necklace she wore during the performance for free. She also called me "The Girl." I'd like to think she meant the talented and beautiful girl.

The Peace Train was a great experience. The message that we wanted to give in each performance was the message of peace and love. We said that it is possible, and it must be a priority to put the "United" back into the USA. [Azhaneet]

Hi, my name is Esmeralda. I am 12 years old. I have been with the Trenton Children's Choirs for the past four years. The Peace Train has been one of the most memorable things I have ever done. It is something I would want to make bigger so that the whole world would have peace. When I first found out I was going to be part of the Peace Train tour, my family was so excited for me. On the way, I met new people and learned so much. I learned that the Peace Train was not just singing from place to place. It was making a difference. After every show, I would see people walk out with a smile on their faces. Some people would walk in and out even if they didn't say anything; I know they left with peace in their hearts. I can't forget to talk about Sharon Katz. She has inspired me to make a difference in the world. I will never forget anything that happened and everyone I met. I will love to do this again and again. I would like to thank Marilyn and Sharon for giving me the opportunity to be here. [Esmeralda]

Twenty-three years after the first Peace Train tour carried its message of unity and peace from city to city in South Africa to bridge the racial divide, the American Peace Train Tour of 2016 embarked on a similar journey from city to city in the United States. The children's testimonies on the 2016 Peace Train Tour suggested themes that were strikingly similar to themes that emerged during my interviews with participants on the 1993 tour. The reference to the rigor of rehearsals, the feelings of excitement and wonder, and the focus on personal growth—all themes reflected through personal experiences in 2016 in America—had a familiar ring from twenty-three years earlier in 1993 on another continent in Africa. Other consistent themes of both the South African Peace Train Tour and the American Peace Train Tour were ideas of reflection, healing, conflict resolution, and hope. Throughout the tour in 2016, participants were encouraged to write, share their thoughts verbally, reflect on their experiences, and ponder their roles in the world. Jeremy, a member of the Trenton Children's Chorus from New Jersey, United States, and an African American child performer on the Peace Train Tour of 2016, writes in his testimony:

Throughout the trip, we had to work on a RAP—Responsible Action Plan—or something that each of us can do to make the world a better place. When I grow up, I want to be a doctor who provides healthcare for people in urban areas. I recently noticed that whenever we go to a doctor, we go to Hopewell, Princeton, or Hamilton. Never in Trenton, where we live. I sometimes wonder about the people who do not have cars and how they get access to healthcare.

With the rising cost of healthcare being a cause for great concern in the United States and the widening gap in funding and resources between richer and poorer communities, it is not surprising that Jeremy highlights this as a part of his "Responsible Action Plan." It is noteworthy that Jeremy, as a young teenager, demonstrates the thoughtfulness and level of compassion that exceeds his years. Paola, another young performer, summarizes the broad themes that emerged. She says:

As a member of the Peace Train, we sang non-violence songs and made Responsible Action Plans to stop hate in the world. We don't need violence and conflict; we just need love and support. That's what the Peace Train is all about; spreading the word to make a change we want for the better.

Katz's first South African Peace Train Tour of 1993 led to a United States Tour in 1995. This tour projected an image of the newly created "rainbow nation" with young people from the Black, White, Colored, and Indian communities of South Africa singing songs of unity, equality, love, peace, and the brotherhood of man. In 2016, the American Peace Train Tour highlighted the themes of reconciliation for Americans amid racial tensions related to police brutality, seen by many as targeting African American people. In an e-mail dated April 25, 2020, Katz shared the details of the song quoted at the beginning of this chapter:

I wrote the song and then collaborated for the recording with Nonhlanhla for the recording that Malcolm Nhleko produced. It was released in 2018 on our album, "Side-By-Side." The English lyrics, the form, and the concept of the song are mine. Nonhlanhla wrote the second verse in Zulu, and as always, we collaborated on the structure of the song, with our musicians and with Malcolm. The latest version has Spanish, and we performed it in Cuba. We are currently creating a music video in Mexico with that song. The Spanish lyrics mean the same as the theme: *Podemos ser el cambio, que queremos en el mundo.*

Katz adds that the chorus is deliberately sung in many languages because it is appropriate for many situations. The creative process that sparked this composition is that Katz "originally wrote it before the 2016 elections hoping the USA could unite and change. Now we sing it because we feel that change is possible if we unify. I mostly use the song to inspire youth, that they can use their voices and feel empowered" (ibid.).

Empowerment among children and youth comes from being civically engaged. This engagement is vital when the policies of a government work against the majority of its people. The Trump administration that came into power in 2016 created a sense of hopelessness in the United States and beyond. One of the dire consequences of its harsh immigration policies was the disintegration of families through the separation of children from their parents. Trump and his administration's disinterest in scientific evidence as a basis for social policy, with climate deniers leading governmental agencies, and a blatant disregard for medical advice during the pandemic, have not served its people well. Then there was a lack of support for public education, the poor, and the disenfranchised. These are only a few examples of how the young and old of the United States saw the chasms of an inequitable society deepen where the lust for power and self-interest trumped public-good.

The empowerment of people comes from reimagining their sociological landscape. The society we inherit does not have to be the one we pass on to our children. Young people must be reminded that as much as they are products of a society, they are also the future producers of society. Empowering youth is where the stoic efforts of Sharon Katz & The Peace Train come into play. The ongoing inter-cultural exchange and the focus on current social issues provide young people with an opportunity for civic engagement through their musical activism.

The dynamic nature of society is already evident in 2021 with the inauguration of President Biden and Vice-President Kamala Harris (the first woman and the first person of color–of South Asian and Jamaican descent–to hold this office). This new political change breathes hope and optimism—both nationally and internationally—into a system of government intended to provide "liberty and justice for all."

NOTES

1. The Brandt Line is named for the West German former Chancellor Willy Brandt who proposed a visual depiction of the world in the 1980s where European countries, the United States, and Russia among others to the North of this line were considered richer while African, South American, and developing Asian countries to the South were seen as poorer countries. This North-South divide based on both socioeconomic and political factors was propagated in the late twentieth and early twenty-first centuries. The BBC reports, however, that since 2014 there has been a

shift with countries such as Mexico, Brazil, South Africa, India, and China demonstrating an increase in wealth and greater industrialization. (Available at: https://www.reference.com/world-view/brandt-line-c935232c3e5b896c)

2. Information accessed April 28, 2017, at http://www.msnbc.com/transcripts/rachel-maddow-show/2015-04-27.

3. Information accessed June 15, 2020, at https://www.theguardian.com/commentisfree/2020/jun/14/these-protests-feel-different-but-we-have-to-be-realistic-theres-a-long-road-ahead.

4. Accessed July 24, 2017, http://trendprivemagazine.com/2016/09/11/jump-aboard-the-peace-train/.

5. For a complete list of raw data, see Appendix D in Ambigay Yudkoff, "When Voices Meet: Sharon Katz as Musical Activist During the Apartheid Era and Beyond," Ph.D. dissertation (University of South Africa, 2018).

6. Information available at https://www.census.gov/quickfacts/table/RHI125215/00.

7. Gumboot dancing was conceived by Black miners in South Africa as an alternative to drumming—which authorities restricted. Another reason for gumboot dancing was for the miners in South Africa as they worked, they sang. [. . .] Gumboot dancing has developed into a South African art form with a universal appeal a world-known dance; in schools [in South Africa], children perform the dance. The dancers expand upon traditional steps, with the addition of contemporary movement, music and song. Extremely physical, the dancing serves as a cathartic release, celebrating the body as an instrument, and the richness and complexities of South African culture. (Accessed November 24, 2017, at www.enigmasa.com/gumboot-dancing/history-of-gumboot-dancing)

8. Stepping is a rising art form and an important part of America's artistic and cultural heritage. In stepping, the body is used as an instrument to create intricate rhythms and sounds through a combination of footsteps, claps, and the spoken word. It draws movements from African foot dances, such as Gumboot, originally conceived by miners in South Africa as an alternative to drumming, which was banned by authorities. The stepping tradition in the United States grew out of song and dance rituals practiced by historically African American fraternities and sororities, beginning in the early 1900s. (Accessed November 24, 2017, at http://www.stepafrika.org/company/what-is-stepping/)

9. Accessed November 21, 2017, https://dlnr.hawaii.gov/mk/files/2016/10/F-5-Witness-Testimony-Hawane-Rios.pdf.

10. Tabla, pair of small drums fundamental (since the eighteenth century) to Hindustani music of northern India, Pakistan, and Bangladesh. (Accessed November 8, 2017, at https://www.britannica.com/art/tabla)

11. Available at http://www.trentonchildrenschorus.org/peace-train-1.html.

Chapter 6

The Peace Train Rolls On

Hamba kahle Mandela (Go Well Mandela)
Rest in Peace
You have done your work
You led us all
Hamba kahle Mandela (Go Well Mandela)
Rest in Peace
Now it's our turn
You taught us well

—*Go Well Mandela* by Sharon Katz (2013)

COACHING FOR CHANGE

The grassroots initiatives of the South African musician and therapist Sharon Katz are her lifelong mission. Katz's endeavors have included the following: The South African Peace Train; the efforts of the nonprofit Friends of The Peace Train; Katz's work with Pennsylvania prisoners and boys at an American Reform School; the documentary *When Voices Meet*; and the American Peace Train Tour of July 2016—these five case studies are examined within the framework of musical activism. This research documents the role of music in social and political change and the grassroots impact of a musician with a vision of making a difference within communities faced with the challenges of overcoming inequities borne of prejudice in South Africa and abroad. Although the case studies demonstrate differing levels of success, they provide another fragment of the ethnomusicological history of grassroots musicians from South Africa. The exploration of multiple case studies is best described by Stake (2006) as a design that does not give "emphasis to attributes for comparison" (p. 83). These cases are a "selected group of instances chosen for a better understanding of the quintain" (ibid.).

Political, Social, and Musical Activism

A central question of this study targets an understanding of the various initiatives of Sharon Katz within a framework of political, social, and musical activism. The South African Peace Train's first initiative grew out of a 500-voice multilingual and multiracial choir with its first performance in 1992. This journey occurred at a time when South Africa had apartheid entrenched in its constitution. In taking 110 children between nine and seventeen years from different racial and socioeconomic backgrounds on a ten-day concert tour traveling by passenger train, Katz challenged the political and social status quo of segregation. She created a racially integrated experience for children who had grown up isolated from one another through the government's policy of separate development.

The formation of what became known as "The Peace Train" interrupted the political order of apartheid and broke down social barriers among children and adults through integration. Children and adults from diverse racial backgrounds shared sleeping cars, ate meals together, and engaged in recreational activities such as card-playing and chess. This interaction culminated in performances of music, song, and dance. From a therapeutic perspective, Katz tapped into the practices of Community Music Therapy.

One of the fundamental tenets of the ongoing Community Music Therapy blueprint described by Stige and Ansdell (2016) is to "relate human needs to the wider perspective on human rights—emphasizing that 'musical justice' is often rightly part of a music therapist's agenda" (p. 616). The authors contend that Community Music Therapy is "a musical call for the universal values of social justice, human potential and mutual care" (ibid). The musical activism of Sharon Katz abides by these principles. Besides, Katz focused on creating an atmosphere of unity through music among South Africans from different backgrounds with the broader goal of assisting a peaceful transition to democracy.

Musical Activities and Social Change

Katz's musical activities address the second broad research question that seeks a connection between music and social change. Chapter 2 provides several examples, from a historical perspective and contemporary society, where music and social change are inexorably intertwined. The work of Jenny Vincent in New Mexico, Barenboim, and Said's experiences with the West-Divan Orchestra, the music of Lennon and Masekela, the contributions of

Ladysmith Black Mambazo and Paul Simon are all reflective of the power of music and musical collaborations as vehicles for social change.

The humanitarian efforts of Katz in South Africa are also inspired by music. This connection between music and humanitarian work addresses the question, *What were the motivating factors that led to the formation of the nonprofit Friends of The Peace Train?* Through her relationship with the South African singer, Dolly Rathebe, Katz grasped the idea of empowering struggling communities through fund-raising. Katz's concerts play a significant role in her outreach efforts to provide resources. By creating a nonprofit organization, Friends of The Peace Train, Katz secures sponsorships from well-wishers in the United States to support her extensive work in rural Black communities of South Africa. Besides concerts, her music workshops at schools and universities in the United States and the release of a documentary, *When Voices Meet*, in 2015 have created an awareness among potential philanthropists in the United States of her efforts to create social change in small rural communities in South Africa.

In an email with the subject heading "News from South Africa," dated November 17, 2017, Katz provided an update of progress being made at the Good Hope Community Centre, run by Mama Mary, through the generosity of Friends of The Peace Train. Katz explains that the money raised was not enough to buy the sturdy vehicle needed for the orphanage. However, in their first two weeks in South Africa, they could repair the 2003 Tazz car. This modest vehicle helps transport children and the farm products they are growing. Moreover, the young adults who have been set up in their business by Mama Mary are using the new sewing machines to make school uniforms for the children and curtains and clothing for other community residents. This information reinforces Katz's commitment to ongoing humanitarian work in South Africa through the support of American donors. The positivity, resilience and determination of Katz and her partners are captured in the words of Nelson Mandela (1994), who maintained:

> I am fundamentally an optimist. Whether it comes from nature or nurture, I cannot say. Part of being an optimist is keeping one's head pointed to the sun, one's feet moving forward. There were many dark moments when my faith in humanity was sorely tested, but I would not and could not give myself up to despair. (341–342)

Strategies of Cultural Activism

The third research question explores strategies for cultural activism. In 1992 when Katz decided to form a 500-voice multicultural and multilingual choir, her primary strategy was to visit schools in the segregated communities (White, Black, Colored, and Indian). She recruited singers from established successful choirs recognized through competitions in their respective areas. In doing so, Katz gathered many school-going children to represent the different race groups who were also culturally diverse. Besides, these children were talented singers since they had all participated in and achieved success in music competitions, albeit confined to competitions among their race groups. This strategy of paying attention to the ethnic and cultural makeup of the choir taps into another subquestion: *To what extent do race, gender, or other factors influence Sharon Katz's activism?*

Although the deliberate recruitment of children for the 500-voice choir was initiated to represent Black, White, Colored, and Indian children in a multiracial choir, this attention to diversity became less critical during auditions for the South African Peace Train of 1993. Katz needed a culturally diverse choir, but this was a two-pronged effort—to ensure diversity while also focusing on musical talent. Fortunately for Katz, both criteria were fulfilled.

The success of the concerts of the 500-voice choir may be attributed in part to another strategy of Katz—presenting a culturally diverse program of music for an audience that represented people from ethnically and culturally diverse backgrounds. Remember, Katz had to obtain special permission from the City Council in Durban to stage this multiracial event and to have a "mixed" audience at the Durban City Hall. Apartheid policies that demanded segregated audiences were still in place at that time.

In 1993, the South African Peace Train departed on its journey from the Durban Train Station. Again, Katz created an opportunity for children, who were culturally different from one another, to interact in proximity while traveling on a passenger train in the same coaches. Commuter trains were segregated by race at that juncture in apartheid South Africa. In placing children from different race groups within the same physical space (with special permission from the authorities again), Katz focused on the children's emotional well-being to enable them to develop relationships with each other. This therapeutic focus created an environment conducive to promoting understanding and tolerance. Closely associated with this strategy of taking care of the children's physical needs are organization and structure. Marilyn Cohen, Katz's American partner, is credited with being the driving force behind taking care of their tours' logistical aspects.

Friendships developed quickly among these young performers. Many of the children were already familiar with one another from the 500-voice choir. Diverse audiences in different cities along the route heard the message of unity, hope, and conflict-resolution intended to bridge the cultural and racial divide. This choir performed an act of cultural activism, enhanced through this multiracial choir's optics as a microcosm of a "rainbow nation."[1]

Related to cultural activism strategies, *How did Sharon Katz arrive at a repertoire of music for The Peace Train project suitable for and indeed accessible to all participants across different social and cultural backgrounds of performers?*

As a South African child growing up in a bilingual household, Katz was fluent in both Afrikaans and English, with conversational knowledge of Xhosa—a popular language in Port Elizabeth where Katz grew up—Sotho and Zulu. Katz was keenly aware of the value of code-switching from one language to another to gain acceptance into different communities. This ability to speak a language, however poorly, is a common practice among many South Africans when communicating with people from diverse language groups. Ndebele (2012, v) states that "Code-switching has become a universal phenomenon among bilingual speakers in most communities in South Africa."

Moreover, Katz had become familiar with a range of music genres from ten or eleven. She played Israeli folk songs and Pete Seeger and Bob Dylan's folk music on the guitar acquired on her eleventh birthday. Katz discovered a love of African music by listening to an African music station on her transistor radio. She further explored her interest in African music and theater when she started going to the townships with John Kani at fifteen. In the 1970s, when Katz completed her first degree at the University of Cape Town, she went to a remote village in Lesotho to work at a mission school there. This decision is only one example of Katz's immersion in African communities that stirred a deep and abiding love for African cultures and their music (Katz, personal communication, October 15, 2016). Through her many musical experiences, Katz always prepares a repertoire of music that showcases her songs (using an eclectic South African idiom), sometimes combining English with African languages. She also taps into the traditional Sotho, Zulu, and Xhosa songs that she arranges for performances.

Recurring Themes

The interviews with participants of the South African Peace Train of 1993 and the testimonials of children performing on the American Peace Train of 2016 reveal similar themes. Although the 1993 participants were adults in their thirties at the time of the interviews in 2015, while the children of 2016 ranged in age from seven to seventeen, all Peace Train participants expressed excitement and wonder. They also spoke of the thoroughness of their preparation through many hours of rehearsals. Katz encouraged participants to express their feelings throughout the tours in a reflective manner, with conflict resolution, healing, and hope as its outcomes. Furthermore, the 2016 participants were encouraged to develop a "RAP" or "Responsible Action Plan" to make a difference in their communities.

The interviews in South Africa with adults who had many years to process the effects of the Peace Train experience were remarkably reminiscent of the Truth and Reconciliation Commission (TRC) headed by Archbishop Desmond Tutu in 1995. The cathartic experience that the TRC provided for victims and perpetrators of the apartheid era came from the ability to be transparent and honest about interactions among people. It was an opportunity for the truth with the ultimate goal of peace and reconciliation. Interview after interview among the South African Peace Train participants revealed that people's misconceptions based on race were dispelled through their daily interactions. It may be argued that these participants provided a microcosm of the Truth and Reconciliation Commission as those who participated discovered their own truths about other South Africans and had to reconcile their own stereotypes with the truths they discovered living and working and traveling together.

Central themes emerged during the interviews with South Africans and the testimonials of Americans who were participants in the Peace Train tours of 1993 and 2016. The responses shed light on the following questions:

How do Sharon Katz's initiatives alter or renegotiate the participants' sense of identity and belonging? Did participants forge long-term connections during their experiences in each endeavor, or did the music-making activity simply bind them at the time?

The impact of the Peace Train tours was significant for all participants who shared their experiences. Since the South African participants had more than twenty years to process the long-term impact of their experiences, they could also reflect on their personal growth over the years as they matured into adulthood. Participants articulated many lessons learned from being a member of the Peace Train, as explained in Chapters 4 and 5. Payton, a member of the Trenton Children's Choir in Philadelphia, describes the impact of the Peace Train tour of 2016 in this description of the final day of being with fellow participants:

> The last day reminded me of senior [refers to grade 12 in the United States] speeches before the last performance of a musical at my school. Not a single dry eye in the room and not a single person uncomforted; all the new friends were hugging each other, promising to text and call once we were all back home.

In an age of social media where the means of communication continue to develop rapidly, it is not surprising that the connections among members of the American Peace Train of 2016, mainly through Facebook, continue to flourish. This engagement is evident through a quick perusal of their messages to which I have access.

This ease of ongoing interaction was unfortunately not available to South Africans more than twenty years ago. In my interview with the participants of the South African Peace Train of 1993, Shandhini lamented the difficulties of keeping in touch with friends from the Peace Train even though she felt that they shared deep emotional connections, not unlike the expressions of affection of the American participants of the 2016 tour:

> I think I had some of the best relationships I had there. I think if it were a different time, I would have maintained a lot of those relationships. It was a different time: we were still stuck in apartheid; we were still stuck in different communities; there weren't cell phones; there wasn't the internet; there were logistical problems, traveling-wise. I know if any of that had happened now, I would probably be in touch with many people because I remember the conversations we'd have, the laughter, the fun, and the serious discussions at that age. (Shandhini)

My interview with Shandhini is a poignant reminder that my South African background has helped me gain access to and establish a rapport with fellow South Africans. They were children, teachers, or chaperones on the South African Peace Train in 1993. As an educator in the American educational system, I was also able to gain the trust and friendship of many students and adults on the American Peace Train of 2016. As I reflect on my own experiences, I am also grateful for my ability as an educator to straddle two different cultures (South African and American) and share the respondents' experiences through my work. My focus was to document the grassroots activism of Katz with attention to the facts. While my experiences as a child and young adult of color in apartheid South Africa are valid, I am always aware of my role as a researcher to present my study through a clear lens, unclouded by my own perceptions.

Activism through Music during the Apartheid Era and Beyond

The question that confronts the heart of Sharon Katz's musical activism: *How does the Peace Train sustain its relevance more than twenty years after its formation in post-apartheid South Africa and other countries?*

In the early stages of my research, I was unaware that Katz was working on the documentary film *When Voices Meet*. This film has enjoyed success winning awards at several film festivals, including the United States and Canada, since its premiere at the Durban Film Festival in 2015. Although Katz has continued to be an active performer and therapist since her first Peace Train tour of 1993, the documentary served as a springboard for the reinvention of the Peace Train in another country. It breathed new life into the concept of creating social and political change through a traveling band of children and adults. Nowhere is the Peace Train's relevance more evident than in the American Peace Train Tour of 2016. Across the Atlantic Ocean in another country, with American children, Katz replicated the South African Peace Train's original concept to address social and political injustices prevalent in American society today.

Mediating Access to Communities

The musical activism of Sharon Katz & The Peace Train through her tours in South Africa and the United States entailed a high degree of collaboration with several role-players. Two women who played significant roles in these initiatives are Nonhlanhla Wanda (South African) and Wendy Quick (American). In *Africanizing Anthropology: fieldwork, networks, and the making of cultural knowledge in Central Africa*, Lyn Schumacher (2001) provides a detailed account of the anthropological fieldwork of the mid-twentieth century based at the Rhodes-Livingston Institute (RLI) in Northern Rhodesia (now called Zambia). This book is ground-breaking in that it places the African assistants and informants of researchers in the spotlight as being central players in the making of anthropological knowledge. Schumacher's work has elicited a range of reactions from champions and critics alike. Gordon (2002) states:

> Schumacher's major innovation is her endeavor to move African agency towards center-stage. Her account of how local people interpreted fieldwork is fascinating, and it is hoped more studies on this topic will be done. By arguing for the importance of field assistants, surely one of her major contributions, she also shows how these assistants reappropriated, digested, and transformed fieldwork and Africanized Anthropology. There is an extensive anthropological literature on interpreters and their practice as culture brokers, and it is a pity that Schumacher does not engage with this body of material. (p. 472)

Parpart (2002) highlights the "research" role of African assistants in Schumacher's account, where their intimate knowledge of a society yielded better results for researchers:

> She [Schumacher] reveals the complex work culture behind RLI research, including the key role played by African research assistants. Indeed, some assistants admit they revised answers to culturally "inappropriate" research questions. The urban research teams were significantly dependent on their African assistants, whose political and social connections shaped research agendas and provided access to key informants in the increasingly politicized and volatile urban centers. While mindful of the power imbalance between European researchers and their African assistants, it is clear that the Institute provided an

unusual site for genuine social and intellectual interaction across racial divides.
(p. 517)

Like the White researchers in Zambia, Katz is fully aware of the role of
teachers of color in gaining access to the children from schools in South
Africa (Black, White, Colored, and Indian) for her 500-voice choir in 1992.
Of interest is the invaluable role of Nonhlanhla Wanda, an African teacher
in South Africa, and other music teachers' roles at each of the racially segregated schools. Children from these segregated schools rehearsed separately
and together. This preparation culminated in two unique multicultural choir
events at the Durban City Hall on May 16 and 26, 1993, followed by a third
concert at the Chatsworth Stadium in Kwa-Zulu Natal (Katz, email communication, July 7, 2017). Nonhlanhla Wanda was born in KwaZulu-Natal
in the 1950s, in apartheid South Africa. She is aware that we (as women of
color) shared the unfortunate circumstances of growing up in apartheid South
Africa. Although Wanda is very matter-of-fact in explaining her personal
story, it is difficult to remain unmoved by the details:

> We were segregated as Black people were regarded as the fourth race in our
> country. I studied under the Bantu Education system, which was an inferior
> education. It happened that as a self-taught musician, I could interact with other
> musicians from different townships. One of the greatest musicians in 1992,
> Mandla Mlotshwa, met Sharon Katz and Marilyn Cohen when they were look-
> ing for musicians. Mandla recommended me, and that is how I met Sharon Katz.
> It was a really tough time for both of us since those days mixing with White
> [people] as a Black person was no good thing as the revolution was at its highest
> point. (Wanda, email communication, July 10, 2017)

Wanda describes her teaching circumstances in a rural community-built
school and the challenges they faced with inadequate facilities that were
not conducive to learning. However, she describes her meeting with Katz
as a "miracle" because of the opportunities it created for her to improve the
school's physical condition and provide enriching learning experiences for
her students (discussed in Chapter 3). The struggle to fulfill one's potential in
an unjust society is evident from Wanda's upbringing and subsequent experiences. The social injustices of apartheid policies resonate in the following
narrative. Roberts (2002) describes Schumacher's account as follows:

> The first Zambian that Schumacher introduces sets her study in crystalline
> focus. While Matshakaza Blackson Lukhero was still a teenager in the 1940s,
> he began working with the archaeologist Desmond Clark; after World War II,
> he served as an interpreter to Max Marwick of the RLI during the first stages of

his work among Ngoni, and to J. A. Barnes soon thereafter. Lukhero was given the nickname "The Water Follows the Stream," a name that might suggest his dependency upon Barnes, yet Lukhero's "following amounted to his leading Barnes to the people, introducing him, interpreting for him, teaching him the language, discussing local traditions, and afterward talking to people about their reactions to the anthropologist and assuring them that Barnes was not a spy. (p. 2)

Roberts is keenly aware of the way Schumacher presents these invaluable relationships. Schumacher applies the useful notion of his being a "culture broker" so as not to lose sight of the politically and economically "inegalitarian relationship between anthropologist and informant" (p. 13). Lukhero's intellectual ability is evident in his "active and conscious role in shaping and elucidating various kinds of knowledge," whether he has been recognized as such by those who have employed him over the years (14–15). Lukhero, like other "culture brokers," has borne the burden of the colonial color bar and more recent iniquities (ibid., 137).

Unlike many of the researchers at RLI who originated from the United Kingdom and Europe, Katz is a South African who had to negotiate access to communities of color in South Africa because of the political circumstances of the apartheid era. She realized as a child that she had been born into a more privileged position by being White. The parallel between Lukhero and Nonhlanhla Wanda is striking. Not only did Wanda forge relationships for and with Katz, but she also served the role of interpreter among African people in the rural areas of Kwa-Zulu Natal. Wanda is also an intellectual, a musician, and a dancer who contributes significantly to Katz's productions. However, during her life, she has been deprived of the same level of access as her White counterparts to both academia and other resources because she is black.

An outline of critical statistics between the Black and White populations in apartheid South Africa sheds some light on Wanda's circumstances. Yudkoff (2016) states that "By 1978 [Wanda was studying under the Bantu Education system], there was little change in the inequities of South African education" (p. 98). Some of the most severe impacts occurred in fundamental rights to education and healthcare. The disparity in educational funding severely hampered the progress of Black students and the upward mobility of Blacks. At the same time, the severe lack of health care directly impacted the mortality rate of Black infants. Table 6.1 from an article by Collett (2017) provides some insights:

Significantly, the current crisis in the United States similarly stems from the deep-rooted iniquities of the economic, educational, and healthcare systems that have led to the disenfranchisement of black and brown communities.

Table 6.1 Inequitable Treatment of Blacks and Whites in South Africa circa 1978. Source: Adapted by author from Leo 80 (Collett, 2017)

Disproportionate Treatment circa 1978	Blacks	Whites
Population	19 million	4.5 million
Share of land	13%	87%
Share of national income	Below 20%	75%
Ratio of average earnings	1	14
Minimum taxable income	360 Rands	750 rands
Doctors per population	1/44 000	1/400
Infant death rate	20%(urban) 40%(rural)	2.7%
Annual expenditure on education per pupil	$45	$696
Teacher pupil ratio	1/60	1/22

In the United States, Katz forged a significant relationship with Wendy Quick, an African American woman from Pennsylvania. In an email communication to the author, dated June 16, 2017, Wendy Quick describes herself as "a performance artist, singer/dancer, educator, and entrepreneur." She has worked as a social worker, teacher, and law enforcement officer. During her tenure as a Philadelphia Police Detective, Quick developed several youth programs as comprehensive community-based programs formulated the understanding that education (or lack thereof), the economy, and crime are all connected (ibid.).

Wendy Quick met Sharon Katz in 2007 when she attended a community education course in South African music and dance offered by Katz. Quick was excited about learning new rhythms and dances from South Africa. In 2008, she traveled to South Africa as part of a tour group with Sharon Katz, Marilyn Cohen, and the Peace Train. She saw first-hand the various community projects with which Sharon Katz and Friends of The Peace Train were involved. The tours, organized by Katz and Cohen, were intended to introduce Americans to the sights, sounds, and history of South Africa, thereby garnering support for Katz's humanitarian work there. Wendy pledged to volunteer her time and talents to the Peace Train projects. While on tour, Wendy was bestowed with the name, Khethiwe, which means "Chosen One." It was one of the tour's many highlights for her. This African name made me think that Wendy Quick was South African when I first saw her perform at Caffè Lena in upstate New York.

During several concerts in South Africa, Katz invited Quick to join her on stage to participate in performing songs she had learned in class with the band. Quick describes this as "a truly a mind-blowing experience" (Quick, email communication, June 16, 2017). Months later, back in the United States, when Katz needed a female vocalist/dancer for her group, she invited Quick to join Sharon Katz & The Peace Train. Quick accepted without hesitation, viewing this opportunity as a "God-given gift" (ibid). After intense training in learning vocal parts, tongue-twisting lyrics in Zulu, Xhosa, other South African languages, and various Southern African dance moves, Quick made her début with the band in September 2008 as a vocalist and dancer. Performing throughout the United States, Canada, and South Africa, Quick thoroughly enjoys spreading the message of peace, love, and harmony through song and dance. Incredibly proud of continuing with her passion for "Peace Education through the Arts," Quick works alongside Katz as a presenter for workshop presentations, school assemblies, Artist-in-Residence programs, and special projects.

Quick states in her email: "I am the only American African female to have had the honor of performing with Sharon Katz & The Peace Train as a vocalist and dancer." Quick waxes poetic when she says: "I bring to the stage: Pride of my Ancestors, shown in my stance; Rhythm of the Motherland portrayed in my dance!" (ibid.) Quick has not only been an asset to Katz on the concert stage, but her aptitude in choreography has been particularly useful. She assists Katz in facilitating many music workshops among American schoolchildren and rehearsing with participants of the American Peace Train Tour of 2016. This production's choreography and vocal quality were achieved in part through the recruitment and participation of several Black youths in America. As an African American herself, Quick played a vital role in forging relationships and creating an atmosphere of trust and level of comfort for these young participants.

"Culture Brokers"—Nonhanhla Wanda (South African) and Wendy "Khetiwe" Quick (American)

After an interview with Sharon Katz at her home in Philadelphia on October 15, 2016, Katz sent me an email the following day in which she provides more significant insights into her close relationships with the two women—Wanda, pictured in Figure 6.1, and Quick, pictured in Figure 6.2—who have served as "culture brokers":

> I wanted to mention in response to your question about my work with Nonhlanhla and Wendy over the years. In the work I do, to build bridges between people who are divided, it is so important to model the opposite of separation, and I've always sought out partners with whom to work. In Israel/ Palestine, I also work with Palestinian and Israeli musicians, and these are critical relationships in getting the work done. I've been so fortunate to form such very strong friendships with these two women to do the work [. . .] I've been privileged on many levels—and that privilege includes in my way of thinking, the privilege of knowing these women, being accepted in their families and communities, and working together, as well as being friends for life.

Figure 6.1 **Nonhlanhla Wanda (Left Microphone) with Sharon Katz (Right Microphone) during the First American Peace Train Concert Performance in New York on July 9, 2016.** Photo courtesy of Brian Klasewitz (photographer).

Figure 6.2 **Sharon Katz (Left Microphone) with Wendy Quick (Right Microphone) during the First American Peace Train Tour Concert in New York on July 9, 2016.** Photo courtesy of Brian Klasewitz (photographer).

Transcending Barriers through the Power of Music

The release of the award-winning documentary *When Voices Meet* that chronicles the journey of Sharon Katz & The Peace Train triggered enthusiasm and support. This positive reaction led to the Peace Train tour of 2016 documented in Chapter 5. The film and the tour captured the imagination of ordinary people—teachers, musicians, activists, youth, and children —to confront the issues that create divisions within our communities and within society and to create a platform for change. This refusal to accept the status quo and this energy to disrupt the forces that work against human rights and social justice is the hallmark of Katz's musical activism. Toward this end, Katz and her team have organized projects, workshops, and concerts in many communities across the United States, in the border region between the USA and Mexico, in Cuba, and in South Africa. Since 2016, Sharon Katz and Marilyn Cohen have joined with local partners to develop musical projects that focus on Transcending Barriers by building mutual understanding, respect, and friendships.

The Peace Train Project in Northern California in 2017

In May 2017, more than a hundred youth and musicians from diverse backgrounds joined forces and paraded through the East Bay area of California. This Peace Train project focused on all children's hopes and rights, especially children from disenfranchised minorities, including Latina, African American, migrant, and immigrant families. Students, teachers, and families from Sacramento, San Pablo, Oakland, and Berkeley traveled for this project. They performed concerts at schools, train stations, and public parks to voice their heartbreak, suffering, and discontent. La Pena Community Chorus singers and musicians joined the Peace Train's band for these special events. Katz shared the details of this tour with me. "The Peace Train Transcending Barriers" tour included their cross-border work between the United States and Mexico as well as a tour to Cuba.

In Mexico, Katz works with choirs in vulnerable areas of Tijuana and in orphanages and safe houses with children who have been rescued from child trafficking. The project also includes training students from the Kroc Center for Peace and Justice at the University of San Diego. These music therapy projects are in partnership with a Tijuana organization called *Promotora de las Bellas Artes*. The major thrust last year was to lead families and singers across the U.S.-Mexican border, hold workshops together with Mexican families and singers and stage a concert in defiance of the Trump-era regulations trying to restrict the movement of Mexicans across the U.S. border. According to Katz, "These goals were beautifully accomplished and realized on July 21, 2018" (Katz, email communication, November 17, 2019).

The Peace Train's Transcending Barriers
Project Across the Border in 2018

In 2018, a partnership with *Promotora de las Bellas Artes* (PBA) in Tijuana, Mexico, was established. Sharon Katz & The Peace Train have collaborated with PBA conducting yearly programs on both sides of the U.S.-Mexico border. Katz has implemented her activism model (based on her work in the 1990s in South Africa), working with schools, community groups, homes for rescued girls and migrants.

Sharon Katz is committed to professionalism in her work. It took many months of rehearsals and preparations on both sides of the border before the Peace Train implemented a binational Transcending Barriers Project in July 2018 to promote intercultural understanding, respect, and friendship. This project's united and purposeful nature was evident from the enthusiasm when participants of all ages boarded the Peace Train Diego Trolley for a ride to the border at San Ysidro. The U.S. group then marched across the border, greeted by hundreds of young singers and their families from Katz's partner organization, *Promotora de las Bellas Artes*. Americans and Mexicans joyously paraded through the streets of Tijuana, Mexico, to the Cultural Center of Tijuana (CECUT). As a prelude to a combined performance, Katz—with her music therapy background—initiated friendship-building workshops followed by a rehearsal. The combined group performed at CECUT with TV cameras rolling, and reporters provided coverage of the event in Mexico and the United States.

Transcending Barriers to Cuba—2019

Katz explains the continually evolving nature of her work:

> This year, 2019, we continued doing the work by spending a lot of time training choirs and teachers in Tijuana. I was able to participate in an event with 1,500 children performing together in a stadium in Tijuana on June 9 [see Figure 6.3]. And as you know, this opportunity of working with a Cuban choral conductor, Daria Abreu Feraud, in Tijuana, resulted in my being invited to stage the Peace Train in Cuba because she is the President of the International Festival of Choirs, which takes place every two years in Santiago de Cuba. (Katz, email communication, November 17, 2019)

An essential part of Katz's activism includes her humanitarian efforts, creating opportunities for less-privileged children. Toward this end, Katz revealed that the Peace Train was able to "sponsor 30 Mexican children to join 150 Cuban children and a fifty-piece symphony orchestra to stage a memorable concert in Santiago de Cuba on November 1, 2019" (ibid.). The International Festival of

Figure 6.3   Sharon Katz Performs as Guest Artist of *Promotora de las Bella's Artes* with 1,500 Children in Concert in Tijuana, Mexico, 2019. Photo courtesy of Gonzalo Gonzalez (photographer).

Choirs was hosted in Santiago de Cuba. According to Katz, it took a month (since October 2019) to train a band, the symphony orchestra, the dancers, and the children's choirs. From her standpoint, "The ripple effect on the city continues to vibrate as people were extremely excited about the social, political, and spiritual impact of our project in their city of Santiago de Cuba. From an ethnomusicology standpoint, we were able to incorporate Afro Cuban rhythms and dance into our South African compositions and expand the scope of our original music" (ibid.). This cultural exchange culminated with a grand performance at the festival on November 1, 2019. Since that collaboration, Sharon Katz & The Peace Train have assisted the Clave de Sol Guitar School in Cuba.

After the tour of 2016 in the United States, Katz continued with the artistic endeavor of recording new songs and rearranging previously written songs. In 2018 Katz and Wanda released "Nonhlanhla Wanda & Sharon Katz—Side-By-Side." Besides, Katz recorded four new songs in Cuba in 2019: Vamos en el Tren de la Paz; Santiago; Afrika y Cuba and a Cuban version of "The Time is Right Today." In response to the COVID-19 Pandemic, Katz has created a "We Know What To Do" song with videos posted online to promote everyone's health and well-being. This ongoing, uplifting musical activism of Katz reminds me that it was feeling bereft as an immigrant in the United States that started this ethnomusicological journey.

Advancing Research in Grassroots Musical Activism

It was a yearning for home that brought me to Caffè Lena in downtown Saratoga Springs, New York, on that fateful day in the Spring of 2013 when I first encountered Sharon Katz. Her program of music in that historic venue exuded hope and optimism. Katz's eclectic musical style supported by her dexterity on guitar filled a nostalgia I had for the familiar sounds of South Africa. The haunting quality of Katz's voice blended with the rich harmonies sung by Wendy Quick, whose graceful movements in African-inspired dress were captivating. This experience was only the beginning.

Discovering and documenting the multifaceted nature of Katz's grassroots activism has been fortuitous as it taps into a gap in the ethnomusicological history of South African musicians. The apartheid era's restrictive policies stymied the preservation of a long history of activism through music in South Africa. Katz provides healing and hope for the people of a country whose recovery from the effects of apartheid policies, fueled by corruption, has a long road ahead.

Katz's activism extends beyond South Africa to broad outreach in the United States, Mexico, and Cuba. This research may inform the analyses and comparisons of grassroots musical activism within a global context in the future. Since the journey of Sharon Katz & The Peace Train is far from over, tracking the trajectory of this activism through its musical collaborations and cultural exchanges lends itself to future documentation as the Peace Train rolls on.

NOTE

1. In apartheid South Africa, two events, the 1927 Liquor Act, which among other restrictions prohibited Africans and Indians from selling alcohol or entering licensed premises, and the Great Depression, were responsible for the emergence of township shebeens. Shebeens played an essential role in South Africa's predemocratic socialand political history. During apartheid, shebeens came to be associated with the townships, where they served as meeting places for political dissidents, but they have since crossed over from makeshift taverns to mainstream venues for relaxing and socializing. Accessed April 6, 2017, http://www.southafrica.net/za/en/articles/entry/article-southafrica.net-shebeens.

Glossary of Musical Styles

The following definitions relate to the variety of musical styles that Katz has incorporated into her compositions. Katz's songs cannot be pigeonholed into a single genre. It is this aspect of her music that speaks to its broad appeal. Katz has used the following term to describe her musical style, or they have been identified as occurring in her songs:

Afro-Pop refers to African pop music that incorporates electric instruments. It originated in the 1980s and references western pop or soul music.

Crossover refers to the music of a genre such as jazz, which does well in other categories of music like "popular" music. This term may also refer to artists. In the most common crossover type, classically trained performers sing popular songs, folk music, or holiday songs.

High-Life Afro-Pop refers to African music comprised of dance styles from English-speaking West Africa where guitar band music is heard with jazzy horn sections or in rural areas with just multiple guitars.

Gumboot Dancing (Isicathulo) originated with South African mineworkers who used it as an alternative to drumming and relaying messages while working in the mines. These rhythms have developed into a popular African dance performed by dancers wearing Wellington boots, called *gumboots*, in South Africa.

Kwela refers to a style of popular music of Central and Southern Africa in which the lead part is usually played on the penny whistle. It is rhythmical and repetitive, resembling jazz.

Marabi is associated with Pretoria's townships' working-class culture during the 1930s that included drinking and dancing. Besides the dancing, it is a term that also refers to the popular music of this culture with a keyboard

and brass dominant sound influenced by ragtime and indigenous folk
music.

Maskanda refers to traditional Zulu music played on Western instruments
such as the guitar and violin or concertina. *Maskanda* also includes voice
and the piano accordion. The origin of the word "maskanda" may be attributed to the Afrikaans word *musikant* (meaning musician). This connection
may also be ascribed to the early emergence of this genre among Dutch
farmers. Muller (2008) describes the birth of maskanda as the outcome of
the following historical process:

1. European music
2. Translated into Afrikaans cultural practices
3. Borrowed and transformed by Zulu-speaking musicians into a musical
   language more consistent with their own (113–114).

Mbaqanga describes the music made by small bands playing the music
popular in Black communities from the 1930s to the present. The style was
featured in much of the protest music theater of the early 1980s and 1990s
(ibid., 87). Mbaqanga developed in the South African shebeens[1] during the
1960s. It used western instruments, which contributed to its development
into a South African version of American jazz. However, the South African
vocal style retained its musical sound as emanating from Africa. Many
Mbaqanga researchers have described this style as a hybrid of marabi and
kwela musical styles.

Township Jive or *Jaiva* refers to South African township music and an African dance style that has influenced Western breakdance. It may be attributed to the shebeen culture of the apartheid era townships. It has its roots
in Mbaqanga, but it has more of an international flair rather than being
rooted in tradition.

R&B or *Rhythm and Blues* refers to popular music, originally by African American artists, that tends to have soul, jazz, funk, and even hip-hop elements.

Funk refers to a music style that emphasizes intensely syncopated rhythmic
groove, a type of popular music, originally by African American artists, that
can have features of soul, jazz, funk, hip-hop, and typically features a repetitive melody and minimal chord changes. It is usually accompanied by dancing.

Folk Music traditionally refers to the music of the people from an area or
region. Some songs of Sharon Katz are reminiscent of American folk music.

Jazz refers to a style of modern music first developed by African Americans
in New Orleans. Besides having syncopated rhythms and rich harmonies,
one of the critical components of jazz is improvisation.

Rap refers to a popular music genre where the words are spoken (not sung)
to a steady rhythmic beat.

Reggae is a popular music style popularized in the 1970s through Bob Marley's songs and lyrics that spoke to Rastafarian ideas. Originating in Jamaica, it is characterized by a strongly accented secondary beat. Reggae evolved in the late 1960s from ska and other local variations on calypso and rhythm and blues.

NOTE

1. In apartheid South Africa, two events, the 1927 Liquor Act, which among other restrictions prohibited Africans and Indians from selling alcohol or entering licensed premises, and the Great Depression, were responsible for the emergence of township shebeens that played an essential role in apartheid South Africa's social and political history. Shebeens came to be associated with the townships, where they served as meeting places for political dissidents, but they have since crossed over from makeshift taverns to mainstream venues for relaxing and socialising. Accessed April 6, 2017, http://www.southafrica.net/za/en/articles/entry/article-southafrica.net-she beens.

Appendices

Compact Discs by Sharon Katz & The Peace Train

SIDE-BY-SIDE

Nonhlanhla Wanda and Sharon Katz celebrate twenty-five years of world-wide touring and musical collaboration with the release of their CD "Side-By-Side." This Afro-Jazz-Contemporary fusion album features all original compositions by Nonhlanhla Wanda, Sharon Katz, and producer Malcolm Nhleko. The recording showcases their distinctive voices and close harmonies with Sharon Katz on guitars, Qhubekani Mthethwa on bass, Charles Boykie Mnomiya on drums, and Sanele Phakathi on piano and synthesizer.

Label: Thando Rhythms

Released: February 25, 2018

WHEN VOICES MEET

This CD is an award-winning soundtrack of the documentary titled *When Voices Meet.*

Upon the release of Nelson Mandela from prison, South African musician and music therapist Sharon Katz joined with singer and educator Nonhlanhla Wanda to form a 500-voice multiracial youth choir. The film *When Voices Meet* documents the trials, tribulations, and triumphs of these musician activists. These are their songs.

Label: Thando Rhythms

Released: September 18, 2015

DOUBLE TAKE

This CD is a musical collaboration of Sharon Katz with Abigail Kubeka and Dolly Rathebe, whom Katz refers to as her soul-sisters.

Label: Thando Rhythms

Released: October 18, 2011

LERATO

Sharon Katz with the legendary Dolly Rathebe

"Lerato" means love, and it is the name South Africa's legendary Dolly Rathebe gave to Sharon as they recorded four jazzy and soulful tracks on this album. The melodic lines combine with catchy rhythms and Sharon's unmistakable guitar and vocal styles.

Label: Thando Rhythms

Released January 1, 2005.

CRYSTAL JOURNEY

Sharon Katz with the *Peace Train's* original 500-voice choir

Label: Thando Rhythms

Released [August 6, 2004] December 13, 2007

IMBIZO

The title means "a Zulu cultural gathering."

Sharon Katz created the music on Imbizo with seventy musicians from South Africa, West Africa, and the United States who fuse traditional and contemporary rhythms, instruments, and harmonies with universally relevant lyrics of political and personal concerns. This is a Grammy-nominated CD.

Label: Appleseed

Released July 9, 2002

APPENDIX 2

NVivo Software Applications

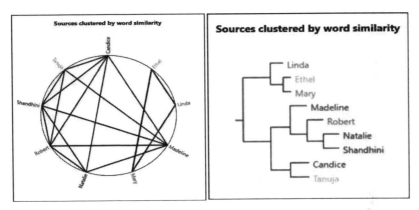

Figure 7.1   Cluster Depictions. Created by Brandon Raidoo.

The NVivo software displayed the frequency of keywords elicited from the raw data of the transcripts as follows:

Table 7.1   Frequency of Keywords and Related References in Interviews. *Created by the author.*

Number	Number of Interviewees	Keywords	Frequency of References
1	9	Cultural and racial differences	239
2	9	Performances/auditions/rehearsals	333
3	9	Peace and unity	347
4	9	Feelings of excitement/wonder	530
5	9	Memories/remember	393
6	9	Impact of experiences	511
7	9	Personal growth and development	419

Keywords	References
Feelings excitement wonder	⬆ 530
Impact of experience	⬆ 511
Personal growth	➡ 419
Memories remember	➡ 393
Peace and unity	➡ 347
Performances auditions	⬇ 333
Cultural racial differences	⬇ 239

Figure 7.2   Selected Keywords of Interviewees and the Frequency of Associated References from Highest to Lowest Using NVivo Software. Created by Brandon Raidoo.

APPENDIX 3

Vocal Scores

Shosholoza

trad. Arr. Sharon Katz

Figure 7.3 The Song *Shosholoza* Arranged by Sharon Katz. Courtesy of Sharon Katz. Used with permission.

Figure 7.3 Continued

We Are The Children

words and music by Sharon Kat

Figure 7.4 *We Are the Children* **Composed by Sharon Katz in 1993/Adapted 2016.**
Courtesy of Sharon Katz. Used with permission.

Figure 7.4 Continued

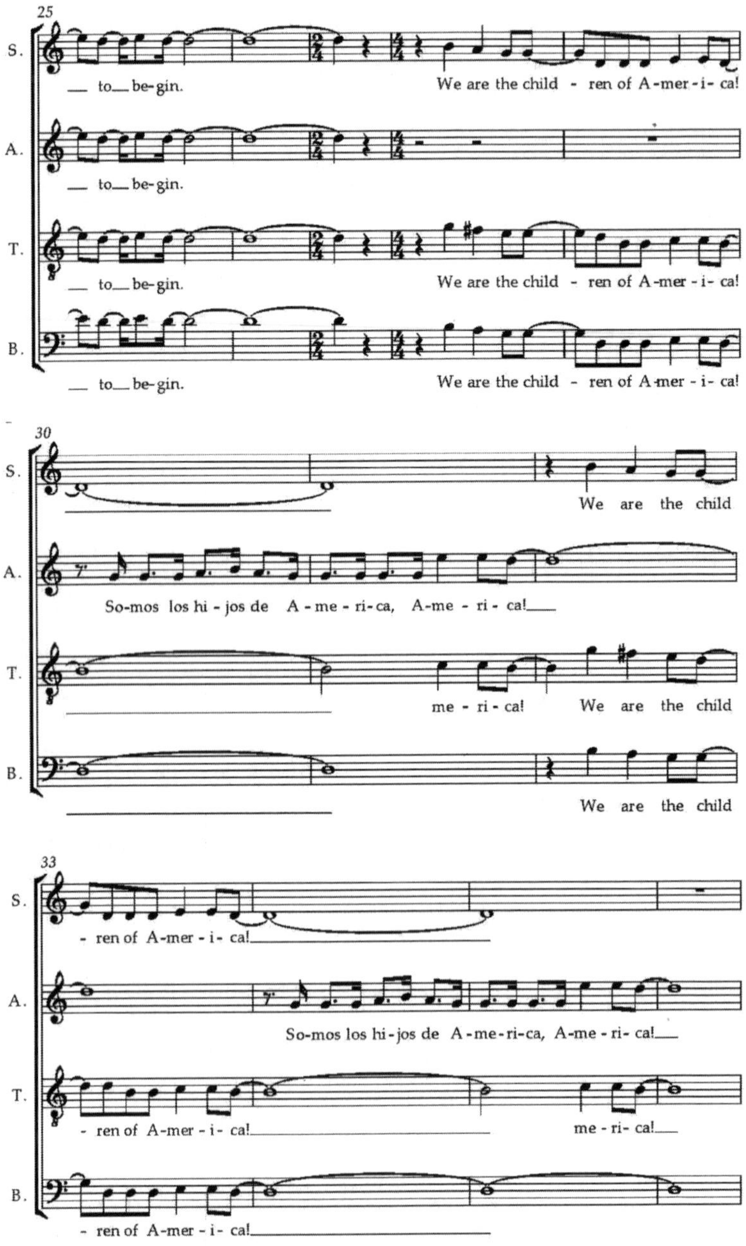

Figure 7.4 Continued

The Time is Right Today

Sharon Katz (1993/2016)

Figure 7.5 *The Time Is Right Today* **Composed by Sharon Katz 1993/Adapted 2016.**
Courtesy of Sharon Katz. Used with permission.

Appendices

Figure 7.5   Continued

Figure 7.5 Continued

SANALWAMI
Traditional Xhosa Song

Figure 7.6 *Sanalwami* **Arranged by Sharon Katz.** Courtesy of Sharon Katz. Used with permission.

Figure 7.6 Continued

182   *Appendices*

VOCAL SCORE   SALA NGOANA

SHARON KATZ

Figure 7.7   *Sala Ngoana* **Composed by Sharon Katz.** Courtesy of Sharon Katz. Used with permission.

2   Sala Ngoana

Figure 7.7 Continued

VOCAL SCORE

Figure 7.8 *The Little We Have We Share* by **Sharon Katz.** Courtesy of Sharon Katz. Used with permission.

Figure 7.8 Continued

APPENDIX 4

Responses to Questionnaire: A Demographic Survey of Adults on Tour

Sharon Katz and Marilyn Cohen were not invited to answer the questionnaire, which brings the women in the forty-five to sixty-four category down to eighteen. Twelve chaperones (ten women and two men) had filled out an "Informed Consent" letter at Catholic University (their accommodations in Washington D.C.), indicating a willingness to answer the questionnaire and demographic survey. Nine female respondents and one male respondent returned their surveys and questionnaires. The demographic survey of these adult respondents revealed the following:

Table 7.2   A Demographic Survey of Adult Respondents on the American Peace Train Tour of 2016. *Created by the author*

Respondent/ Chaperone	Gender	Age	Race	Marital Status	Education	Occupation	Performer on tour
1	F	60	W	M	T	P	N
2	F	51	W	M	T	P	Y
3	F	56	W	M	T	P	Y
4	F	55	W	M	T	P	Y
5	F	70	W	M	T	P	Y
6	F	50	W	S	T	P	Y
7	F	53	B	S	T	P	N
8	F	54	B	S	T	P	Y
9	F	58	B	S	T	P	Y
10	M	68	W	S	T	P	Y

Key (created following responses received):

Gender—F (Female); M (Male)
Race—W (White); Black (B)
Marital Status—M (Married); S (Single)
Education—T meaning Tertiary Education (College or University)
Occupation—P (Professional); W (white-collar job); B (blue-collar job)
Performed on Tour—Y (Yes); N (No)

References

Activism, [online]. Accessed May 28, 2017, https://en.oxforddictionaries.com/defini tion/activism.

Alford, R. R. et al. 1995. "Designing Social Inquiry: Scientific Inference in Qualitative Research." *Contemporary Sociology*, 24 (3): 424.

Allan, Jani. 2016. "Afrikaner pride and passion mix with fun and laughter for the new era boere punks." Posted in *South Africa, Sunday Times, The Eighties*, March 18, 2016. http://janiallan.com/2016/03/18/afrikaner-pride-passion-mixed-fun-laug hter-new-era-boere-punks/#more-.'

Anderson, B. 2002. "A Principle of Hope: Recorded Music, Listening Practices and the Immanence of Utopia." *Geografiska Annaler. Series B, Human Geography*, 84 (3/4): 211–227. http://www.jstor.org/stable/3554317.

Ansdell, G. 2014. "Revisiting 'Community Music Therapy and the Winds of Change' (2002): An Original Article and A Retrospective Evaluation." *International Journal of Community Music*, 7(1): 11–45.

Ansdell, G. & Stige, B. 2016. "Community Music Therapy." In *The Oxford Handbook of Music Therapy*, edited by Edwards, J. Oxford, UK: Oxford University Press.

Ansell, G. 2004. *Soweto Blues: Jazz, Popular Music and Politics in South Africa.* London: Bloomsbury Academic.

Asch, T., Marshall, J. & Spier, P. 1973. "Ethnographic Film: Structure and Function." *Annual Review of Anthropology*, 2: 179–187. http://www.jstor.org/stable/2949268.

Aspden, P. & Minamore, B. 2017. "Is John Lennon's Imagine Patronizingly Sappy, or a Moving Meditation on Hope?" *The Guardian*, June 26, 2017. https://www.the guardian.com/commentisfree/2017/jun/26/head-to-head-imagine-john-lennon-sop py-meditation-hope.

Baines, G. 2008. "Popular Music and Negotiating Whiteness in Apartheid South Africa." In *Composing Apartheid: Music For and Against Apartheid*, edited by G. Olwage, 99–113. Johannesburg, South Africa: Wits University Press.

Ballantine, C. 2004. "Re-thinking 'whiteness'? Identity, change and 'white' popular music in post-apartheid South Africa." *Popular Music*, 23/2: 105–131. https://

www.researchgate.net/publication/231980297_Re-thinking_%27whiteness%27_I
dentity_change_and_%27white%27_popular_music_in_post-apartheid_South_A
frica.

Barenboim, D. 2004. "An Art of Sound That Crosses All Borders." *Le Monde Diplomatique*, June 7, 2004. http://mondediplo.com/2004/06/07barenboim?

Barenboim, D. 2006. *Reith Lectures.* Accessed February 25, 2014, http://www.bbc.co.uk/radio4/featulectures/transcripts/2000/#y2006.

Bar-Tal, D. 2001. "Why Does Fear Override Hope in Societies Engulfed by Intractable Conflict, as it Does in the Israeli Society?" *Political Psychology*, 22 (3): 601–627.

Baxter, P. & Jack, S. 2008. "Qualitative Case Study Methodology: Study Design and Implementation for Novice Researchers." *The Qualitative Report*, 13 (4): 544–545. Accessed December 9, 2017, http://www.nova.edu/ssss/QR/QR13-4/baxter.pdf.

Belafonte, Shari. 2016. "Jump Aboard the Peace Train." *Trend Privé Magazine.* September 11, 2016. http://trendprivemagazine.com/2016/09/11/jump-aboard-the-peace-train/.

Benarde, S. R. 2003. *Stars of David: Rock 'n Roll's Jewish Stories.* Waltham, MA: Brandeis University Press.

Bender, W. 1991. *Sweet Mother: Modern African Music.* Chicago: The University of Chicago Press.

Blacking, J. 1973. *How Musical is Man?* Seattle: University of Washington Press.

_____. 1980. "Trends in the Black Music of South Africa, 1959–1969." In *Music of Many Cultures,* edited by Elizabeth May, 95–215. Los Angeles, CA: University of California Press.

Booth, D. & Nauright, J. 2007. "Embodied Identities: Sport and Race in South Africa." *Contours: A Journal of the African Diaspora*, 1 (1): 16–36.

Boxill, E. H. 1988. "Continuing Notes: Worldwide Networking for Peace Editorial." *Music Therapy,* 7 (1): 80–85.

_____.1997. *The Miracle of Music Therapy.* Gilsum, NH: Barcelona Publishers.

Brantley, Ben. 1997. "When Birnam Wood Comes to South Africa, Look Out." Review in the *New York Times*, July 23, 1997. https://www.nytimes.com/1997/07/23/theater/when-birnam-wood-comes-to-south-africa-look-out.html).

Braun, V. & Clarke, V. 2006. "Using thematic analysis in psychology." *Qualitative Research in Psychology*, 3: 77–101. Accessed July 9, 2015, www.QualResearchPsych.com.

Browne, D. 2017. "Joan Baez's Fighting Side: The Life and Times of a Secret Badass." *Rolling Stone.* Accessed August 29, 2017, https://www.rollingstone.com/music/features/joan-baez-the-life-and-times-of-a-secret-badass-w474962.

Byerly, I. B. 2008. "Decomposing Apartheid: Things Come Together. The Anatomy of a Music Revolution." In *Composing Apartheid: Music For and Against Apartheid* edited by Grant Olwage. Johannesburg, South Africa: Wits University Press.

Chang, H. 2015. "Self-Narratives for Christian Multicultural Educators: A Pathway to Understanding Self and Others." *A Journal of the International Christian Community for Teacher Education*, 1(1). Accessed June 6, 2018, https://www.researchgate.net/profile/Heewon_Chang/publication/238086361_Self-Narratives

_for_Christian_Multicultural_Educators_A_Pathway_to_Understanding_Self_an
d_Others/links/55b9183e08aed621de086175.pdf.

Cheah, E. 2009. *An Orchestra beyond Borders: Voices of the West-Eastern Divan
Orchestra*. London: Verso.

Collett, D. 2017. "International Day for the Elimination of Racial Discrimination."
Accessed August 24, 2017, https://learnenglish.britishcouncil.org/en/magazine/int
ernational-day-elimination-racial-discrimination.

Cohen, R. D. 2013. "Peace Songs of the 1960s." *Smithsonian Folkways Magazine*.
Accessed August 30, 2014, http://media.smithsonianfolkways.org/docs/folkways/
magazine/2013_spring_summer/Cohen_Peace-Songs-of-the-1960s.pdf.

Collett, Dave. 2017. "International Day for the Elimination of Racial Discrimination."
Accessed August 24, 2017, http://learnenglish.educ.ar/files/attachment/learnengli
sh-central-articles-racial-discrimination.pdf.

Coplan, David B. 1985. *In Township Tonight*. New York, NY: Longman.

Crabtree B. & Miller, W. Eds. 1999. *Doing Qualitative Research*, 2nd ed. London:
Sage.

Creswell, J. W. 1998. *Research Design: Qualitative, Quantitative, and Mixed
Methods Approaches*, 2nd ed. Thousand Oaks, CA: Sage.

_____. 2013. *Qualitative Inquiry & Research Design*. 3rd ed. Thousand
Oaks, CA: Sage Publications.

Danielson, Virginia. 1998. *"The Voice of Egypt": Umm Kulthum, Arabic Song,
and Egyptian Society in the Twentieth Century*. Chicago: University of Chicago
Press.

Davhula, M. J. 2008. *Malombo Musical Arts in Vhavenda Indigenous Healing
Practices*. Unpublished Doctoral Thesis. Pretoria: University of Pretoria.

de Caro, F. 2012. "Stories and 'Oral History' Interviews: A Thematic Analysis of
'Embedded' Narratives." *Western Folklore*, 71 (3–4): 275–276.

De Beer, R., & Shitandi, W. 2012. "Choral Music in Africa: History, Content, and
Performance Practice." In *The Cambridge Companion to Choral Music*, edited by
A. De Quadros, 185–200. Cambridge: Cambridge University Press. doi:10.1017/
CCOL9780521111737.015

DeNora, T. 2003 [2000]. *Music in Everyday Life*. Cambridge, UK: Cambridge
University Press.

Dolly Rathebe. n.d. *South African History Online*. Accessed March 14, 2017, http://
www.sahistory.org.za/people/dolly-rathebe.

Doyle, J. 2009. "Four Dead in O-hi-o, 1970." *The Pop History Dig*. Accessed
September 9, 2017, http://www.pophistorydig.com/topics/tag/crosby-stills-nash-o
hio/.

Dylan, Bob. *The Times They Are A-Changin'* [online]. Accessed August 28, 2017,
https://www.bobdylan.com/songs/times-they-are-changin/.

Edmondson, J. & Weiner, R. G. 2013. "Radical Protest in Rock: Zappa, Lennon,
and Garcia." In *Social Protest in Popular Music* edited by Jonathan Friedman,
142–156. London and New York: Routledge.

Elsila, M., Lloyd & Marcos. 1998. "Music Behind Bars: Learning to Teach Radically
in Prison." *The Politics of Music Education,* 52 (Spring): 4–8.

Erlmann, Veit. 1991. *African Stars: Studies in Black South African Performance.* Chicago and London: The University of Chicago Press.

Etuk, U. A. 2002. *Religion and Cultural Identity.* Ibadan, Nigeria: Hope Publication.

Eyerman, R. & Jamison, A. 1998. *Music and Social Movements: Mobilizing Traditions in the Twentieth Century.* Cambridge, UK: Cambridge University Press.

Fabian, J. 1990. *Power and Performance: Ethnographic Explorations through Proverbial Wisdom and Theatre in Shaba, Zaire.* Madison, WI: University of Wisconsin Press.

Fischlin, D. & Heble, A. (eds) 2003. *Rebel Musics.* London, UK: Black Rose Books.

Flick, U. 2014. "Theorization from Data. In *The SAGE Handbook of Qualitative Data Analysis,* edited by U. Flick, 554–568. London: Sage. DOI:10.4135/9781446282243. n38

Fosnot, C. T. (ed.) 1996. *Constructivism: Theory, Perspectives, and Practice.* New York and London: Teachers College, Columbia University Press.

Friedman, J. C. (ed.) 2013. *Social Protest in Popular Music.* New York, NY: Routledge.

Froehlich, H. 2002. "Tackling the Seemingly Obvious—A Daunting Task Indeed: An Essay Review of Music in Everyday Life." *Action, Criticism, and Theory for Music Education,* 1 (2): 2–11. Accessed July 24, 2017, http://act.maydaygroup.or g/articles/Froehlich1_2.pdf.

Furman, R. 2007. "Poetry and Narrative as Qualitative Data: Explorations into Existential Theory." *Indo-Pacific Journal of Phenomenology,* 7 (1): 1–9. http://dx. doi.org/10.1080/20797222.2007.11433939.

Gabriel, Peter. n.d. "Biko" (the song). *Genius.* Accessed September 11, 2017. https:/ /genius.com/Peter-gabriel-biko-lyrics.

Gans, C. J. 2014. "Hugh Masekela Celebrates 75th Birthday." *Mail & Guardian.* April 6, 2014, https://mg.co.za/article/2014-04-06-hugh-masekela-celebrates-75th -birthday.

Garfias, Robert. 2004. *Music: The Cultural Context.* Osaka: National Museum of Ethnology.

Gay, L. R. et al. 2009. *Educational Research: Competencies for Analysis and Applications.* New York: Merrill/Pearson.

Gilbert, S. 2008. "Singing Against Apartheid: ANC Cultural Groups and the International Anti-Apartheid Struggle." In *Composing Apartheid: Music For and Against Apartheid* edited by Grant Olwage, 155–184. Johannesburg: Witwatersrand Press.

Glaser, Barney G. & Strauss A. 1967. *The Discovery of Grounded Theory: Strategies for Qualitative Research.* New York: Aldine.

Gordon, R. 2002. *Journal of Southern African Studies,* 28 (2): 471–473.

Gordimer, N. 2004. *Telling Tales.* New York: Picador.

Gorlinski, V. n.d. "Johnny Clegg: South African musician." *Encyclopedia Britannica.* Accessed May 28, 2018, https://www.britannica.com/biography/Johnny-Clegg.

Gouk, P. (ed) 2016. *Musical Healing in Cultural Contexts.* London and New York: Routledge.

Gould, H. 2000. "Creative Exchange: Culture for Peace and Stability." *Development,* 43 (30): 79–80.

Greenwald, Matthew. n.d. "Bring Him Back Home (Nelson Mandela): Song Review." *AllMusic.* Accessed September 11, 2017, http://www.allmusic.com/song/bring-him -back-home-nelson-mandela-mt0030437954.

Grundlingh, A. 2004. "Rocking the Boat" in South Africa? Voëlvry Music and Afrikaans Anti-Apartheid Social Protest in the 1980s." *The International Journal of African Historical Studies,* 37 (3): 483–514. Accessed June 18, 2017, http:// www.jstor.org/stable/4129042.

Hartwig, G. 2001. "Explorations in the Changing Form, Theory and Practice of Documentary." *New Media Documentary.* Accessed September 25, 2016, http:// www.gunthar.com/gatech/digital_documentary/Database_Documentary.pdf.

Hendrickson, T. 2011. "Sharon Katz and the Peace Train preview: Nearly two decades after the momentous event, Peace Train remains a force for change." *The Star-Ledger.* June 17, 2011, https://www.nj.com/entertainment/music/2011/06/sha ron_katz_and_the_peace_trai.html.

Hess, J. 2019. *Music Education for Social Change.* New York and London: Routledge.

Hirsh, L. 2003. *Amandla! A Revolution in Four-Part Harmony.* [DVD] Santa Monica, CA: Artisan. http://woodstockpreservation.org/Gallery/NYTCompilation.html.

Hopkins, P. 2006. *Voëlvry: The Movement That Rocked South Africa.* Cape Town: Zebra Press.

Idang, G. E. 2015. "African Culture and Values." *Phronimon* [online], 16 (2): 97–111.

Ishak, N. & Bakar, A. 2012. "Qualitative Data Management and Analysis using NVivo: An Approach Used to Examine Leadership Qualities in Student Leaders." *Education Research Journal,* 2 (3): 94–103.

Jolaosho, Tayo. n.d. "Anti-Apartheid Freedom Songs Then and Now." *Smithsonian Folkways Magazine.* Accessed August 22, 2014, http://media.smithsonianfolkways .org/docs/folkways/magazine/2014_spring/Anti_apartheid_Freedom_Songs_Jola osho.pdf.

Jardine, D. 1992. "Reflections on Education, Hermeneutics, and Ambiguity: Hermeneutics as a Restoring of Life to Its Original Difficulty." In *Understanding Curriculum as Phenomenological and Deconstructed Text,* edited by Pinar and Reynolds, 116–130. New York: Teachers College Press.

Jimi Hendrix *Machine Gun* (Live). [online] Accessed August 20, 2017, https://www .youtube.com/watch?v=AJw_XqvsSIs.

"Joe's Pub Remembers Pete Seeger; Concert Set for 2/17 to Benefit Rocking the Boat." Accessed August 16, 2017, https://www.broadwayworld.com/article/Joes -Pub-Remembers-Pete-Seeger-Concert-Set-for-217-to-Benefit-Rocking-the-Boat -20140206.

John-Hall, A. 2002. "Pounding a Peace Beat Sharon Katz & Peace Train, Activists with a Beat." www.Philly.com.

Johnston, H. & Aarelaid-Tart, A. 2000. "Generations, Microcohorts, and Long Term Mobilization: The Estonian National Movement, 1940–1991." *Sociological Perspectives,* 43: 671–698.

Jury, B. 1996. "Boys to Men: Afrikaans Alternative Popular Music 1986–1990." *African Languages and Cultures*, 9 (2): 99–109.

Katz, S. 2011. "The Peace Train." *Voices: A World Forum for Music Therapy*, 11 (1). Accessed March 26, 2014, https://voices.no/index.php/voices/article/viewArt icle/284/439.

Katz, S. & Cohen, M. n.d. *African Music Therapy: Toward the Development of a Model for the African Continent.* Unpublished Manuscript.

Kivnick, H. Q. 1990. *Where is the Way: Song and Struggle in South Africa.* New York: Penguin Books.

Kuntz, A. M. 2015. *The Responsible Methodologist: Inquiry, Truth-Telling, and Social Justice.* Walnut Creek, CA: Left Coast Press.

Lather, P. 1992. "Critical Frames in Educational Research: Feminist and Post-Structural Perspectives." *Theory into Practice*, 31 (2): 87–99.

Lavrakas, P. J. 2008. "Demographic Measure." In *Encyclopedia of Survey Research Methods.* Sage. DOI: 10.4135/9781412963947.

Lebaka, M. E. K. 2018. "The Art of Establishing and Maintaining Contact with Ancestors: A Study of Bapedi Tradition." *HTS Teologiese Studies/Theological Studies*, 74 (1): 4871. https://doi. org/10.4102/hts.v74i1.4871.

Lengyel, P. 1982. "Makings of Music." *International Science Journal*, 34 (4): 570–581. http://unesdoc.unesco.org/images/0005/000547/054739eo.pdf.

Long Walk to Freedom. 2002. [2 CD] n.p. Wrasse Records Limited.

Louw, A. 1997. "Surviving the Transition: Trends and Perceptions of Crime in South Africa." *Social Indicators Research*, 41 (1/3): 137–168.

Ludski, Warren. 2019. "Touring Dixies Paved Way 60 Years Ago—And Some Never Came Back." *Music Legends of Cape Town.* Accessed April 29, 2020, https://wa rrenludskimusicscene.com/interviews-3/touring-dixies-paved-way-60-years-ago -and-some-never-came-back/.

Malisa, M. & Malange, N. 2013. "Songs for Freedom: Music and the Struggle against Apartheid." In *The Routledge History of Social Protest in Popular Music* edited by J. C. Friedman, 314. New York: Routledge.

Maluleka, R. J. 2020. "The Status of Traditional Healing in the Limpopo Province of South Africa." *HTS Teologiese Studies/Theological Studies* 76 (4): a6103. https:// doi. org/10.4102/hts.v76i4.6103.

Mandela, N. 1994. *Long Walk to Freedom: The Autobiography of Nelson Mandela.* New York: Little, Brown and Co.

_____.1995. *Long Walk to Freedom: The Autobiography of Nelson Mandela.* London: Abacus.

Marshall, S. 2017. *Bob Dylan: A Spiritual Life.* California: WND Books, Incorporated.

Mashabela, J. K. 2017. "Healing in a Cultural Context: The Role of Healing as a Defining Character in the Growth and Popular Faith of the Zion Christian Church." *Studia Historiae Ecclesiasticae*, 43 (3): 1–14.

Maultsby, P. K. 1983. "Soul Music: Its Sociological and Political Significance in American Popular Culture." *The Journal of Popular Culture*, 17 (2): 51–60.

McAdam, D. 1986. "Recruitment to High-Risk Activism." *American Journal of Sociology*, 92: 64–90.

McCollum, J. & Hebert, D. G. (eds.) 2014. *Theory and Method in Historical Ethnomusicology.* New York: Lexington Books.

Merriam, A. 1967. *Ethnomusicology of the Flathead Indian.* Chicago: Aldine Press.

_____. 1982. *African Music in Perspective.* New York: Garland.

Merriam, S. B. 1995. "What Can I Tell You from an N of 1: Issues of Validity and Reliability in Qualitative Research." *PAACE Journal of Lifelong Learning,* 4: 51–60.

Meintjies, L. 1990. "Paul Simon's Graceland, South Africa, and the Mediation of Musical Meaning." *The Society for Ethnomusicology,* 34 (1): 37–73.

Miles M. B., Huberman A. M. & Saldaña, J. 2013. *Qualitative Data Analysis: A Methods Sourcebook.* 3rd ed. Thousand Oaks, CA: Sage.

Modisenyane, S. 2017. "Mama Mary Lwate Recognized Vastly!" *Winterveld News.* March 3, 2017.

Moll, L. C. 2014. *L.S. Vygotsky and Education.* New York and London: Routledge.

Monson, I. 2007. *Freedom Sounds: Civil Rights Call Out to Jazz and Africa.* Oxford, U.K.: Oxford University Press.

Mugovhani, N. 2015. "Emerging trends from indigenous music and dance practices: a glimpse into contemporary Malende and Tshigombela." *Southern African Journal for Folklore Studies,* 25: 1–16.

Muller, Carol A. 2008. *Music of South Africa.* 2nd ed. New York, NY: Taylor & Francis.

Ndebele, H. 2012. "A Socio-Cultural Approach to Codeswitching and Code-Mixing Among Speakers of IsiZulu in KwaZulu-Natal: A Contribution to Spoken Language Corpora." Ph.D. diss., The University of Kwa-Zulu Natal.

Nelson Mandela's Address to Rally in Cape Town On His Release from Prison. Accessed January 30, 2015, http://db.nelsonmandela.org/speeches/pub_view.asp?pg=item&ItemID=NMS016.

Nelson Mandela's Five Most Memorable Speeches. 2013. *FirstPost.* Accessed February 7, 2017, https://www.firstpost.com/world/nelson-mandelas-five-most-me morable-speeches-1270759.html.

Nettl, B. 2005. *The Study of Ethnomusicology: Thirty-One Issues and Concepts.* 2nd ed. Champaign, IL: The University of Illinois Press.

Ng, W. F. 2005. "Music Therapy, War Trauma, and Peace: A Singaporean Perspective," *Voices: A World Forum for Music Therapy,* 5 (3). https://voices.no/index.php/voices/article/view/231.

Nichols, B. 1991. *Representing Reality.* Indianapolis, IN: Indiana University.

Nyairo, J. 2016. "Blowin' in the Wind: Why the Nobel Committee made the right call on Dylan." *Daily Nation, Kenya.* Accessed August 28, 2017, http://www.nati on.co.ke/lifestyle/weekend/Why-Nobel-team-was-right-to-choose-Dylan/1220-34 25392-vhtmrp/index.html.

Nzewi, M. E. 1991. "Backcloth to Music and Healing in Traditional African Society." *Voices,* 2 (1): 1–4.

_____. 2003. "Acquiring Knowledge on Musical Arts in Traditional Society." In *Musical arts in Africa: Theory, practice and education* edited by A. Herbst, M. Nzewi and K. Agawu, 13–37. Pretoria, South Africa: Unisa Press.

Olwage, G. (ed.) 2008. *Composing Apartheid: Music For and Against Apartheid.* Johannesburg, Witwatersrand University Press.

Omibiyi-Obidike, M. A. 1998 "African musical resources and African identity in the new African art music." In *African Art Music in Nigeria*, edited by M. A. Omibiyi-Obidike, 150–160. Ibadan, Nigeria: Stirling-Horden Publishers.

One Love by Bob Marley and The Wailers. *Songfacts.* [online]. Accessed 27 August 2017, https://www.songfacts.com/facts/bob-marley-the-wailers/one-love.

Oppenheim, C. E. 2012. "Nelson Mandela and the Power of Ubuntu." *Religions*, 3 (2): 369–388. http://dx.doi.org/10.3390/rel3020369.

Pavlicevic, M. 1994. "Between Chaos and Creativity: Music Therapy with 'Traumatised Children' in South Africa." *Journal of British Music Therapy,* 8 (2): 4–9.

_____. 2002. "Fragile Rhythms and Uncertain Listenings: Perspectives from Music Therapy with South African Children." In *Music, Music Therapy and Trauma: International Perspectives* edited by J. P. Sutton, 97–118. London, UK and Philadelphia, PA: Jessica Kingsley Publishers.

Qureshi, Regula. 2001. "In Search of Begum Akhtar: Patriarchy, Poetry, and Twentieth-Century Indian Music." *The World of Music*, 43 (1): 97–137.

Ramanna, N. 2013. "Shifting Fortunes: Jazz in (post) Apartheid South Africa." [Online] *Researchgate*, Accessed December 3, 2017, https://www.researchgate.net /publication/321110573.

Reed, D. B. & Daniel B. 2004. "Performing the Nation: Swahili Music and Cultural Politics in Tanzania (review)." *Africa Today*, 50 (3): 139–140.

Rees, Helen (ed.) 2009. *Lives in Chinese Music*. Urbana, IL: University of Illinois Press.

Rice, Tim. 1994. *May It Fill Your Soul: Experiencing Bulgarian Music*. Chicago and London: The University of Chicago Press.

Riiser, S. 2010. "National Identity and the West-Eastern Divan Orchestra." *Music and Arts in Action*, 2 (2): 19–37.

Rios, H. 2016. *Written Direct Testimony of Hawane Rios*. Accessed November 21, 2017, https://dlnr.hawaii.gov/mk/files/2016/10/F-5-Witness-Testimony-Hawane-Rios.pdf.

Roberson, J. E. 2009. "Memory and Music in Okinawa: The Cultural Politics of War and Peace." *Positions: East Asia Cultures Critique*, 17 (3): 683–711.

Roberts, A. F. 2002. "Africanizing Anthropology: Fieldwork, Networks, and the Making of Cultural Knowledge in Central Africa (review)." *Africa Today*, 49 (3): 136–138.

"2017 Rock & Roll Hall of Fame Joan Baez Complete Induction Speech." *Rolling Stone,* [online]. Accessed August 20, 2017, http://www.rollingstone.com/music/n ews/read-joan-baezs-moving-rock-hall-of-fame-speech-w475770.

Rosenthal, R. & Flacks, R. 2012. *Playing for Change: Music and Musicians in the Service of Social Movements*. Boulder, CO: Paradigm Publishers.

——. 2013. "Playing for Change: Music and Musicians in the Service of Social Movements." *American Journal of Sociology,* 119 (3): 868–870.

Roy, William G. 2013. *Reds, Whites, and Blues: Social Movements, Folk Music, and Race in the United States* (Princeton Studies in Cultural Sociology). Princeton, NJ: Princeton University Press.

Rural Project Partners. *Stellenbosch University.* Accessed March 24, 2017, http://www0.sun.ac.za/music/rural-project-partners/.

Sanders, T. 2003. *American Anthropologist*, 105(2): 461–462.

Seeger, C. 1977. *Studies in Musicology 1935–1975.* Berkeley & London: University of California Press.

Schumacher, L. 2001. *Africanizing Anthropology.* Durham & London: Duke University Press.

Scribner, S. 1990. "Reflections on a model." *Quarterly Newsletter of the Laboratory of Comparative Human Cognition*, 12(2): 90–94.

Seidman, G. 1999. "Is South Africa Different? Sociological Comparisons and Theoretical Contributions from the Land of Apartheid." *Annual Review of Sociology*, 25: 419–440.

Seidman, I. 2006. *Interviewing as Qualitative Research.* New York, NY: Teachers College Press.

Sharkey, P. 2001. "Hermeneutic Phenomenology." In *Phenomenology* edited by R. Barnacle, 16–37. Melbourne: RMIT Publications.

Sharon Katz & Masande—Serantabole (Umbrella Song), [online]. Accessed March 24, 2016, https://www.youtube.com/watch?v=3fBIWOBJ1Ug.

Sharon Katz and the Peace Train [online]. Accessed November 8, 2015, http://sharonkatz.com/bio/.

Shimoni, Gideon. 2003. *Community and Conscience: The Jews in Apartheid South Africa.* Waltham, MA: Brandeis University Press.

Smith, Jonathan A. & Osborn, M. 2007. *Qualitative Psychology: A Practical Guide to Research Methods.* Thousand Oaks, CA: Sage.

Soweto Student Uprising. *South Africa: Overcoming Apartheid.* Accessed September 10, 2017, http://overcomingapartheid.msu.edu/sidebar.php?id=65-258-3.

Stake, R. E. . 1995. *The Art of Case Study Research.* Thousand Oaks, CA: Sage.

——— 2006. *Multiple Case Study Analysis.* New York: The Guilford Press.

Stewart, K. (ed.) 2010. *Music Therapy and Trauma: Bridging Theory and Clinical Practice.* New York: Satchnote Press.

Stige, B. 2003. *Elaborations Toward a Notion of Community Music Therapy.* Norway: Oslo Academic Press.

Storhoff, Tim. 2015. "Under African Skies by Joe Berlinger." *Ethnomusicology*, 59(1): 117–119. http://www.jstor.org/stable/10.5406/ethnomusicology.59.1.0170.

Stoutenborough, J. W. 2011. "Demographic Measure." In *Encyclopedia of Survey Research Methods*, edited by P. J. Lavraks. Sage Publications Inc. http://dx.doi.org/10.4135/9781412963947.

TCC Rides the Peace Train. *Trenton Children's Chorus.* Accessed July 23, 2017, http://www.trentonchildrenschorus.org/peace-train-1.html.

The History of 'Ohio.' *Ultimate Classic Rock* [online]. Accessed September 9, 2017, http://ultimateclassicrock.com/csny-ohio/.

The History Place—Great Speeches Collection: Nelson Mandela, [online]. Accessed August 22, 2014, www.historyplace.com/speeches/mandela.htm.

The Rachel Maddow Show, Transcript 04/27/15, [online]. Accessed July 23, 2017, http://www.msnbc.com/transcripts/rachel-maddow-show/2015-04-27.

Thompson, L. 2001. *A History of South Africa*, 3rd ed. New Haven & London: Yale University Press.

Township Uprising 1984–1985. *South African History Online.* Accessed May 20, 2018, http://www.sahistory.org.za/article/township-uprising-1984-1985.

United States Census Bureau, [online]. Accessed April 12, 2017, https://www.census.gov/quickfacts/table/RHI125215/00.

Urbain, O. (Ed.). 2015. *Music and Conflict Transformation.* Croydon, UK: I.B. Tauris & Co. Ltd.

Vershbow, M. E. 2010. "The Sounds of Resistance: The Role of Music in South Africa's Anti-Apartheid Movement." *Inquiries Journal/Student Pulse,* 2 (6). Accessed September 18, 2016, http://www.inquiriesjournal.com/a?id=265.

Washington, S. 2012. "Exiles/Inxiles: Differing Axes of South African Jazz during late Apartheid." *SAMUS,* 32 (1): 91–111.

Watkins, L. 2008. "Review. Composing Apartheid: Music For and against Apartheid by Grant Olwage." *African Music,* 8 (2): 117–118. Accessed July 10, 2017, http://www.jstor.org.oasis.unisa.ac.za/stable/pdf/30250019.pdf?refreqid=search%3Abace5d66a1f1c45020f4f95db836f723.

Webb, Darren. 2008. "Exploring the Relationship between Hope and Utopia: Towards a Conceptual Framework." *Politics,* 28 (3): 197–206. https://doi.org/10.1111/j.1467-9256.2008.00329.x.

Weinstein-Moser, E. 2003. "Emissary of Peace: An Interview with Sharon Katz." *New Visions Magazine,* February: 9–10, 16, 18, 20, 24, 34.

When Voices Meet. *Durban International Film Festival.* Accessed July 10, 2015, http://www.durbanfilmfest.co.za/index.php/film/item/599-when-voices-meet.

Williams, L. 1993. "Mirrors without Memories: Truth, History, and the New Documentary." *Film Quarterly,* 46 (3): 9–21. Accessed September 25, 2016, http://www.jstor.org/stable/1212899.

Willson, R. B. 2009a. "The Parallax Worlds of the West-Eastern Divan Orchestra." *Journal of the Royal Musical Association,* 134 (2): 319–347.

_____. 2009b. "Whose Utopia: Perspectives on the West-Eastern Divan Orchestra." *Music & Politics,* 3 (2): 1–21.

Wilson, H. & Hutchinson, S. 1991. "Triangulation of Qualitative Methods: Heideggerian Hermeneutics and Grounded Theory." *Qualitative Health Research* 1: 263–276.

Wong, L. P. 2008. "Data Analysis in Qualitative Research: A Brief Guide to Using NVivo." *Malaysian Family Physician,* 3 (1): 14–20. http://www.emfp.org/old/2008v3n1/pdf/NVivo_in_Qualitative_Research.pdf.

Woodstock, *Joni Mitchell,* [online]. Accessed August 20, 2017, http://jonimitchell.com/music/song.cfm?id=75.

Yawney, R. 1993. "Music Therapy in Gaza: An Occupational Hazard?" *Canadian Journal of Music Therapy,* 3 (1): 1–17.

Yin, R. K. 2009. *Case Study Research: Design and Methods,* 4th ed. Thousand Oaks, CA: Sage.

_____. 2003. *Case study research: Design and Methods*, 3rd ed. Thousand Oaks, CA: Sage.

_____. 1994. *Case study research: Design and Methods.* Thousand Oaks, CA: Sage.

Yudkoff, A. 2016. "Nationalism and Patriotism: The Experience of an Indian Diaspora in South Africa." In *Patriotism and Nationalism in Music Education*, edited by Hebert and Kertz-Welzel, A, 95–110. London and New York: Routledge.

Zeitlin, M. 1970. *Revolutionary Politics and the Cuban Working Class.* New York: Harper Torchbooks.

Zelizer, C. 2003. "The Role of Artistic Processes in Peacebuilding in Bosnia-Herzegovina." *Peace & Conflict Studies,* 10 (2): 62–75.

Index

Italicized pages refer to figures and tables.

Aarelaid-Tart, A., 134
activism: cultural, 149–51; defined, 21;
    Kuntz on, 21; music and, 21, 22. See
    also musical activism
activist-musicians, 22
Adler, Franklin, 25, 26
Africa Cup of Nations, 102
African American, 7–8; police brutality
    against, 116–17, 143
Africanizing Anthropology
    (Schumacher), 154
African National Congress (ANC), 4–5,
    25–26, 49, 103
Afrikaners, 35
Akhtar, Begum, 2–3
Albert, Don, 109
Alhambra Theatre, 5
Allan, Jani, 35, 37
Amandla! A Revolution in Four-Part
    Harmony, 47–48, 124
Amandla Cultural Ensemble, 49
American Peace Train Tour (2016),
    115–44; Belafonte connection, 117–
    18; children's reflections, 139–44;
    demographic data, 120; demographic
    survey, 133–35; impact on
    participants, 130–33; inclusiveness,
    121–22; itinerary, 118–19;
    performers, 119–20; questionnaire
    and responses, 133–39; racial mix
    of participants, 120; songs, 122–30.
    See also Peace Train (South African
    Tour)
Ansdell, G., 62, 148
antisemitism, 24
apartheid, 23; brutality of, 44–45;
    dehumanizing effects, 13; Jews/
    Jewish people and community, 23,
    24–30. See also South Africa
Arenstein, Rowley, 26
Arthur, Brooks, 27
Asch, T., 101
Aspden, Peter, 43
awards to When Voices Meet, 109–13,
    110–11

Baez, Joan, 41, 42, 46–47, 77
"Baggage" (Pollack-Johnson), 132–33
Ballad of Sharpeville, 44
Ballantine, Christopher, 23, 39
bands, 38
Bapedi people, 6
Barenboim, Daniel, 53–54, 148
Batweni, Zandile, 91

Beastie Boys, 27–28
Belafonte, Harry, 21, 45, 46, 103, 113n4, 117
Belafonte, Shari, 117–18
Bellamy, Ziare, 131
Benarde, S. R., 26, 27, 28, 29
Berlinger, Joe, 102, 103, 105
Biden, Joe, 144
Biko, 45
Biko, Steve, 45
biographical availability, 134
black gold, 15, 19n18
Blacking, John, 40
"Black Magic Woman," 27
"Blinded by the Light," 27
boeremusiek, 38
Boesman and Lena (Fugard), 30
Boxill, Edith, 78
Boyoyo Boys, 28
Bra Gib: Father of South Africa's Township Theatre (Solberg), 11
Bra Gibson Kente Theatre, 11
Brandt, Willy, 144n1
Brandt Line, 116, 144n1
Braun, V., 66
Bridgewater, Pamela E., 108
Bring Him Back Home, 45
Broadway World, 17
Brown, Michael, 116
Browne, David, 47
Buthelezi, Mangosuthu, 16, 19n20
Byerly, I. B., 48

Caffè Lena, 1, 2
California, Peace Train project in, 160
The Call (Kente), 10
Cape Town Jazz Festival, 107
CD compilations, 16
"Chanukah Song," 27
Chartock, Alan, 117
Cheah, Elena, 54
children: American Peace Train Tour (2016), 139–44; Cuban, 161–62; Mexican, 161; South African Peace Train, 69

choir music, 8
choral competitions, 64–65
Christianity, 6–7
Christy Minstrels, 7
churches, 14
Civil Rights Movement, 41
Clarke, V., 66
Clave de Sol Guitar School in Cuba, 162
Clegg, Johnny, 28–29, 38–39
Clover Mama Afrika, 88
CNN, 16
Cohen, Leonard, 29–30
Cohen, Marilyn, 23, 53, 64, 73–74, 84, 85, 89, 90, 107, 111, 118, 133, 138, 150, 155, 157, 160, 186
collaborations. *See* musical collaborations
collective memory, 22
Collett, D., 156
communal singing, 6
community music, 6; music therapy and, 62–63
Community Music Therapy, 14, 62–63, 148
COVID-19, 162
Crystal Journey, 125–26
Cuba, 160, 161–62
cultural activism, 149–51
Cultural Center of Tijuana (CECUT), 161
culture brokers, 158
cultures/cultural influences, 5–6

Danielson, Virginia, 2
Da Silva, Howard, 52
Davhula, M. J., 14
Davis, Peter, 81
De Beer, R., 6–7
de Klerk, F. W., 63
Dent, Floyd, 116
Dhlamini, Ezekiel "King Kong," 8
Diamond, Neil, 26, 27
"Diamonds On the Soles of Her Shoes," 28

Double Take, 50
Drexel University College of Medicine, 61
"Drums of Africa," 8
Du Bois, W. E. B., 8, 18n7
Dutch Reformed Church, 35
Dutch settlers, 7
Dylan, Bob, 2, 23, 27, 29, 36, 41–42, 46, 151

edgewalker, 94, 96–97n12
Elba, Idris, 25–26
Elizabeth Sneddon Theatre, 67
Elsila, Mikail, 61
empowerment of people, 144
entertainment industry in South Africa, 10
Erlmann, Veit, 2
ethnomusicology, 2, 162
Etuk, U. A., 14
Eurocentric influence in music, 7
Eyerman, R., 22

Fassie, Brenda, 10
film festivals, 52–53
First, Ruth, 25, 26
Fisk Jubilee Singers, 8
Flathead music, 40
Fleetwood Mac, 27
Floyd, George, 116–17
folk music and songs, 2, 5, 23–24; international, 51; Jewish Israeli, 23; musicians, 49–50
freedom songs, 41–50
Friends of the Peace Train, 16, 59, 68, 80, 82, 84, 85, 86–87, 89, 91, 92, 95, 147, 149
Fugard, Athol, 30, 32
Furman, R., 133

Gabriel, Peter, 45
Gandhi, Mohandas Karamchand, 15
Gans, C. J., 45
Garner, Eric, 116
German Jewish refugees, 24

Gershwin, George, 30
Ghana, 81
Gilbert, Shirli, 49
Gillies, Arthur, 9–10
Glaser, Barney G., 86
Goldberg, Whoopi, 12
Golden City Dixies, 9
Goldreich, Arthur, 8, 26
Good Hope Community Centre, 149
Good Hope Community Organization, 82–83
Good Shepherd Organization, 59
Gordimer, Nadine, 25
Gordon, R., 154
Gore, Al, 52
Gouk, P., 13, 62
Graceland, 28, 102–3, 104
Grammy Foundation, 2
Greenbaum, Peter, 27
Greenwald, Matthew, 45–46
Grierson, John, 100–101
Group Areas Act, 4, 54n1, 101–2
"Group Therapy Music Model," 62
The Guardian, 43
"Gumboota"/"Gumboots," 28
gumboot dancing, 121
Guthrie, Arlo, 2
Guthrie, Woody, 52
Gwangwa, Jonas, 49

Hahnemann University Hospital, Philadelphia, 61
"Hallelujah," 29
Hampton Institute in Virginia, 8
Hampton Male Quartette, 8
Harris, Eric, 116
Harris, Kamala, 144
Hartwig, Gunthar, 101
healing: music therapy, 60–63; Peace Train, 78–80; traditional (indigenous practices), 13–14
Hendrix, Jimi, 42, 47
Hess, J., 22
Hillbrow, 37
Hindu festivals, 5

Hirsch, Lee, 47–48
A History of South Africa (Thompson), 4
"Homeless," 28
Hopkins, P., 37
How Long (Kente), 10
How Musical is Man? (Blacking), 40
humanitarian efforts, 16–17, 80–96
"Hush Little Baby," 5

Ibrahim, Abdullah, 48
"Ich bin ein kleiner Judenbub" (I am a little Jewish boy), 30
Idang, G. E., 14
Imagine (Lennon), 42–43
Imbizo, 28
Independent Electoral Commission, 16
Indian culture, 5, 6
infanticide, 61
Institute for the Study of Nonviolence, 47
International Festival of Choirs, 161–62
"It Ain't Necessarily So," 30
"I've Got Rhythm," 30

Jamison, A., 22
jazz musicians, 50
"Jericho," 28
"Jerusalem," 28
Jewish Israeli folk songs, 23
Jews/Jewish people and community, 23, 24–30; ANC and, 25–26; apartheid, 24–26; as Communists, 25; double marginality, 25; earliest emigration, 24; as Europeans, 24; German refugees, 24; Mandela and, 24, 25–26; musicians and musical influence, 26–30; Nationalist government and, 24–25
Joel, Billy, 26
"Joe's Pub Remembers Pete Seeger," 17
Johnston, H., 134
Judaism, 29–30
Juluka, 38–39

The Just Assassins (Fugard), 30

Kani, John, 30–32, 51, 55n12, 106, 151
Katz, Sharon, 1, 2, 3, 8; African musical style, 7; awakening, 30–32; CD compilations, 16; childhood, 23; CNN coverage, 7; humanitarian efforts, 16–17, 80–96; international audience, 16; interview with, 22–54; Jewish upbringing and life, 23, 24; Mandela and, 13; Marxism and, 23; musical activism, 6, 14; musical collaborations, 102–6, 154–58; music therapy and, 13, 60–63; presentations/teaching experiences, 32–33; professionalism, 161; Transcending Barriers Project, 161; Western music and, 7; Zionist Youth Movement, 23. *See also* American Peace Train Tour (2016); musical activism; Peace Train; *When Voices Meet* (documentary)
Kayamandi township music project, 90–91
Kente, Gibson, 10–11
Kent State Massacre, 43
Kerkorrel, Johannes, 34, 35, 37
Khumalo, Leleti, 12
King Kong: An African Jazz, 8–9
Klein, Carole, 27
Koos Kombuis. *See* Letoit, André
Kubeka, Abigail, 17, 50, 52, 106
Kulthum, Umm, 2
Kuntz, A. M., 21
KwaNgcolosi school project, 91–96, 104

Ladysmith Black Mambazo, 28, 49, 67, 70, 77, 89, 103–8, 149
La Pena Community Chorus, 160
Lawrence, D. H., 51
Lee, Harper, 131
left-leaning intellectuals, 23
Lennon, John, 42–43

Letoit, André, 34–35, 37
Levine, Adam, 26
Library of Congress, 2
Lilieslief, 26
"The Little We Have, We Share"
    (Katz), 129
Loeb, Lisa, 26
Long Walk to Freedom (Mandela), 25,
    26
Lucey, Roger, 50
Ludski, Warren, 9
Lwate, Mama Mary, 59, 82–89, 95, 149

Ma, Yo Yo, 113, 130
Maasai people and music, 6
Macbeth (Shakespeare), 11
MacColl, Ewan, 44
Machine Gun (Hendrix), 42
Maddow, Rachel, 116
Madonna, 16, 27
Mahlasela, Vusi, 48
Makeba, Miriam, 8–9, 10, 17, 48–49
Maki, Busi, 91
Maliwa, Thobela, 91
"Mama Mary Lwate recognized vastly!"
    (Modisenyan), 87–88
Manana, The Jazz Prophet (Kente), 10
Mandela, Nelson, 8, 10, 12–13, 45–46,
    52, 54, 57n32, 80, 102, 113, 119,
    121, 124, 130, 149, 169; concert in
    the honor of, 63; imprisonment of,
    4–5, 42, 44; Jews and, 24, 25–26;
    Long Walk to Freedom, 25, 26, 48,
    49; released from prison, 63, 77
Mandela, Winnie, 46, 47
Mandela Day Celebrations, 54
Mandela: Long Walk to Freedom,
    25–26
Mann, Manfred, 27
March on Washington, 42, 47
Marley, Bob, 43
Marshall, J., 101
Marshall, Scott, 29
Marxism/Marxist ideologies, 23

Marxist ideologies, 23
Masekela, Hugh, 8, 45–46, 48, 124, 148
Mashabela, J. K., 13
Matisyahu. *See* Miller, Matthew Paul
Mayibuye Cultural Ensemble, 49
Mbulu, Letta, 10
McAdoo, Orpheus, 7–8
Mchunu, Sipho, 38, 39
Mdledle, Nathan, 9
"Meeting in Music" (Barenboim), 53
Merriam, A., 13, 40
Merriam, S. B., 100
Mexican children, 161
Mexico, 14, 160–61
Middle East model, 54
Midler, Bette, 26
"Mighty Quinn," 27
Miller, Matthew Paul, 27
Minamore, Bridget, 43
minstrel group and shows, 7–8
Mirrors without Memories: Truth,
    History and the New Documentary
    (Williams), 102
missionaries, 6–7, 14
Mitchell, Joni, 42, 46, 47, 109
Modisenyane, Seiso, 87–88
Monson, Ingrid, 95–96
Mqoma, Phyllis, 8
Msomi, Welcome, 11
Mtwa, Percy, 12
Mugovhani, N., 13
Muller, Carol A., 104
music: activism and, 21, 22. *See also*
    musical activism; African societies
    and, 21; political and social change
    through, 34–50; and resistance in
    South Africa since 1948, 3–17;
    songs, 21
musical activism, 6, 59–96; advancing
    research in, 163; freedom and
    peace songs, 41–50; as a global
    phenomenon, 50–54; humanitarian
    efforts, 80–96; music therapy, 60–63;
    performance, 63–80; relevance,

153–54; social change and, 148–49. *See also* Katz, Sharon
musical collaborations, 102–6, 154–58
musicians: folk, 49–50; Jewish, 26–30; in social and political landscapes (Monson's views), 95–96
The Music of Strangers: Yo-Yo Ma and the Silk Road Ensemble, 113
music therapy, 60–63
Muslims, 6

National Folk Festival, 52
National Guardsmen in the United States, 43
Nationalist Party, 15
Nazi, 24, 30
Ndebele, 124, 125
Ndlovu, Hastings, 44
necklacing, 37
Nelson Mandela Bay, 23, 30
Nene, Nomsa, 10
Nettl, B., 3, 40
New Mexico State Historic Preservation Division, 53
New York Times, 11
Ngema, Mbongeni, 10, 11–12, 93, 96n10
Ng, Wang Feng, 78
Nhleko, Malcolm, 89, 90, 91, 104–5, 108, 143
Nichols, Bill, 101
Nixon, Richard, 43
Nketia, Joseph Hanson Kwabena, 81, 96n3
"Nkosi Sikelele iAfrica," 30
"Nonhlanhla Wanda & Sharon Katz—Side-By-Side," 162
NVivo, 66–67, 69, 171
Nyairo, J., 42
Nzewi, M. E., 13

Ohio (Young), 43–44
Olwage, Grant, 40, 49
One Love (Marley), 43
open universities, 25

orchestra: Middle East model, 54; as a "utopian republic," 54; West-Eastern Divan Orchestra, 53–54
An Orchestra Beyond Borders: Voices of the West-Eastern Divan Orchestra (Cheah), 54

Pan Africanist Congress, 44
Patel, Sarreshbay, 116
peace songs, 41–50
Peace Train (South African Tour), 63–80; children, 69; family and community support, 76–78; feelings, 69–70; formation of, 2, 3, 12–14; healing power of music, 78–80; impact of experiences, 70–71; interviews with South African Tour, 65–67; organization and structure, 73–74; performance preparation, 73; personal growth, 71–73; racial and cultural differences, 74–76; recurring themes, 151–53; relevance, 153–54; sociological implications, 80; teachers' experiences, 67–69. *See also* American Peace Train Tour (2016); *When Voices Meet* (documentary)
Phillips, James, 34
Phiri, Ray, 28
Pieterson, Hector, 44
Pink, 26
poetry and narratives, 133
political change through music, 34–41. *See also* social change
Pollack-Johnson, Linda, 132–33
Popular Problems, 29
Population Registration Act, 4
Porgy and Bess, 30
Prince Theatre, London, 9
Progressive Party, 30, 55n13
Promotora de las Bellas Artes (PBA), 160, 161
protest consciousness, 44

Quick, Wendy Khetiwe, 1, 2, 111, 130, 154, 157–58
Qureshi, Regula, 2–3

Rabbitt, 27
Rabie, Ralph. *See* Kerkorrel, Johannes
Rabin, Trevor, 27
Rabinowitz, Gershon, 27
racial segregation, 13
Rand Afrikaans University, 37
Rathebe, Dorothy (Dolly), 50, 52, 81, 82, 85, 95, 96n4, 149
Rees, Helen, 3
Reform School in Philadelphia, 62
Representing Reality (Nichols), 101
research in grassroots musical activism, 163
"Responsible Action Plan" (RAP), 143, 151
Reynolds, Malvina, 52
Rhodes-Livingston Institute (RLI), 154
Rice, Tamir, 116
Rice, Timothy, 2
Riiser, Solveig, 53–54
Rios, Hāwane, 121, 122
Robinson, Earl, 52
Rocky Mountain Farmers Union (RMFU), 52
Rolling Stone, 46, 47
Roth, David Lee, 26
Royal Schools of Music in London, 5
Ruud, 62
Ryan Prison in Detroit, Michigan, 61

Sachs, Albie, 26
Said, Edward, 53, 54, 148
Sala Ngoana, 129
Sala Ngoana Sala, 129
Sanalwami, 41, 126–28
Sandler, Adam, 27
Santiago de Cuba, 162
Sarafina!, 11–12, 84, 96n10
Satyagraha, 15
"Scatterlings of Africa," 39
Schoenberg, Arnold, 30
Schumacher, Lyn, 154–56
screenings of *When Voices Meet*, 109–13, *110–11*
Seeger, Peggy, 44

Seeger, Pete, 2, 16–17, 23–24, 40–41, 44, 46, 52, 151
Seidman, Gay, 80, 85–86
Shabalala, Joseph, 28, 104, 107
Shakespeare, William, 11
Sharpeville Massacre of 1960, 4, 44, 50
Shitandi, W., 6–7
Shosholoza, 121, 123–25
Shukla, Priya, 65
Sikalo (Kente), 10
Simmons, Gene, 26
Simon, Barney, 12
Simon, Carly, 26
Simon, Paul, 16, 23, 26, 28, 45, 102–5, 117, 149
Sing My Whole Life Long: Jenny Vincent's Life in Folk Music and Activism (Smith), 51
"Skylarks," 17
Slovo, Joe, 25, 26
Smith, Craig, 51, 52
Smith, Nancy Sutton, 99, 100, 101, 102, 105
Smith, Sandra Susan, 117
Smithsonian Folkways Recordings, 44
social change, 34–41; freedom and peace songs, 41–50; musical activism and, 148–49
Solberg, Rolf, 11
songs, 21
South Africa: anti-apartheid songs, 45–50; antisemitism, 24; Eurocentric influence in music, 7; first democratic election, 16; Gandhi and, 15; Jews/Jewish people, 23, 24–30; left-leaning intellectuals, 23; Marxist ideologies, 23; music and resistance since 1948, 3–17; racial segregation, 13; transition to democracy, 13; traveling musical groups, 7–12; urban culture, 7. *See also* Peace Train (South African Tour); *When Voices Meet* (documentary)
South African Broadcasting Corporation, 35

South African Jewish Board of Deputies, 24
South African Native National Congress. *See* African National Congress (ANC)
Soweto uprising of June 16, 1976, 44–45
Spektor, Regina, 26
Spier, P., 101
spirituality, 29
Springsteen, Bruce, 27
Stake, R. E., 60, 148
Stars of David: Rock 'n Roll's Jewish Stories (Benarde), 26
Stige, B., 62, 148
Sting, 16
Storhoff, Tim, 104
Strauss A., 86
Streisand, Barbra, 26
"Summertime," 30
"Suncoast," 68
Sunday Times, 35
Suzman, Helen, 25, 55n13
Swart September, 35–36
Sweden, 9
Symphony Orchestra, 81

Tambo, Dali, 103, 114n6
Tambo, Oliver, 114n6
Taylor, Jeremy, 50
teachers' experiences of Peace Train, 67–69
Temple University, 60, 61
thematic analysis, 66
Thirty Meter Telescope (TMT), 120
Thompson, Leonard, 4
"Thula Baba," 5
Tijuana, Mexico, 160–61
The Time is Right Today, 50, 59, 125–26
The Times They Are A-Changin (Dylan), 23, 41
To Kill A Mocking Bird (Lee), 131
traditional healing, 13–14
Transcending Barriers Project, 161
Transkei, 23, 55n3

traveling musical groups, 7–12
Treason Trial, 9, 18–19n10
Trenton Children's Chorus, 139–42, 152
triangulation, 100
A Tribute to Gibson Kente, 11
Trump administration, 144
Truth and Reconciliation Commission (TRC), 102, 113n2, 152
Turner, Tina, 16

Umabatha, 11
UMkhonto we Sizwe, 25, 55n8
Under African Skies (documentary), 102–6, 113
United States (US), 3, 14, 106, 107, 108, 115–44, 161, 162, 163; atrocities/brutality against minorities, 115–16, 120; Belafonte, 116–17; Brandt line, 116; Caffè Lena, 2; peace songs in, 41–44; population, 120; workshops and performances in, 95. *See also* American Peace Train Tour (2016)
Universal Men (Juluka), 39
University of Cape Town, 25
University of Ghana, 81
University of Natal's Music Department, 23
University of New Mexico, 53
University of South Africa, 25
urban culture, 7
U.S. Census Bureau, 120
U.S.-Mexican border, 160, 161

"Variety," 8
Vaudeville Theatre, 8
Vershbow, M. E., 5
Vietnam War, 41–42, 46, 47
Vincent, Jenny, 51–53, 148
Virginia Jubilee Singers, 7–8
Virginia Minstrels, 7
Vlok, Elain, 88
Voëlvry, 34, 35, 37
Voices: A World Forum for Music Therapy, 62, 94

Wallace, Henry, 52
Wanda, Nonhlanhla, 68–69, 96, 100, 107, 111, 115, 121, 130, 155, 156, 158, 162
Waren, 134
Warren, Diane, 26
"Warsaw 1943," 28
Washington, S., 48, 50
We Are the Children of South Africa, 47
We are the Children of South Africa (America), 125
"We Know What To Do," 162
Welcome Msomi, 11
Wembley Stadium in London, 63
West-Eastern Divan Orchestra, 53–54
Western music, 7
When Voices Meet (documentary), 13, 14, 30–31, 51, 52–53, 59–60, 65, 66, 69, 76, 79, 99–113, 115, 117, 118, 135, 136, 147, 149, 153, 160; activism and, 106–9; musical collaborations compared, 102–6; screenings and awards, 109–13, *110–11*; understanding, 100–102

"When Will It All Change" (Bellamy), 131
Where Have All the Flowers Gone? (Seeger), 23
Williams, L., 102
Willson, Rachel Beckles, 54
Witkin, Sidelskey, and Eidelman (law firm), 25
Wits University, 25
Wolpe, Harold, 25
Woodstock, 47
Woodstock Festival, 42, 47
Woza Albert, 11–12

Yes, 27
Young, Neil, 43–44
Yudkoff, A. Ashgate, 156

Zambrano-Montez, Antonio, 116
Zeitlin, M., 134
Zionism, 23
Zionist Youth Movement, 23
"Zonk!", 8

About the Author

Ambigay Yudkoff is a South African-born educator, musician, and conductor. She holds a PhD in Musicology from the University of South Africa and a masters degree in ethnomusicology from the University of Natal in Durban. She has served as guest conductor of the *Sai* Movement's youth choir of Isipingo in South Africa and the Battenkill Chorale of Vermont in the United States, each boasting notable performances for Nelson Mandela. Since immigrating to the United States, she has worked at the University of Massachusetts, Amherst, where she devised a world music course. In recent years, she has held a fulltime, tenured position as a high school chorus director in New York State. Ambigay has performed for television specials and Christmas productions at the iconic Carnegie Hall and is a vocal adjudicator for the New York State School Music Association. She released an album of popular music titled *Legacy* in 2020 and is currently working on an album of Indian devotional music. She has authored chapters for the books *Patriotism and Nationalism in Music Education* (2016) and *Ethnomusicology and Cultural Diplomacy* (Lexington, forthcoming).